MW01280124

Construction Funding

Wiley Series of Practical Construction Guides
M. D. Morris, P.E., Editor

Jacob Feld
CONSTRUCTION FAILURE

William G. Rapp
CONSTRUCTION OF STRUCTURAL STEEL BUILDING
FRAMES

John Philip Cook
CONSTRUCTION SEALANTS AND ADHESIVES

Ben C. Gerwick, Jr.
CONSTRUCTION OF PRESTRESSED CONCRETE
STRUCTURES

S. Peter Volpe
CONSTRUCTION MANAGEMENT PRACTICE

Robert Crimmins, Reuben Samuels, and Bernard Monahan
CONSTRUCTION ROCK WORK GUIDE

B. Austin Barry
CONSTRUCTION MEASUREMENTS

D. A. Day
CONSTRUCTION EQUIPMENT GUIDE

Harold J. Rosen
CONSTRUCTION SPECIFICATION WRITING

Gordon A. Fletcher and Vernon A. Smoots
CONSTRUCTION GUIDE FOR SOILS AND
FOUNDATIONS

Don A. Halperin
CONSTRUCTION FUNDING: WHERE THE MONEY
COMES FROM

Construction Funding

Where the Money Comes From

Don A. Halperin, AIC

Chairman, Department of Building Construction
University of Florida

A Wiley-Interscience Publication

JOHN WILEY & SONS   *New York • London • Sydney • Toronto*

Library of Congress Cataloging in Publication Data

Halperin, Don A

   Construction funding.

   (Wiley series of practical construction guides)

   "A Wiley-Interscience publication."

   1. Construction industry—Finance. 2. Mortgage loans. 3. Leases. I. Title.

HD9715.A2H3   338.4'3   74-11188

ISBN O-471-34570-9

Printed in the United States of America

10 9 8 7 6 5 4 3

Series Preface

The construction industry in the United States and other advanced nations continues to grow at a phenomenal rate. In the United States alone construction in the near future will exceed ninety billion dollars a year. With the population explosion and continued demand for new building of all kinds, the need will be for more professional practitioners.

In the past, before science and technology seriously affected the concepts, approaches, methods, and financing of structures, most practitioners developed their know-how by direct experience in the field. Now that the construction industry has become more complex there is a clear need for a more professional approach to new tools for learning and practice.

This series is intended to provide the construction practitioner with up-to-date guides which cover theory, design, and practice to help him approach his problems with more confidence. These books should be useful to all people working in construction: engineers, architects, specification experts, materials and equipment manufacturers, project superintendents, and all who contribute to the construction or engineering firm's success.

Although these books will offer a fuller explanation of the practical problems which face the construction industry, they will also serve the professional educator and student.

M.D. MORRIS, P.E.

Contents

Chapter 1 Sources of Money   *1*

   1.0 *Short-Term and Permanent Financing*   *1*

   1.1 *The Mortgage Loan*   *2*

       1.1.1 *Lending Institutions*   *2*
       1.1.2 *Mortgage Brokers*   *2*
       1.1.3 *Smaller Loans*   *4*
       1.1.4 *Closing Costs*   *5*
       1.1.5 *Commitment*   *7*

   1.2 *Construction Loan*   *44*

       1.2.1 *Sources of Construction Loans*   *44*
       1.2.2 *Commercial Loans*   *45*
       1.2.3 *Conformity of Commitments* *46*
       1.2.4 *Entrepreneur*   *46*
       1.2.5 *Effect of Discount*   *47*
       1.2.6 *Amount of Construction Loan*   *48*
       1.2.7 *Stand-by Commitment on the Gap* *48*
       1.2.8 *Cost of Gap Financing*   *49*
       1.2.9 *Construction Loan Application* *50*
       1.2.10 *Single Home Loans*   *51*
       1.2.11 *FHA Loans*   *52*

   1.3 *Front Money*   *54*

       1.3.1 *Sources of Front Money*   *55*
       1.3.2 *Cost of Front Money*   *55*

        1.3.3   *FHA Obviates Front Money*   55

    1.4   *Retainage on Construction Draw*   56

        1.4.1   *Last Draw*   56
        1.4.2   *Required Capital*   57
        1.4.3   *Borrowing on the Contract*   57

    1.5   *Holdback on Subcontractors*   59

        1.5.1   *Fairness of Holdback on Subs*   59
        1.5.2   *Extra Holdback on Subs*   59
        1.5.3   *Numerical Example*   60

    1.6   *Summary*   61

Chapter 2   Capitalization and the Importance of Money   **63**

    2.0   *Corporate Thinking*   63

    2.1   *Money as a Company Tool*   64

        2.1.1   *The Use of Money*   64
        2.1.2   *Liquid Assets*   64

    2.2   *Capitalization*   65

        2.2.1   *Individual Ownership*   65
        2.2.2   *Partnership*   67
        2.2.3   *Corporation*   71
        2.2.4   *Combinations*   73
        2.2.5   *Subsequent Capitalization*   74

    2.3   *Summary*   75

Chapter 3   Site Selection and Development   **77**

    3.0   *Importance of Location*   77

    3.1   *Site Selection*   77

        3.1.1   *Market*   77
        3.1.2   *Factors*   78

    3.2   *Land Purchasing*   90

3.3 Land Financing   *90*

    3.3.1 Appraisal   *90*
    3.3.2 Loan Application Requirements   *91*
    3.3.3 Good Faith Deposits   *91*

3.4 Land Development Financing   *93*

    3.4.1 Land Development Loan Draws   *93*
    3.4.2 Title X   *93*

Chapter 4 Preparing the Request for Funds   **96**

4.0 Importance of the Application   *96*

4.1 Equity   *97*

4.2 Requirements   *97*

4.3 Income Approach to Value   *97*

    4.3.1 An Analogy   *98*
    4.3.2 The Value of a Business   *98*
    4.3.3 The Bank's Attitude   *99*
    4.3.4 Numerical Example   *99*

4.4 Cost Approach   *114*
    4.4.1 Construction Cost   *115*
    4.4.2 Replacement Cost   *116*
    4.4.3 Financing Fees   *116*
    4.4.4 "Sources of Cash": First Mortgage   *117*
    4.4.5 "Sources of Cash": Cash Flow   *117*

4.5 Income Feasibility   *118*

    4.5.1 Debt Service   *118*
    4.5.2 Cash Flow   *119*
    4.5.3 Rate of Return   *119*
    4.5.4 Making the Equity   *120*
    4.5.5 Builder's Fee   *120*
    4.5.6 Developer's Fee   *120*
    4.5.7 Other Professional Fees   *121*

4.6   Building Budget Feasibility   121

    4.6.1   Example   121
    4.6.2   Preliminary Considerations   121
    4.6.3   Ground Rent   123
    4.6.4   Losses   123
    4.6.5   Net Income   123
    4.6.6   Economic Value of Example   123
    4.6.7   Amount of Mortgage   124
    4.6.8   Debt Service of Example   124
    4.6.9   Profit   124
    4.6.10   Return on Investment   124
    4.6.11   Cash Needed   125
    4.6.12   Building Budget   125
    4.6.13   Increased Equity   126

Chapter 5   Draw Schedules   **127**

5.0   The Builder's Goal   127

5.1   Residential Draws   127

    5.1.1   Amount of Each Draw   127
    5.1.2   Certification   129
    5.1.3   Location Description   129
    5.1.4   Ambiguity of the Example   129
    5.1.5   Variations   130
    5.1.6   Lien Release Form   130
    5.1.7   Value of Efficiency   130

5.2   Monthly Draws   131

    5.2.1   The Estimate   131
    5.2.2   Draw Schedules   135
    5.2.3   Required Payments   135
    5.2.4   Reasons for Holdback   137
    5.2.5   Avoiding Difficulties   138
    5.2.6   Alternative Draw Schedule   138
    5.2.7   Front End Loading   140

Chapter 6   Cash Forecasting   **142**

6.0   Planning Expenditures   142

6.1   *Bar Charts*   *142*

    6.1.1   *Example*   *143*
    6.1.2   *Cost Per Month*   *144*
    6.1.3   *Purpose of Bar Charts*   *144*

6.2   *S-Curve*   *145*

    6.2.1   *Plotting Bank Draws*   *146*
    6.2.2   *The First Draw*   *146*
    6.2.3   *Step Curves*   *147*

6.3   *Cash Forecasting*   *147*

    6.3.1   *Difference Between Curves*   *147*
    6.3.2   *Net Actual Cost*   *147*
    6.3.3   *Developer's Cost*   *148*
    6.3.4   *Effect of Time Lag*   *148*
    6.3.5   *Predicting Construction Interest*   *149*

6.4   *Summary*   *150*

Chapter 7   Time Value of Money   **151**

7.0   *Money as a Company Tool*   *151*

7.1   *Why Interest?*   *151*

7.2   *Interest Defined*   *152*

    7.2.1   *Rate of Interest*   *152*

7.3   *Plans for Paying Back a Loan*   *153*

    7.3.1   *Short Term Notes*   *153*
    7.3.2   *Uniform Principal Payments*   *153*
    7.3.3   *Level Constant Payments*   *155*
    7.3.4   *Paying Off Loan*   *156*
    7.3.5   *Compound Interest*   *156*

7.4   *Equivalence*   *157*

    7.4.1   *Commonality of Plans*   *157*
    7.4.2   *The Borrower's Viewpoint*   *158*
    7.4.3   *Superiority of Plans*   *158*

7.5   *Present Worth*   *159*

    7.5.1   *Interest Rate vs Present Worth*   *159*

7.5.2	Time vs Present Worth	159
7.5.3	Meaning of "Present"	160
7.6	$S = P(1 + i)^n$	160
7.7	Level Constant Payments	162
7.7.1	Capital Recovery Factor	164
7.8	Nominal and Effective Rates	166
7.8.1	Periods Shorter Than One Year	167
7.8.2	Effective Rate	168
7.9	Examples of Problems	168
7.9.1	Add-On Interest	178
7.10	Loss of Interest as a Cost	179
7.10.1	Risk Profit	179
7.10.2	Example	179
7.10.3	Equipment Cost	180
7.11	Leasing	182
7.11.1	Cost Per Hour	183
7.11.2	Consideration of Alternatives	184
7.12	Applications to Real Estate Problems	184
7.12.1	Equity Build-Up	185
7.12.2	Depreciation	186
7.12.3	Time-Adjusted Return	187
7.12.4	Depreciation Fallacies	188

Appendix   **189**

Index   **223**

Construction Funding

1

Sources of Money

1.0 Short-Term and Permanent Financing

The financing of a construction project can be divided into two stages, the short-term funding and the long-term funding. The short-term funding is paid off either on completion of construction or before that date, whereas the long-term financing is obtained from a mortgage loan that will not be repaid for a number of years and is, therefore, often called permanent financing.

Short-term financing has many different forms and phases and includes such loans as land purchase loans, land development loans, "front money," construction payroll loans, "gap" financing, and the construction loan itself. All of these terms will be explained later under their various headings. But, in every case, all short-term financing is provided by some lender because he has the assurance that each and every part of it will eventually be repaid by some other loan, and the ultimate assurance of all the loans is the mortgage loan. Hence the mortgage loan will be discussed first, because it constitutes the keystone of all construction financing. Without the certain knowledge that a mortgage loan will be forthcoming, no other loans can be obtained, and the project cannot be built unless the owner pays all of the bills with his own money.

1

1.1 The Mortgage Loan

There are several sources from which a developer can obtain permanent financing for his project. The source to approach depends on the size and nature of his project. In some instances a particular lending institution can handle any type and size of real estate venture. But there are some insurance companies, for example, that will not lend less than several hundred thousand dollars on any one package, while certain small savings and loan banks cannot lend more than $50,000 on any one job, being restricted by law because of their total financial status. However, even when a certain small bank is incapable of handling a larger loan, it can join forces temporarily with several other such banks, and each will participate in a given loan, thus forming a joint venture in financing. In that case the originating bank handles the details of getting together the total sum requested by the developer. It is not at all necessary, therefore, for the developer to approach all of the participating banks separately to arrange the details of the joint venture—all of this is worked out for him by the originating bank.

1.1.1 Lending Institutions

Although all of the various institutions that lend money for a long term on real estate projects are often called banks, there are actually five types of lending institutions:

1. Savings and Loan Associations.
2. Insurance Companies.
3. Quasi-governmental corporations.
4. Pension funds and other trusts.
5. Real estate investment trusts (REIT's).

1.1.2 Mortgage Brokers

Each of the five sources enumerated above has certain advantages and disadvantages when compared with the other four, and within each type there are several companies. To avoid the guesswork of trying to choose the specific company that has the funds for the particular project being proposed, and to save considerable time, it is usually advisable to employ the services of a mortgage broker. In fact, it is sometimes impossible to approach certain companies without going through a broker. A mortgage broker does not provide his own funds for any project. He is a professional whose job it is to obtain mortgages and then to service these mortgages after construction is completed.

1.1.2.1. The mortgage broker has several sources of funds and is in constant touch with the money market. As stated above, not only are there several types of sources of funds, but also within each type, such as insurance companies, there are a large number of banks to choose from, any one of which may or may not be interested in a specific project in a certain location. Furthermore, every one of them has slight variations in the information required for approval of a loan application and can turn down a request if the wrong data is presented, if there is insufficient data, or if the data is not presented in a form approved by the institution. The mortgage broker is thoroughly familiar with all of their vagaries and idiosyncrasies and can not only choose the proper source for any given project at any given time but can also greatly expedite the request directed toward that source.

1.1.2.2. The broker must be fair to both the lender and the borrower. If, for example, he persuades the bank to put too much money into a given project, that project will find itself in grave financial difficulty. The mortgage payments will be so large that other obligations cannot be met, and the owner, unable to pay all his bills, will abandon the project, turning it back to the mortgagor. Lending institutions do not want to be landlords—they are in the money business, not in the real estate business. Therefore, if the broker is overly optimistic and presents figures that are not realistic, the lenders will soon quit trusting him and will refuse to finance any projects coming from his office. This means that all of his sources of funds will dry up, and he will be out of business. On the other hand, the broker cannot be too pessimistic either. If a prospective borrower has enough confidence in his project to invest a large sum of his own money in it and can show that it will be successful if he gets the proper financing, it is the broker's job to obtain that amount of money for his client rather than some lesser amount. If the broker can rarely get enough money to do the job, he soon will not have any customers, and, again, he will be out of business.

1.1.2.3.   Before the broker approaches one of the lending institutions with which he is associated, he will visit the site of the proposed project and give his opinion of the venture. If he is not favorably impressed, he will refuse to do any more work. It is then sometimes possible to persuade him that the project is a worthwhile one by presenting strong arguments in its favor. These arguments should include "a pretty picture and a price"—that is, (*a*) preliminary designs by an architect which show the layout in sketch form, the appearance of the various buildings, and an overall view of the project; and (*b*) a detailed explanation of cost and value. (The presentation of cost and value will be explained in Chapter 4.) Once the broker is convinced in his own mind as to the feasibility of the proposal, he will work hard toward obtaining adequate financing for it. His fee will generally be about 2% of the mortgage.

1.1.2.4.   In the event that the broker remains unconvinced, another broker should be contacted. If it is not possible to find even one who likes the project, in all likelihood the idea should be abandoned, and the land should be considered for some other use or should be sold as fast as possible.

1.1.3 Smaller Loans

It is not always necessary to work with a mortgage broker. For a mortgage on a small project, be it a house or a group of houses, a small apartment building, or a relatively small office building or warehouse, for example, it is probably advantageous to go to a savings and loan bank and present the request directly to the mortgage loan officer. The advantage of this procedure over going through a mortgage broker lies in a saving in time and money. Particularly on larger projects, an application for a loan made through a mortgage broker requires about 30 days for approval or disapproval. But not only does the mortgage loan officer of a savings bank do his work without a broker's fee, he can also determine within a few days whether or not the bank's loan committee has approved the application. He himself does not have the authority to make a loan in the name of the bank, but he can and will either encourage or discourage the making of an application after the proposition has been explained to him. In that sense he acts somewhat in the role of the mortgage broker. Similarly, at the time he is approached, he will state the going rate of interest and the length in years of the indebtedness, and he will explain all the fees that will have to be paid.

1.1.3.1.   An application for a loan on a smaller real estate project should include *plans, specifications*, and often a *financial statement* of the borrower. The architectural plans should be fairly complete. In the case of a single house they can be drawn by the builder, but for all other projects they must be drawn by an architect. The term "plans" is meant to include the plot plan, as made by a surveyor, and should also include a legal description of the land. The lot number, block number (if any), and name of the subdivision will generally suffice for a house or other relatively small building. The specifications on houses and certain other projects can be rather skimpy, but on an office building, for example, they are usually precise and extensive, even though the building itself is not very large. The financial statement of the borrower should be presented on a standard form furnished by the bank.

1.1.3.2.   The bank is generally familiar with the area, because a loan for a small project is usually made with a bank in the same locale. The banker will then know the borrower, and he will also be familiar with the site, so that he will have a far greater "feeling" for the project than some banker far removed geographically would have. Because of this intimacy, so to speak, the bank can make a decision quite rapidly. Usually, the bank's loan committee meets once or twice each week to decide on all applications, so the answer to a request for a well documented loan rarely takes more than one week.

1.1.4 Closing Costs

All of the fees mentioned in Section 1.1.3 are included in the closing costs. For a comparatively small project they consist of *discount, legal*, and *recording fees*. For larger real estate ventures other items would also be included, as will be seen later.

1.1.4.1 DISCOUNT.   The discount is a percentage of the loan that must be paid to the bank for the privilege of borrowing the money.

It is sometimes called the *origination fee*, and may have even other names, but it simply amounts to an increase in the effective interest rate. For example, if the loan officer states that the discount will be 2 points, what he means is that for every $100 that is borrowed, the borrower will actually receive only $98, "2 points" being the equivalent of 2%. But the borrower will have to pay back $100, plus the interest on $100 rather than the interest on the $98 actually received, thus, in effect, raising the true interest rate about $\frac{1}{2}$ of 1%. The bank's justification for an origination fee is that the money so obtained is used to pay for the time of the loan officer and the time of the loan committee and for setting up a file on the loan. The banks could just as well eliminate the discount and increase the interest rate slightly, but perhaps they believe that the loans are more palatable this way. In any event, the discount is unavoidable; it is a way of life and must be paid wherever this type of business is transacted.

1.1.4.2 LEGAL FEE. The legal fee is paid to the bank's attorney. Here again there is no choice. The bank will not accept work done by the borrower's attorney, nor will it permit substitutions of title insurance for a part of the legal work, nor will it accept an opinion of title to the land by anyone else, even if he is the world's leading authority on real estate law. The opinion of title, together with all other necessary documents, must be prepared by the bank's attorney, and the borrower must pay the fee that he sets. In all fairness, it must be said that his fee will not be exorbitant and that he and the bank have worked together on so many jobs that the paperwork will go along much more smoothly if he is the attorney of record. Furthermore, it is always fair and ethical for one attorney to have two clients when he draws up an agreement between two parties that are in accord, and the processing of a loan is consistent with this practice. Although the borrower and the bank share the services of the same attorney, the borrower pays his entire fee. The various papers that the attorney draws up are called "legal instruments."

1.1.4.3 NOTE VERSUS MORTGAGE. The borrower will be required to sign two legal instruments, a *note* and a *mortgage*. The note is evidence of indebtedness and constitutes a personal pledge to pay back the amount borrowed. As an example, look at any paper money. Notice on the front of the bill the words "Federal Reserve Note" along the top, and near the top notice the sentence "This note is legal tender for all debts, public and private." A note, then, is transferrable and can be given or sold from one party to another. A mortgage, on the other hand, is evidence of security. It shows that, if the party who issued the note cannot pay it when it falls due, he has a tangible item of equal value which can be taken as payment in full as, for example, an automobile or furniture or a piece of land, any of which must be described in great detail. If part of the note has been paid and there remains only a balance at the time of default, the property would be auctioned or sold and the proceeds of the sale used to pay off the balance of the note, with any excess cash from the sale, after the note and legal fees are paid, going to the original owner. The security instrument known as a mortgage is recorded in an appropriate book at the county courthouse, so that any future holder of the note can always be assured of value, without any misunderstandings or prior claims against the asset that is mortgaged.

1.1.4.4 RECORDING FEES. The recording fees include the charges levied by the appropriate county officer for recording the mortgage, as well as any taxes levied by the state and federal governments on such transactions. Like all other parts of the closing costs, these fees and taxes must be paid solely by the borrower. The total amount of all the closing costs can be as much as 4% of the value of the property.

1.1.4.5. All of the closing costs mentioned above will be present in every kind of real estate transaction, whenever money is borrowed from a bank as part of that transaction.

1.1.5 Commitment

Let us suppose now that the application for a mortgage loan has been submitted to a mortgage broker. He has put it into a form acceptable to a certain bank and has forwarded it to that institution, perhaps even appearing in person to plead the case. Suppose further that after careful consideration the loan committee of the lender has approved the application. At this point no money will change hands. Instead, the bank will issue a formal statement which commits it to lending a specified sum of money to a specified borrower, provided the borrower fulfills the several conditions set forth in the statement. That document (the statement) is called a *commitment* and is sent from the bank to its agent, the mortgage broker, who then puts it into his own form and transmits it to his client, the borrower.

1.1.5.1.   The commitment shown as Figure 1.1 will now be explained in detail. This is a form that was used by one particular broker. It is not universal, each company having its own approach, but it is typical and contains almost everything that every other commitment would have. Once the commitment is signed by the borrower, it becomes a binding contract: the borrower must construct the project according to the plans he submitted and according to any modifications contained in the commitment, and the lender must then furnish the stipulated sum of money at the stated interest rate for the stated period of time.

1.1.5.2.   As can be seen in the heading of the commitment (Figure 1.2) the mortgage broker in this case was the Jacksonville National Bank. The borrower was the Prime Meridian Corporation, whose president was Mr. James Rhoden. The lender was the Metropolitan Life Insurance Company. The lender's file number is C-1817, which has no significance whatsoever.

1.1.5.3 FIRST MORTGAGES AND OTHER MORTGAGES.   The application was made for a *first* mortgage loan. It is possible to have any number of mortgages on the same property. There could be a first mortgage, a second mortgage, a third mortgage, and so on, or there could be a first mortgage and two second mortgages. As an example, a motel might have a first mortgage on the building, a second mortgage on the land, and a third mortgage on the furnishings. The difference between a first mortgage and a second mortgage is not explained by timing; that is, it is not necessarily an indication of which mortgage was placed first on the property and which one was put on later. It is, rather, a ranking of importance. The second mortgage is beneath or junior to the first mortgage rather than alongside it and is subsidiary to the first mortgage; that is, the first mortgage takes precedence over the second mortgage. Payments are made first to the first mortgage, then to the second mortgage, and then to any other bills that have to be paid. Of course, payments could be made

JACKSONVILLE NATIONAL BANK

TELEPHONE (904) 355-2881 / 47 WEST FORSYTH STREET / P. O. BOX 2017 / JACKSONVILLE, FLORIDA 32203

MORTGAGE LOAN COMMITMENT

TO: Mr. James Rhoden
Prime Meridian Corporation
823 Thomasville Road
Tallahassee, Florida

BORROWER: Prime Meridian Corporation

RE: Metropolitan Submission No. C-1817

Your application for a 1st mortgage loan has been approved and we have received a commitment from
METROPOLITAN LIFE INSURANCE COMPANY
for the permanent financing of property described below, containing the following provisions, and attached Special
Conditions:

LOCATION OF PROPERTY: NE/C Ocala Road and Continental Avenue, Tallahassee, Florida

SIZE OF PLOT: Approx. 433,870 square feet irregular

IMPROVEMENTS: 12 - 2 story, brick veneer with plywood, stucco finish apartment buildings, 140 families, 623 rooms, 178 full baths and 20 1/2 baths. On-lot parking for 286 cars.

LOAN AMOUNT $1,450,000   INTEREST RATE: 7.500   TERM: 22   4 months   YEARS

REPAYABLE: Monthly installments of $ 11,177.00 including interest. Such installment shall commence not later than the first day of the 3rd month following the closing of the loan to the Borrower. Interest only shall be paid on the first day of each month, prior to the commencement of amortization. Commencing with the closing of the loan, and thereafter until otherwise elected by the investor, the Borrower (XX) shall ( ) shall not be required to make deposits for taxes, assessments and similar charges with each installment.

PREPAYMENT PRIVILEGE: Closed 1st 10 years from date amortization begins; payment in full 11th year at 3% prepayment fee declining 1/2% per year thereafter to par. 60 days written notice.
INSURABLE VALUE: $1,600,000 including fixtures and personalty valued at $107,000.

SPECIFIC FIXTURES &
PERSONALTY ON WHICH LIEN
IS REQUIRED:
140 Ranges
140 Refrigerators
140 Dishwashers
All carpeting approximately 10,800 square yards

Deadline for Acceptance
of this Commitment: March 29, 1968   LIQUIDATED DAMAGES: $14,500.00 *
* See Reverse Side

TERM OF COMMITMENT: Expires: 9/13/69: It is understood and agreed if this loan is to be closed within the term of this commitment, all closing documents shall be submitted to Jacksonville National Bank's Legal Representatives for approval on or before 21 days prior to the expiration date of the Commitment:

SPECIAL CONDITIONS: It is understood and agreed this Commitment is subject to the 15 printed conditions on Page 2 of this Commitment, as well as the 16 thru 29 Special Conditions on the following pages.

This commitment is not assignable without the expressed written approval of Jacksonville National Bank
This Commitment will expire 9/13/69 as indicated above, by which time the final advance must
be made and the loan assigned to

METROPOLITAN LIFE INSURANCE COMPANY

In order that our records may be complete we would appreciate your acknowledging your acceptance of the terms
and conditions of this commitment on the duplicate of this commitment and return same to this office.

Very truly yours,

ACCEPTED: Date March 29, 1968
BERKSHIRE MANORS, Ltd.
BY:
as amended by letter attached

JACKSONVILLE NATIONAL BANK

Real Estate Officer

Fig. 1.1 Commitment for a loan.

1. **Assignment of Security; The Mortgage; Absence of Liens.** The evidence of indebtedness (herein called the "Note"), the security instrument (herein called the "Mortgage") and each other instrument required by us as security for the Loan shall be transferred to us in form and manner satisfactory to us. The Note shall be secured by a Mortgage which shall be a first lien on the unencumbered, marketable, fee simple absolute title to the real property, to easements appurtenant thereto (if any) and to all improvements to the property described in this Commitment and in the Loan Submission (herein collectively called the "Real Property"), free of the possibility of any (a) prior mechanics' liens, (b) prior materialmen's liens or (c) special assessments for work completed or under construction on the date of our purchase of the Loan. Any title exceptions will be subject to the approval of our Law Division.

2. **Chattel Mortgage.** If the first page hereof requires a lien to be obtained on specific fixtures and personal property, a Chattel Mortgage (or other lien satisfactory to our Law Division) constituting a first lien on all fixtures and personal property used in the operation of the Real Property (other than trade fixtures of space tenants) shall be assigned to us. Such fixtures and personal property shall be free of conditional sales contracts and other title retention arrangements and we shall be furnished with an opinion of our local attorney, or other evidence satisfactory to us, to that effect.

3. **No Adverse Change.** Except as may be otherwise required by this Commitment, the Loan, the rental income of the Real Property, the credit of the Borrower and all other features of the transaction shall be as offered in the Loan Submission without material, adverse change. No part of the Real Property shall have been damaged and not repaired to our satisfaction nor taken in condemnation or other like proceeding, nor shall any such proceeding be pending. Neither the Borrower nor any tenant under any assigned lease, nor any guarantor of the Loan or any such lease, shall be involved in any bankruptcy, reorganization or insolvency proceeding.

4. **No Default.** No default shall have occurred and be continuing in the performance of any obligation in the instruments evidencing, securing, supporting or transferring the Loan.

5. **Hazard Insurance.** Original paid-up fire and extended coverage insurance policies of companies, and in form, acceptable to us containing the non-contributory New York Standard Mortgagee Clause or its equivalent in our favor shall be delivered to us. Unless a greater amount is required by a typewritten condition of this Commitment, the insurance shall be in an amount not less than the greater of (a) the Loan Amount shown on the first page hereof or (b) the amount obtained by multiplying the insurable value shown on the first page hereof by any applicable coinsurance percentage. If the Loan Amount exceeds such insurable value the amount of insurance shall be not less than such insurable value.

6. **Survey.** A survey and licensed surveyor's certificate dated not more than six months prior to the date of our purchase of the Loan and after the completion of all improvements shall be furnished to us. The survey shall show the dimensions and total square foot area of the plot, interior lot lines, if any, the dimensions and location of all improvements, parking areas, and easements, and the location of adjoining streets and the distance to and name of the nearest intersecting street.

7. **Title Policy.** An American Title Association Additional Coverage (or Revised if Additional Coverage cannot be obtained) form of title policy for the Loan Amount (or other form of title evidence acceptable to us) shall be delivered to us insuring us as the holder of the Mortgage as described in paragraph 1 above. Such policy shall be issued by a title company acceptable to us.

8. **Taxes and Assessments.** All taxes and assessments affecting the Real Property or any part thereof due and payable on the date of our purchase shall have been paid. Unless otherwise expressly permitted by this Commitment, all special assessments affecting the Real Property or any part thereof shall also have been paid and discharged, whether or not (a) confirmed, (b) payable in instalments or (c) constituting a lien against the Real Property or any part thereof.

9. **Compliance with Governmental Regulations.** Certificates of Occupancy, if obtainable, and other evidence satisfactory to us shall be furnished that all improvements and their use comply fully with all applicable zoning, building and other governmental laws and requirements. The Loan and our purchase thereof shall in all respects be legal and shall not violate any applicable law or other requirement of any governmental authority.

10. **Other Documents.** The full amount of the Loan that we are requested to disburse shall have been paid to the Borrower and an estoppel affidavit signed by the Borrower shall be furnished to us stating the amount then unpaid on the Note and that no defenses or set-offs exist with respect thereto. A Certificate as to Disbursement and such other documents and certificates as we shall require shall also be furnished.

11. **Mortgage to Provide for Tax Deposits.** The Mortgage shall require the Borrower, at the election of the mortgagee, to pay concurrently with each instalment of principal and interest payable on the Note, such amount as in the mortgagee's discretion will enable the mortgagee to pay (out of the monies so paid to the mortgagee) at least 30 days before due, all taxes, assessments and similar charges affecting the Real Property. No interest shall be payable on such deposits.

12. **Approval by our Law Division.** Each document required in connection with our purchase of the Loan shall be delivered to, and shall be in form and substance acceptable to, our Law Division. Without limiting the generality of the foregoing, the detailed legal description of the Real Property set forth in the Mortgage shall be acceptable to our Law Division. The survey, title report and drafts of all documents shall be submitted to our Law Division before execution.

• 13. **Expenses.** Unless otherwise expressly provided in this Commitment letter, you by your acceptance hereof agree that, regardless of whether or not we purchase the loan, we shall not be liable for any, and you will arrange for the payment of all, expenses, fees and charges in respect of the Loan and its transfer to us, or in any way connected therewith, including, without limiting the generality thereof, survey costs, brokerage commissions, title costs, recording charges, mortgage taxes and revenue stamps. Your obligation for expenses, fees and charges under this Commitment shall be in addition to your obligation to pay the amount of liquidated damages, if any, referred to on the first page hereof.

14. **Subject to Contract; Assignability.** This Commitment is, and the Loan shall be after its purchase by us, subject to the terms and provisions of your correspondent contract with us and the Loan shall be serviced by you pursuant to the terms and provisions of said contract. This Commitment may not be assigned without our written consent.

15. **Oral Changes; Paragraph Titles.** This Commitment cannot be changed, discharged, or terminated orally, but only by an instrument in writing signed by the party against whom enforcement of any change, discharge or termination is sought. Paragraph titles herein are for convenience only and shall not affect the construction hereof.

The undersigned has obligated itself to pay to Jacksonville National Bank the sum of $14,500.00 as liquidated damages in the event the loan contemplated hereby is not made before the expiration date hereof. If the loan contemplated hereby is not made before the expiration date hereof you agree to pay to the Jacksonville National Bank the amount shown above as liquidated damages.

Fig. 1.1 (*Continued*)

10

Correspondent: _____Jacksonville National Bank_____

Submission Number____C-1817____ Page __3__ of Commitment Letter Dated ____March 13, 1968____

As recited in the first paragraph on page 1 of this Commitment, the following conditions are also to be satisfied prior to or concurrently with our purchase of the Loan:

~~15.~~

16. PLANS AND SPECIFICATIONS. Detailed plans and specifications for all improvements shall be submitted to our Architect.

17. COMPLETION OF CONSTRUCTION. The building or buildings and all other improvements contemplated by this Commitment and the Loan Submission (including any grading, seeding, and landscaping and all other on-site and off-site improvements) shall be completed in accordance with plans and specifications to be approved in writing by our Architect and shall be equipped and paid for to our satisfaction, and each such building shall be ready for occupancy. Our representatives shall have the right to inspect all such improvements periodically during and after construction. Periodic inspections during construction shall be made, and construction shall be approved, by our Architect.

18. AGREEMENT WITH CONSTRUCTION LENDER. At the time of execution of the construction loan documents, the construction lender shall agree to sell the Loan to you and you shall agree, subject to all the terms, including the satisfaction of each of the conditions, of this Commitment, to buy the Loan from the construction lender and both the Borrower and you shall consent to such agreement.

19. COMBINED CONSTRUCTION - PERMANENT LOAN. The terms of the construction loan documents shall be such as to meet all the requirements in this Commitment which are to be complied with on the date of our purchase of the Loan. Prior to the commencement of construction, the combined construction and permanent mortgage shall be recorded or filed for record.

20. RENT ROLL. The annual rental (including rental for parking) from not more than 81 percent of the apartments in the buildings on an unfurnished basis with the landlord paying for cold water only, shall be not less than $226,000, and the space rented shall be rented on a basis so that if the buildings were 100% rented, the annual rental would be at least $280,000. Such apartments shall be occupied by tenants on a current, rent-paying basis under written leases or rental agreements of at least 1 year terms. The Borrower shall have given to you a rent roll certified to be correct indicating the apartments and annual rentals therefrom relied upon to satisfy this condition. You shall send the rent roll to us and certify to us that you have examined the rent roll and the leases or rental agreements and have checked the occupancy of the Real Property to establish the accuracy of the rent roll statement. No rental concessions to tenants shall have been made and your certificate should so state.

If on the date of our purchase of the Loan said annual rental has not been achieved on the foregoing basis, the maximum amount of the Loan will be $1,200,000 and there shall be appropriate adjustments in the instalment payments, cash fee and net interest rate.

21. STREET DEDICATION. Evidence shall be submitted that all streets adjoining the Real Property have been completed, dedicated and accepted for maintenance and public use by the appropriate governmental authorities.

22. If, at any time, during the term of this commitment, the property, in our judgment, has been sufficiently completed and has otherwise complied with the terms of our commitment, including rental achievements if any, the loan is to be tendered to us for purchase within 60 days of such completion and compliance, and amortization is to commence in accordance with the terms of our commitment.

(continued)

Fig. 1.1 *(Continued)*

Correspondent: Jacksonville National Bank

Submission Number C-1817 Page 4 of Commitment Letter Dated March 13, 1968

As recited in the first paragraph on page 1 of this Commitment, the following conditions are also to be satisfied prior to or concurrently with our purchase of the Loan:

23. At our option, this commitment may be terminated unless within 30 days from the date of your acceptance hereof, we receive a letter, in form and substance satisfactory to us, from a bank that it will furnish sufficient funds so that the building or buildings will be completed in accordance with the terms and conditions of this commitment.

24. At our option, this commitment may be terminated unless actual construction is started within 90 days from the date of the above required letter from the construction lender, and is diligently pursued thereafter, except for circumstances beyond the borrower's control.

25. ADDITION TO CONDITION #2 - CHATTEL MORTGAGE. In addition to the first lien which we require on items of equipment specified on Page 1 of this commitment, we require a lien upon the borrower's equity in all other personal property at any time located on the mortgaged premises or used in connection with the operation of said premises.

26. INTEREST EQUALIZATION TAX. We shall not be obligated to purchase the loan unless we are furnished with evidence, satisfactory to our Law Department that the transaction is not subject to the Interest Equalization Tax.

27. The Borrower shall submit to the Metropolitan an annual statement of the gross rents collected. The statement shall be certified by a C.P.A. and the Borrower shall submit to the Metropolitan 10% of the gross rents collected in excess of $280,000. The statement and payment shall be submitted annually within 90 days from the closing of the books.

28. In the event of any conveyance or transfer of any of the property covered by the lien of our mortgage or in event of any internal change in the members of the Borrower corporation, Borrower shall, at the option of the lender, make an additional payment of principal in accord with the amortization schedule within 30 days thereafter, so as to reduce the unpaid principal balance of the loan to an amount not in excess of $1,350,000.

29. In addition to any requirements of our Architect we shall require:

    1. Reversal of the fixture wall or adequate sound proofing of the interior bath/dinning area wall in the F, K, & L units.

    2. Marble or ceramic tile window sills.

    3. Vinyl wallpaper or ceramic tile on bath fixture walls and ceramic tile base moulding.

    4. Cast iron tubs.

Fig. 1.1 (*Continued*)

JACKSONVILLE NATIONAL BANK

TELEPHONE (904) 355-2881 / 47 WEST FORSYTH STREET / P. O. BOX 2017 / JACKSONVILLE, FLORIDA 32203

MORTGAGE LOAN COMMITMENT

TO: Mr. James Rhoden   BORROWER: **Prima Meridian Corporation**
Prime Meridian Corporation
823 Thomasville Road
Tallahassee, Florida

RE: **Metropolitan Submission No. C-1817**

Your application for a 1st mortgage loan has been approved and we have received a commitment from
METROPOLITAN LIFE INSURANCE COMPANY
for the permanent financing of property described below, containing the following provisions, and attached Special
Conditions:

Fig. 1.2

to both mortgages simultaneously. However, if there is a default in payments to the first mortgage, the bank that owns this mortgage takes possession of the property after due process in the courts. The property is then usually sold at auction, and the proceeds from the sale are used to pay off the first mortgage. If there is any additional cash left, it is to used to pay off the second mortgage; if there are two second mortgages, the money is divided between them. If any money still remains, it goes to the former owner. By extension, one could add a third mortgage behind the second mortgage, before the owner.

1.1.5.4.   On the other hand, if the first mortgage is paid in full but there is a default on the second mortgage, the bank that owns the second mortgage cannot take over the property and sell it at auction. That course of action is the sole prerogative of the bank that has the first mortgage. The bank or person who holds a bad second mortgage or third mortgage may be able to protect his investment only by buying up the position of the owner. The second lender thus becomes the owner of the property in order to protect his holdings. This is an expensive, difficult operation which involves a lot of legal work.

1.1.5.5.   It is possible to have two first mortgages, but this is highly unlikely. Generally, any bank which places a first mortgage requires that there be absolutely no other first mortgages.

1.1.5.6 SUBORDINATION.   In all cases of multiple mortgages on one piece of property, the mortgages other than the first mortgage are called *subordinated*. In fact, the lender of the first mortgage will demand that all other mortgages be subordinated to his position, and they will be so entered in the county records. The term "subordinated" means that these mortgages are inferior in value and junior to the claims of the first mortgage. A third mortgage is subordinate to the second mortgage, which is, in turn, subordinate to the first mortgage.

1.1.5.7.   Again, bear in mind that the numbering of the mortgages indicates not timing, but rather importance or subordination. It is even possible to obtain a second mortgage before getting a first one. In such a case the lender of the second mortgage will agree to subordination to a future first mortgage. Sometimes this is done when land is being purchased. If the seller agrees to it, such an arrangement has a beneficial result for the developer, since he thus ties up only a minimal amount of working capital. The mortgage so obtained is recorded immediately in the county records as a second mortgage, subordinated to a future first mortgage. If no first mortgage is ever placed on the property, then the second mortgage, being the only debt on the land, is a first mortgage. However, sometimes first mortgage lenders require that the developer own the land outright, free and clear of all debts and encumbrances, as will soon be seen in the commitment being studied. In such a case, the procedure outlined above cannot be followed, and the land must be purchased for cash, because a recorded second mortgage, even if subordinated, will not do. Methods of buying land will be discussed in Chapter 3.

1.1.5.8.   The next items in the document constitute a description of the project (Figure 1.3), consisting of the location of the property, the size of the plot, and the proposed construction. Although the property location is sometimes given in a full legal description,

LOCATION OF PROPERTY: NE/C Ocala Road and Continental Avenue, Tallahassee, Florida

SIZE OF PLOT: Approx. 433,870 square feet irregular

IMPROVEMENTS: 12 - 2 story, brick veneer with plywood, stucco finish apartment buildings, 140 families, 623 rooms, 178 full baths and 20 1/2 baths.   On-lot parking for 286 cars.

Fig. 1.3

involving township, range, bearing, and length, in this case it is simply described as the Northeast Corner of Ocala Road and Continental Avenue, Tallahassee, Florida, which really establishes it quite well, particularly when the size of the plot is included. This is the parcel that was inspected by the broker, and the lender is requiring that the project be built on that approved site. Although no drawings are contained in the commitment, drawings were submitted in order to obtain it. Therefore, the commitment states that the project must be built with 12 buildings containing the 140 dwelling units that were shown on the designs submitted.

1.1.5.9. It can now be seen that the preliminary plans should not be off-the-cuff rough sketches of some idealistic dream; they should, rather, be thoroughly thought out and carefully presented, showing only that which is actually going to be built. In one case, for example, an architect sketched a beautiful oak tree in front of an office building on the preliminary design. The bank later insisted that this oak tree be planted by the builder, claiming that it had been induced to make the loan because of the appearance of that tree in front of the building. The builder had to put it in, at a large unplanned expense. The mortgage is granted for a specific project, and the project must be built just as it was submitted for approval.

1.1.5.10 DISCOUNTS AND FEES. The document next shows a description of the loan and the method of repayment (Figure 1.4). The interest rate is shown as $7\frac{1}{2}\%$ but is actually somewhat higher because of discount points. Large lenders require points just as does a small savings and loan bank. Often on a large loan the fee will be 1% of the mortgage, which is above and beyond the 2 points charged by the broker. Thus, for this mortgage of $1,450,000, the Metropolitan Life Insurance Company charges 0.01 × $1,450,000 =

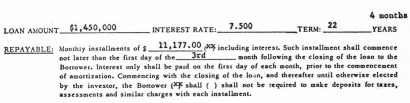

LOAN AMOUNT __$1,450,000__ INTEREST RATE: __7.500__ TERM: __22__ __4 months__ YEARS

REPAYABLE: Monthly installments of $ __11,177.00__ (x) including interest. Such installment shall commence not later than the first day of the __3rd__ month following the closing of the loan to the Borrower. Interest only shall be paid on the first day of each month, prior to the commencement of amortization. Commencing with the closing of the loan, and thereafter until otherwise elected by the investor, the Borrower (x) shall ( ) shall not be required to make deposits for taxes, assessments and similar charges with each installment.

Fig. 1.4

$14,500, and the broker, the Jacksonville National Bank, will charge an additional fee of $29,000.

1.1.5.11 IMPORTANCE OF TIME OF MORTGAGE. The term of the mortgage is just as important to the financial success of a project as the interest rate. The same interest rate will require smaller monthly payments for a long than for a short period of time. For example, an interest rate of $7\frac{1}{2}\%$ for a term of 30 years when applied to the mortgage of $1,450,000 would require monthly payments of $10,231 rather than the $11,177 shown, whereas a rate of $7\frac{1}{2}\%$ and a time of 15 years would mean monthly payments of $13,689 on the same mortgage.

1.1.5.12 THE CONSTANT. The commitment shows a term of 22 years and 4 months, which comes to 268 months and payments of $11,177 per month. This means that the mortgage will be amortized, that is, paid off in full at the end of 268 months. Meanwhile the total paid each year will be $12 \times \$11,177 = \$134,124$, which is $9\frac{1}{4}\%$ of the loan amount of $1,450,000. This percentage is called *the constant;* that is, this mortgage has a 9.25 constant. This means that there is the same constant payment, or level constant payment, each and every year for the life of the mortgage. If the term had been for 30 years with a $7\frac{1}{2}\%$ interest rate, the constant would have been 8.47; whereas, if the term had been for 15 years, the constant would have been 11.33. In all cases the payments include both interest and principal when a level constant payment is called for.

1.1.5.13. Not very many years ago most developers felt that the highest constant a project could safely sustain was 9; that is to say, 9% of the face amount of the mortgage could safely be paid as the yearly installment. In other words, if the mortgage were for $100, the yearly payment would be $9 including principal and interest. Of course, a lower constant would be preferable. Yet today it is not unusual to see constants of $9\frac{1}{4}$, $9\frac{1}{2}$, or even 10 or more. Apparently, developers now feel that the rate of repayment on a mortgage is immaterial, provided that the net cash profit is satisfactory. This change is due, in part, to a realization of a higher apparent constant for inflation. In other words, the lender is getting back dollars in later years that are worth less in terms of purchasing power than they were when the loan was made. But the developer is gambling that he can rent the property at a higher rate later on, and still have good occupancy. That is a risky position to adopt.

1.1.5.14 BALLOON NOTES. Most first mortgage loans today require a uniform payment over the life of the debt, but it is possible, particularly on secondary mortgages, to obtain a *balloon note*. This is one on which only the interest is paid for a given period of time; at the end of that time the principal is paid in one lump sum. With a partial balloon note, some reduction in principal is made, but there still remains a relatively large principal payment due at final maturity. In some kinds of balloon notes no money is paid at all for the duration of the note; at the end of the period of time all of the accrued interest plus the principal is paid in one grand sum. The level constant payment, a balloon note type of repayment, and two other methods of debt repayment will be discussed more fully in Chapter 7.

1.1.5.15 GRACE PERIOD. In the commitment of Figure 1.1, in the paragraph labeled "REPAYABLE," notice that the installments of $11,177 will commence no later than the first day of the third month following the closing of the loan to the borrower. For the first 3 months the lender requires that only the interest be paid; nothing has to be paid against the principal. In other words, for the first 3 months the interest rate of $7\frac{1}{2}\%$ per year requires payments of $0.075 \times \$1,450,000 \div 12$ (months per year) $= \$9062.50$ per month, instead of $11,177 per month. This provision is intended to help the owner achieve a solid cash position and survive the initial rent-up period when he is trying to get enough tenants to make the project profitable. Furthermore, it will help the borrower to pay off any cost overruns and to have money available for advertising and rental expenses. In certain commercial ventures the period of interest-only payments is much longer than 3 months, sometimes extending for 1 or even $1\frac{1}{2}$ years before payments have to be made on both principal and interest.

1.1.5.16 ESCROWED ACCOUNTS. The commitment paragraph under consideration goes on to say that the borrower shall be required to make deposits for taxes, assessments, and similar charges with each installment. This means that every month the owner, instead of paying $11,177, must pay an additional amount sufficient to cover the taxes when they come due. If, for example, the real estate taxes on this project are $24,000 per year, then $\frac{1}{12}$ of $24,000 = $2000 additional will have to be paid each month, making the total monthly payment $11,177 + $2000 = $13,177. This tax money will be collected by the broker acting as agent for the lender. The broker will put the tax money into a separate bank account, called an *escrow account*. An escrow account is one that cannot be used by anybody for any purpose except the stated purpose for which it is intended. It cannot be lent out by the bank in which it is deposited. It cannot be used to cover delinquent mortgage payments. It cannot be used for anything except taxes, assessments, and similar charges. Quite often, mortgage lenders also require that insurance premiums be escrowed, so as to guarantee that the necessary money will be on hand when the insurance bill comes due.

1.1.5.17.   The requirement of an escrow account is made simply as protection for the lender. Regardless of what mortgages are recorded, real estate taxes always take first priority. Even if all mortgage payments are made on time, the government can take possession of the property and sell it at auction if the taxes have not been paid as required. The proceeds of the sale are used to pay first the back taxes and then the mortgage. This would be a rare and extreme situation, but it could happen. For this reason the lender insists that sufficient money be in the bank when the taxes come due. The necessity of fire and extended coverage insurance is obvious, as is the deed to have the money on hand to meet these premiums.

1.1.5.18 PREPAYMENT PRIVILEGE.   During the course of time interest rates fluctuate because money is a commodity, just like wheat or oil. When there is a lot of it in the banks and the demand by borrowers is light, the interest rate drops because the banks must rent out the money that is on deposit in order to realize a profit. Conversely, in times of short supply, the interest rate will rise. Since the lender in the commitment shown (Figure 1.5) wants to be sure of a return of $7\frac{1}{2}\%$ for a reasonable period of time, he states that the

---

PREPAYMENT PRIVILEGE: Closed 1st 10 years from date amortization begins; payment in full 11th year at 3% prepayment fee declining 1/2% per year thereafter to par.   60 days written notice.

Fig. 1.5

loan cannot be paid off in any shorter period than 10 years. It is, therefore, stated that the loan is "closed" for 10 years. A vernacular phrasing would be that the borrower is "locked in" for 10 years. If the borrower wants to pay off the balance remaining on the principal of the loan during the eleventh year, he will have to pay a penalty of 3% of that balance. If, for example, an unpaid balance of $800,000 remains on the loan at that time, he will have to pay the lender $800,000 + (0.03 × $800,000) = $824,000 to completely discharge his obligation. In the twelfth year, the penalty would be $2\frac{1}{2}\%$ of whatever the balance then is; in the thirteenth year it would be 2%; and so on, with no penalty after the sixteenth year. If the going rate of interest 5 years from the date on which the loan was funded is only 6%, the borrower still must pay $7\frac{1}{2}\%$—the payments remain level constant, and no change in terms is possible during the first 10 years. On the other hand, if after the first 5 years others are charged 10% on new loans, the borrower has the advantage of maintaining the original rate of $7\frac{1}{2}\%$. The constant payment does not fluctuate, nor does the interest rate. The bank insists only that the total loan cannot be paid off in less than 10 years. In any event, the bank demands that it be given 60 days' written notice before the balance of the loan can be paid off.

1.1.5.19 EQUITY. Suppose that the actual total cost of the entire project is estimated at $1,650,000. The total cost is called the *replacement cost*, and consists of the cost of the buildings, land, architect's services, mortgage broker's fee, and all other fees, points, and closing costs. The mortgage loan amount is to be $1,450,000, which is $200,000 less than the replacement cost. This balance of $200,000 in capital must be contributed by the developer and is called his *equity*. It is occasionally possible to obtain a mortgage that is greater than the replacement cost; in this case the owner has a negative equity position, and it is said that he "mortgaged out."

1.1.5.20 INSURABLE VALUE. The point is that the amount of the permanent loan is based not on the replacement cost, but rather on the economic value of the project. The economic value is determined by considering the project as a business rather than as a building or a collection of buildings sitting on a piece of land. As a business, the project will produce a certain number of dollars of profit each year, and it is these future dollars per year which are worth a present value.

This concept will be developed in Chapter 4. Meanwhile, suppose that the present project has a theoretical economic value of $1,866,250, on which the lender is willing to place a first mortgage of $1,450,000. His money will be used to pay for the construction of the buildings and for some of the fees. The equity money will pay for the land and the rest of the fees and costs. In order that his investment in the buildings be protected, the lender requires in this commitment (Figure 1.6) that the project be insured for approximately 80% of the economic value, that is, $0.80 \times \$1,866,250 = \$1,493,000$, plus additional insurance in the amount of $107,000 to cover movable items, for a total insured value of $1,600,000. Thus, if all the buildings burn to the ground, the amount of the mortgage will be covered, with a little to spare. Even in that case some value will remain in the land and in the underground utilities, among other things. So, at least in theory, the insurance will be enough to rebuild all the buildings to their original state, and the business will then continue to flourish. (It is advisable for the owner to get additional loss of income insurance, to cover the mortgage payments during the time that the buildings are being rebuilt.)

1.1.5.21 PERSONALTY. Personalty consists of all the items that are removable or replaceable, or that will wear out after a short period of time. For this apartment development, the personalty consists of ranges, refrigerators, dishwashers, and carpeting. The bank is insisting that it has a first mortgage on all these items by the clause "on which lien is required," and if the owner accepts the terms of the commitment, he is agreeing to this condition, even if he pays for some or all of these items with his own capital.

1.1.5.22. When preparing an application for a mortgage it is generally best to show as little as necessary—just enough to cover all the essentials, that is, just enough to make the project work. In this commitment no mention is made of furniture or drapes,

INSURABLE VALUE: $1,600,000 including fixtures and personalty valued at $107,000.

SPECIFIC FIXTURES & PERSONALTY ON WHICH LIEN IS REQUIRED:	140 Ranges 140 Refrigerators 140 Dishwashers All carpeting approximately 10,800 square yards

Fig. 1.6

because the developer did not show them on his plans. Thus the developer is now free to obtain a second mortgage on these items, thus giving him greater flexibility in his financing. All of the personalty that was shown, however, is included in the first mortgage with a specific restriction against placing a second mortgage on it, as will be seen later. The reason for such a restriction is that apartments cannot be rented, at least in Tallahassee, unless they contain ranges, refrigerators, dishwashers, and carpeting. Thus, if the bank must take over the property in case of default, it will be able to rent the units or will find it easier to sell the project.

1.1.5.23 DEADLINE FOR ACCEPTANCE (Figure 1.7). Generally the lender will give the borrower about 1 month to decide whether or not he wants to accept the proposed terms. During that time the borrower must arrange for construction financing and any other requisite short-term financing. The various types and methods of financing will be discussed later. If the short-term financing is unobtainable for any reason, the commitment cannot be accepted.

1.1.5.24 GOOD FAITH DEPOSIT. If the commitment is accepted, the borrower is required to deposit 1 point, that is, 1% of the mortgage, with the lender's agent at the time of acceptance. If the borrower then abandons the project or wants to take a loan from a different bank, this deposit is forfeited. In this case, a binder of $14,500 must be deposited with the mortgage broker as a guarantee that the borrower is neither playing games nor trying to "shop" the mortgage for the best possible terms. The broker will keep the deposit as payment for his time and effort in obtaining the commitment. Should the project proceed, this binder becomes part of the points and fees that must be paid. Sometimes at least one of the additional points will be accepted in the form of a note that is due and payable upon completion of the project, that is, when the funds from the permanent financing are issued.

1.1.5.25 TIME OF COMPLETION. Notice (Figure 1.8) that the term of commitment expires September 13, 1969. This means that all

Deadline for Acceptance
of this Commitment: March 29, 1968   LIQUIDATED DAMAGES: __$14,500.00__ *

Fig. 1.7

TERM OF COMMITMENT: Expires: 9/13/69___: It is understood and agreed if this loan is to be closed within the term of this commitment, all closing documents shall be submitted to Jacksonville National Bank's Legal Representatives for approval on or before 21 days prior to the expiration date of the Commitment:

Fig. 1.8

conditions of the commitment must be met on or before that date— in other words, the entire project must be substantially completed by then. Since the commitment was accepted on March 29, 1968, as shown by the signature of the president of the Prime Meridian Corporation, the developer had about $1\frac{1}{2}$ years to obtain clear title to the land, record the mortgage, complete the architectural work, start building, and finish all building. If the construction were not completed by September 13, 1969, the bank could review the case and decide against lending anything; or if it wished it could then raise the rate of interest, increase the constant, or even call for a penalty payment. Therefore, before a decision is made to accept a commitment, a developer should be quite certain that the proposed project can be completed within the stipulated time period, to avoid making a very expensive mistake.

1.1.5.26 NOT ASSIGNABLE.   Near the bottom of the first page of the commitment (Figure 1.9) the statement is made that this commitent is not assignable without approval of the mortgage broker. In other words, it has been made to the Prime Meridian Corporation because of the background, record of experience, managerial personnel, and financial responsibility of the corporation. In this respect a commitment is not a piece of merchandise that can be bought, sold, or traded. It is evidence of an agreement or contract that is to be made between two specific parties and only those two, unless the agent for the lender approves of a substitution for the

SPECIAL CONDITIONS: It is understood and agreed this Commitment is subject to the 15 printed conditions on Page 2 of this Commitment, as well as the 16 thru 29___ Special Conditions on the following pages.

This Commitment is not assignable without the expressed written approval of Jacksonville National Bank. This Commitment will expire 9/13/69___ as indicated above, by which time the final advance must be made and the loan assigned to

METROPOLITAN LIFE INSURANCE COMPANY

In order that our records may be complete we would appreciate your acknowledging your acceptance of the terms and conditions of this commitment on the duplicate of this commitment and return same to this office.

Fig. 1.9

borrower. This clause is inserted to eliminate promoters who put together a package and then sell it before construction without any substantial investment or involvement on their part, leaving the lender with a financially weak developer. The loan is not being made to the site or to the project, but to the developer, who has himself been approved by the mortgage broker.

1.1.5.27 CONSTRUCTION LOAN ASSIGNMENT. The next sentence in the commitment contains the clause "by which time the final advance must be made and the loan assigned to." This clause refers to the money coming from the construction lender, which is disbursed monthly in accordance with the progress of the work. From the time construction starts, the job may take several months or even a year or more to reach completion. During all this time no money will be forthcoming from the permanent lender. All the money necessary for construction must come either from the developer himself or from a construction lender. Some banks specialize in such loans; they will be discussed in section 1.2.

When the work is completed, the construction lender will issue the balance of his loan ("the final advance"). Note that this must take place on or before September 13, 1969. Shortly thereafter, the construction loan will be incorporated into the mortgage loan. The lender of the permanent financing will pay off the construction loan in full and issue a check for the balance to the borrower. (There will always be a balance, because the mortgage loan is always greater than the construction loan.) The borrower then has a long-term debt with the mortgage lender, and the construction loan is canceled.

1.1.5.28 SUBSIDIARY COMPANIES. Notice at the bottom of the page (Figure 1.10) that James L. Rhoden signed for Berkshire Manors, Ltd., rather than as president of Prime Meridian Corporation,

Very truly yours,

ACCEPTED: Date____March 29, 1968____

BERKSHIRE MANORS, Ltd.

BY: ____

(As amended, his letter attached)

JACKSONVILLE NATIONAL BANK

Real Estate Officer

Fig. 1.10

despite the clause regarding assignability. This was done because the original company set up a second company as a wholly owned subsidiary, solely for the purpose of building and managing this project. Undoubtedly there were certain advantages to this procedure for the parent company in the areas of accounting, taxes, and management. Since the ownership of both companies was identical, there was no problem in Mr. Rhoden's signing as he did.

1.1.5.29 ABSENCE OF LIENS. The various numbered paragraphs of the commitment will now be discussed. Paragraph 1 (Figure 1.11) explains quite clearly the difference between a note and a mortgage, and the reason why both are needed. It also emphasizes that their wording is quite important and therefore must be done in accordance with the requirements of the lender. The statement "The Note shall be secured by a Mortgage which shall be a first lien," means that in the case of default the lender has a prior claim to the property, before all others, with the possible exception of a tax lien, and the lender has protected himself against that contingency by the clause in the first page of the commitment which requires that taxes be deposited in an escrow account. In fact, in a legal sense, an owner does not have complete ownership of his property until all debts against that property have been paid. He has the use of it, and he has nominal ownership; however, the lien holder can snatch it away if a debt which has come due remains unpaid.

The commitment then goes on to require that the title to the land be "unencumbered, marketable, fee simple absolute." All this means simply that there should be no debts or claims outstanding against the land, that it can be easily sold if need be, and that the borrower has outright ownership of it. At the time the commitment is issued there exists only a piece of raw land under consideration; therefore the sentence goes on to require that the mortgage include any improvements, that is, any construction that is going to be put

1. Assignment of Security; The Mortgage; Absence of Liens. The evidence of indebtedness (herein called the "Note"), the security instrument (herein called the "Mortgage") and each other instrument required by us as security for the Loan shall be transferred to us in form and manner satisfactory to us. The Note shall be secured by a Mortgage which shall be a first lien on the unencumbered, marketable, fee simple absolute title to the real property, to easements appurtenant thereto (if any) and to all improvements to the property described in this Commitment and in the Loan Submission (herein collectively called the "Real Property"), free of the possibility of any (a) prior mechanics' liens, (b) prior materialmen's liens or (c) special assessments for work completed or under construction on the date of our purchase of the Loan. Any title exceptions will be subject to the approval of our Law Division.

Fig. 1.11

on or in the land, such as all paving, underground utilities, swimming pool, laundry, and the twelve buildings containing 140 dwelling units. Furthermore, after all construction is completed, all moneys owed for the construction shall have been paid; in other words, all workmen and material suppliers shall have been completely paid, and if the local government has put in any streets or utilities for the project, these too shall have been paid for completely, all before the mortgage money is issued. The final money will be turned over to the developer only if he can prove that there are no debts whatsoever outstanding against the property.

1.1.5.30 CHATTEL MORTGAGE. Whereas a real estate mortgage binds a piece of land and the building thereon, a chattel mortgage (Figure 1.12) is placed against movables, such as an automobile or a refrigerator. The chattel mortgage is one of the "other instruments" referred to in paragraph 1. In this case, it would encompass the 140 ranges, 140 refrigerators, 140 dishwashers, and the 10,800 square yards of carpeting to be included in the project. Carpeting is not *easily* movable, but is removable covering nonetheless. The lender is requiring that all of these items be owned outright by the developer and that there be no second mortgages on any of them. Thus all items necessary to the successful operation of the project will be there in case the bank has to take it over in the event of default.

1.1.5.31 TRADE FIXTURES. In the first sentence of paragraph 2 there is a clause that refers to "trade fixtures of space tenants." Such items could be display cases or freezer chests belonging to a tenant in a shopping center. In an apartment complex they would include the furniture of the tenants. These things are not owned by the project, nor are they included in the rent, nor is it essential that they be there before the space can be rented. Since the developer is not responsible for them and they should not be expected to remain on the premises, they are excluded from the chattel mortgage.

2. Chattel Mortgage. If the first page hereof requires a lien to be obtained on specific fixtures and personal property, a Chattel Mortgage (or other lien satisfactory to our Law Division) constituting a first lien on all fixtures and personal property used in the operation of the Real Property (other than trade fixtures of space tenants) shall be assigned to us. Such fixtures and personal property shall be free of conditional sales contracts and other title retention arrangements and we shall be furnished with an opinion of our local attorney, or other evidence satisfactory to us, to that effect.

Fig. 1.12

1.1.5.32 NO ADVERSE CHANGE. About 1 year, perhaps a little longer, will be required to complete the project from the day that work starts. The terms of the commitment will be satisfied even if it takes up to $1\frac{1}{2}$ years to complete the job. Now this commitment pledges the bank to come up with almost \$1,500,000 at some time in the future, which would be after 1 to $1\frac{1}{2}$ years from the date of signing. The lender wants to be sure that, when he finally funds the loan and produces the money, the borrower will be in a good financial condition and will not use the cash to pay off a stack of bills that have absolutely nothing to do with the project. Therefore the lender insists (Figure 1.13) that the financial statement of the borrower still be a sound one. After all, the bank was induced to make the loan partly because of the credit rating of the developer at the time the application for the loan was made.

The application of the loan also contained a certain rental schedule which led to an economic value, and this in turn was the basis for the size of the loan. Therefore the lender requires that the proposed rental schedule be adhered to or improved, with lowering of rents being a prohibited adverse change.

The bank also requires, as shown in the second sentence of paragraph 3, that the property be in good shape at the time the money is forthcoming. Anything damaged has to be repaired and put into first-class condition.

Finally, paragraph 3 speaks of bankruptcy and the like. Should the borrower, his company, or any of his partners ever get into grave financial difficulty, his other creditors will try to take anything of value that they can find. In such a situation, this first mortgage lender will immediately claim this property in order to preserve his investment, that is, his loan. In other words, the bank wants to make sure that no third party can take this property before the bank gets hold of it, in case of any financial disaster on the part of the borrower.

3. No Adverse Change. Except as may be otherwise required by this Commitment, the Loan, the rental income of the Real Property, the credit of the Borrower and all other features of the transaction shall be as offered in the Loan Submission without material, adverse change. No part of the Real Property shall have been damaged and not repaired to our satisfaction nor taken in condemnation or other like proceeding, nor shall any such proceeding be pending. Neither the Borrower nor any tenant under any assigned lease, nor any guarantor of the Loan or any such lease, shall be involved in any bankruptcy, reorganization or insolvency proceeding.

Fig. 1.13

4. No Default. No default shall have occurred and be continuing in the performance of any obligation in the instruments evidencing, securing, supporting or transferring the Loan.

Fig. 1.14

1.1.5.33 NO DEFAULT. Paragraph 4 (Figure 1.14) speaks of default, which is a failure to pay a financial obligation. The bank here requires not only that all labor and material bills shall have been paid, but also that all points or discounts, all legal fees, and all other "soft" costs associated with the project shall have been paid before the bank disburses any funds for which it has committed itself. This sentence is inserted to continue to insure that all moneys for the project go to the project, that all bills get paid, and that the proposition is a "clean" one.

It is possible that some of the bills will not have been paid at the time of final closing. This should be honestly stated by the developer at the final closing and can easily be handled at the time the cash passes across the table. A default is a special case—a bill which is so long past due that the debtor has taken legal action to collect it.

1.1.5.34 INSURANCE. The lending institution wants to protect itself in the best and fairest way possible. As pointed out previously, the insurance requirement is enough to rebuild the project in the case of total loss by fire. But in paragraph 5 (Figure 1.15) the bank demands that the insurance premium be paid in full before the permanent financing money reaches the borrower. This protects the bank in case a fire breaks out the very day the money changes hands. The lender is not taking any chances whatsoever!

Although the initial premium must be paid in full before the mortgage is funded, thereafter monthly payments would generally have to be paid into an escrow account to cover the next premium when it falls due. This escrow is not required here. But, as is done in this case, most banks will require that the insurance be taken out in their name ("in our favor"), so that, should any catastrophe

5. Hazard Insurance. Original paid-up fire and extended coverage insurance policies of companies, and in form, acceptable to us containing the non-contributory New York Standard Mortgagee Clause or its equivalent in our favor shall be delivered to us. Unless a greater amount is required by a typewritten condition of this Commitment, the insurance shall be in an amount not less than the greater of (a) the Loan Amount shown on the first page hereof or (b) the amount obtained by multiplying the insurable value shown on the first page hereof by any applicable coinsurance percentage. If the Loan Amount exceeds such insurable value the amount of insurance shall be not less than such insurable value.

Fig. 1.15

occur, the insurance company will pay the lender, not the borrower. This will guarantee that the money is used only to repair the damage, and for no other purpose.

Sometimes a 3-year policy can be obtained at a savings in the premium. In such an insurance, the entire amount is paid in advance.

1.1.5.35 SURVEY.   A survey (Figure 1.16) is vitally important in residential construction, particularly for one-family dwellings. This point will be discussed later in Chapter 5, which includes residential draw schedules. In the case of an apartment project, an office building complex, or the like, a survey is needed to prove that all buildings are properly located. If one building has not been set back far enough from the street, the building inspector is within his rights to deny the owner an occupancy permit; this means that no one can move into the building. Since it is almost impossible— certainly extremely expensive and gravely difficult—to move a building back, it usually remains unoccupied and useless. The survey will also show whether all improvements have been made in accordance with the design that was submitted to obtain the loan. In part, the attractive disposition of the buildings, the parking lot, and all other construction was the reason the loan was committed, and this is the reason why all the dimensions are requested in the second sentence of paragraph 6.

The survey after completion, when compared with the survey submitted with the loan application, will also indicate whether any part of the land has been sold during construction. The lender wants all the land that he bargained for.

1.1.5.36 TITLE INSURANCE.   Title insurance (Figure 1.17) is a single-payment policy. The premium is collected only once and will amount

6. Survey. A survey and licensed surveyor's certificate dated not more than six months prior to the date of our purchase of the Loan and after the completion of all improvements shall be furnished to us. The survey shall show the dimensions and total square foot area of the plot, interior lot lines, if any, the dimensions and location of all improvements, parking areas, and easements, and the location of adjoining streets and the distance to and name of the nearest intersecting street.

Fig. 1.16

7. Title Policy. An American Title Association Additional Coverage (or Revised if Additional Coverage cannot be obtained) form of title policy for the Loan Amount (or other form of title evidence acceptable to us) shall be delivered to us insuring us as the holder of the Mortgage as described in paragraph 1 above. Such policy shall be issued by a title company acceptable to us.

Fig. 1.17

to about $\frac{1}{3}$ of 1% of the mortgage. It must be paid in full before any construction can start. The reason for having such a policy can best be explained by an example. The abstract of title, which goes along with real property every time it is sold, traces the ownership from the present to sometime in the past, in some instances for as far back as 300 years or more. Occasionally, although not very often, there was an error in recording a transfer of title at some bygone date, and that error can lead to great difficulties in the future. For instance, suppose that the records show that in 1875 John Abernathy gave a half interest in the land to his brother Joe, who promptly moved to Australia without recording anything. Now, after construction is complete, along comes Joe's grandson, who claims ownership of the land. Being good-hearted, he'll settle for $500,000. The whole legal mess becomes the problem of the title insurance company, which must fight the case, settle it, or pay a judgement if one is awarded. Meanwhile, both the owner and the bank are well protected.

1.1.5.37 TAXES AND ASSESSMENTS. Obligations due any governmental body take precedence over all other debts, as mentioned previously. Since the project will take about 1 year or more to complete, a not insubstantial amount of taxes will be owed on the land for that time. The bank is asking (Figure 1.18) not only that these taxes be paid, but also that the owner pay for any government-sponsored inprovements, such as street paving, before any mortgage funds are disbursed.

1.1.5.38 CERTIFICATE OF OCCUPANCY. Paragraph 9 (Figure 1.19) speaks of a certificate of occupancy, which would be issued by the

8. Taxes and Assessments. All taxes and assessments affecting the Real Property or any part thereof due and payable on the date of our purchase shall have been paid. Unless otherwise expressly permitted by this Commitment, all special assessments affecting the Real Property or any part thereof shall also have been paid and discharged, whether or not (a) confirmed, (b) payable in instalments or (c) constituting a lien against the Real Property or any part thereof.

Fig. 1.18

9. Compliance with Governmental Regulations. Certificates of Occupancy, if obtainable, and other evidence satisfactory to us shall be furnished that all improvements and their use comply fully with all applicable zoning, building and other governmental laws and requirements. The Loan and our purchase thereof shall in all respects be legal and shall not violate any applicable law or other requirement of any governmental authority.

Fig. 1.19

building inspector of the local governing body—the township, city, or county, as the case may be. The certificate indicates that the construction complies with all pertinent building codes and all government ordinances of the city, county, and state having jurisdiction over the site, and that the buildings may be used for the purpose for which they were intended. This would serve as evidence that the building permit had been issued, that the requirements of all governing bodies had been followed, and that the apartments were built in apartment zones, the offices were built in office zones, or whatever the case may be. There have been instances in which a permit was issued to an unscrupulous builder who then constructed something other than what was shown on his plans; he would be denied a certificate of occupancy. Others have built what was supposed to be an office building and then converted it into apartments before completion. Again a certificate of occupancy was denied; this meant that no one could move into and use such a building until the difficulty was settled, even though the building was structurally sound and otherwise well built. Sometimes the matter can be settled by a special use permit or a petition to change the zoning. Obtaining the requisite approval can take a long time, however; and if the governing body is angry with the builder for some reason, they will deny the request, and the entire investment will go down the drain.

Alternatively, the builder may have built the proper structures but violated the setback requirements and placed a building too close to one of the lot lines. Another condition which has nothing to do with the quality of the building, its type, or its location is a landscaping requirement which is contained in an ordinance that many communities have recently adopted. Even though all other requirements have been met, occupancy can be denied if the land does not have sufficient planting or paved offstreet parking. For all these reasons the bank protects itself with paragraph 9 of the commitment.

1.1.5.39 ESTOPPEL. Paragraph 10 (Figure 1.20) speaks of an "estoppel" affidavit. An estoppel is a bar or impediment preventing

10. Other Documents. The full amount of the Loan that we are requested to disburse shall have been paid to the Borrower and an estoppel affidavit signed by the Borrower shall be furnished to us stating the amount then unpaid on the Note and that no defenses or set-offs exist with respect thereto. A Certificate as to Disbursement and such other documents and certificates as we shall require shall also be furnished.

Fig. 1.20

a party from asserting a fact or claim inconsistent with a position he previously took. In other words, the borrower must truly state that he is responsible for the payment of the note that he agreed to previously and that, even if he made some arrangements between times which transferred his obligation to pay to someone else, or if he made some deals that would get him out of paying, these transactions become null and void. He agreed to the terms of the commitment, and he now must follow through with them, regardless of anything he did to negate these terms between the time he signed the commitment and the time the money is handed to him.

1.1.5.40 ESCROW OF TAXES. The escrow provisions of paragraph 11 (Figure 1.21) were discussed in Section 1.1.5.16.

1.1.5.41 APPROVALS. The bank has a legal division (Figure 1.21) in its home office which it maintains at its own expense. Part of the origination fee (Section 1.1.4.1) is used to cover such expenses. Generally the attorney used by the broker, whose fee is paid by the borrower, will prepare all documents in a matter satisfactory to the home office, and there is usually no trouble on this score.

1.1.5.42 EXPENSES. In the first sentence of paragraph 13 (Figure 1.22) mention is made of "purchase [of] the loan," an expression which refers to the relationship between the permanent lender and the construction lender. To be legally correct and to avoid certain expenses in closing costs, the mortgage lender pays off the construction loan by buying that loan. For the borrower, this action

---

11. Mortgage to Provide for Tax Deposits. The Mortgage shall require the Borrower at the election of the mortgagee, to pay concurrently with each instalment of principal and interest payable on the Note, such amount as in the mortgagee's discretion will enable the mortgagee to pay (out of the monies so paid to the mortgagee) at least 30 days before due, all taxes, assessments and similar charges affecting the Real Property. No interest shall be payable on such deposits.

12. Approval by our Law Division. Each document required in connection with our purchase of the Loan shall be delivered to, and shall be in form and substance acceptable to, our Law Division. Without limiting the generality of the foregoing, the detailed legal description of the Real Property set forth in the Mortgage shall be acceptable to our Law Division. The survey, title report and drafts of all documents shall be submitted to our Law Division before execution.

Fig. 1.21

13. Expenses. Unless otherwise expressly provided in this Commitment letter, you by your acceptance hereof agree that, regardless of whether or not we purchase the loan, we shall not be liable for any, and you will arrange for the payment of all, expenses, fees and charges in respect of the Loan and its transfer to us, or in any way connected therewith, including, without limiting the generality thereof, survey costs, brokerage commissions, title costs, recording charges, mortgage taxes and revenue stamps. Your obligation for expenses, fees and charges under this Commitment shall be in addition to your obligation to pay the amount of liquidated damages, if any, referred to on the first page hereof.

Fig. 1.22

simply amounts to a transfer of indebtedness. It is a simple operation, without any complications. Almost all of the items of cost enumerated will have to be paid before construction can start, so that
upon completion of construction there remain only the cost of a
final survey and perhaps some expense on legal fees. In paragraph
13 the bank is demanding that the borrower pay all of these costs,
even if the permanent loan is not funded for some reason. For example, if the construction is not completed within the stipulated
time shown in the "term of commitment," the bank could refuse
to issue the mortgage loan, and the borrower could not collect his
out-of-pocket expenses incurred in conjunction with the financing
thereof.

1.1.5.43 ASSIGNABILITY.   Paragraph 14 (Figure 1.23) refers again
to the fact that the commitment to lend a large sum of money was
made to a certain man, specific company, or a particular group
of people who demonstrated both financial substance and past
experience. It is not a commitment made to a piece of land or a set
of drawings, and is not a piece of mechandise that can be sold like
a washing machine. However, if the developer finds someone
equally acceptable to the bank, the bank will lend the money to
the second party. In other words, the project cannot be sold as a
package, either before construction starts or during the course of
construction, unless the bank first approves of the buyer.

1.1.5.44.   As any experienced builder can testify, it is always a
good policy to put in writing any change in a contract. This avoids
misunderstandings and future litigation. Hence oral changes are
forbidden (Figure 1.24) in this commitment.

The subject of liquidated damages was discussed in Section 1.1.5.24.

1.1.5.45 ARCHITECTURAL APPROVAL.   The architect on the staff
of the lender will review the final working drawings for complete-
ness and practicality (Figure 1.25) but not for design. He does not
have the right to say anything about design, which is something that

---

14. Subject to Contract; Assignability. This Commitment is, and the Loan shall be after its purchase by us, subject to the terms and
provisions of your correspondent contract with us and the Loan shall be serviced by you pursuant to the terms and provisions of said contract. This Commitment may not be assigned without our written consent.

Fig. 1.23

15. Oral Changes; Paragraph Titles. This Commitment cannot be changed, discharged, or terminated orally, but only by an instrument in writing signed by the party against whom enforcement of any change, discharge or termination is sought. Paragraph titles herein are for convenience only and shall not affect the construction hereof.

The undersigned has obligated itself to pay to Jacksonville National Bank the sum of $14,500.00 as liquidated damages in the event the loan contemplated hereby is not made before the expiration date hereof. If the loan contemplated hereby is not made before the expiration date hereof you agree to pay to the Jacksonville National Bank the amount shown above as liquidated damages.

Fig. 1.24

16. PLANS AND SPECIFICATIONS. Detailed plans and specifications for all improvements shall be submitted to our Architect.

Fig. 1.25

the developer has decided upon while working with his architect. If he wants his project to look like an Old English manor house, or like a modern, even futuristic concrete cube, that is his decision, which was probably based on a market appraisal. It would be both insulting and unfair for the bank to insist upon changes in external appearance. However, the lender may well require some design changes based on preliminary submission before the commitment is made, as shown later on in paragraph 28, but these concern either the materials of construction or the planning, not the exterior appearance. For example, the lender could ask for more parking spaces, for a laundry room to be moved from a corner of the site to a more central location, or for a change in wall finish in a public corridor, but he should not require that there be a pitched roof instead of a flat roof. Furthermore, if the preliminary submission is presented in a professional manner, using color, ink, and other artistic media, it may so impress the lender that he will make no demands whatsoever. The first impression is most important. Since any required changes will generally cost thousands of dollars, a little money spent early on a competent architect will save a lot of money later.

It should be pointed out that, although lenders generally do not make demands in regard to external appearances, they can do so. After reviewing the preliminary submission the lender might require that the exterior be changed from stucco to brick veneer, for example. If the cost would thus be raised beyond the point of feasibility, the borrower should refuse the commitment, and it then becomes the broker's task to find another lender who will not make such demands.

The Federal Housing Administration set forth in its Minimum Property Standards rules that must be followed for apartment projects whose mortgages are insured by the FHA.

1.1.5.46 COMPLETION.   Paragraph 17 (Figure 1.26) concerns plans and specifications for the landscaping as well as the buildings and other improvements. These should be done by a qualified landscape architect. A good landscape design can greatly enhance any project; in fact, a mediocre architectural design can often be salvaged by a good design of the surroundings. Cases have been documented in which intensive landscaping has saved a project economically, causing a barren project to suddenly attract tenants. A reasonable landscaping budget can well be as much as 10% of the cost of the land.

1.1.5.47.   The second and third sentences of paragraph 17 are clarifications of paragraph 3. They indicate that the lender has a right to inspect, not only during construction but also after it. In other words, should the porperty be damaged at any time, the lender reserves the right to come to the project and make sure that everything has been restored to first-class condition. Furthermore, if the case is one not of damage, but just of negligence, such as the need for a coat of paint, the lender can require the owner to have the painting done. If the owner does not provide the necessary maintenance within a reasonable amount of time, the lender will make sure that it is done and will charge the cost thereof to the owner, adding it to the mortgage if need be.

1.1.5.48.   The lender's representative will make these inspections from time to time, not necessarily daily or even weekly. Usually they are made monthly during construction, and yearly thereafter. The inspections made during construction are done to insure that

17. COMPLETION OF CONSTRUCTION. The building or buildings and all other improvements contemplated by this Commitment and the Loan Submission (including any grading, seeding, and landscaping and all other on-site and off-site improvements) shall be completed in accordance with plans and specifications to be approved in writing by our Architect and shall be equipped and paid for to our satisfaction, and each such building shall be ready for occupancy. Our representatives shall have the right to inspect all such improvements periodically during and after construction. Periodic inspections during construction shall be made, and construction shall be approved, by our Architect.

Fig. 1.26

the plans and specifications that were submitted and approved are being adhered to.

1.1.5.49. Paragraphs 18 and 19 (Figure 1.27) should probably be considered together. In the case of a small project the construction loan becomes the permanent loan upon completion of the job, but for a large project two lenders are involved, as previously explained. Because of state and federal taxes, the cost of recording a large mortgage can be several thousand dollars. To avoid spending such a sum twice, the permanent lender buys the construction loan. The mortgage lender therefore requires herein that the construction loan meet the specifications of his commitment.

1.1.5.50. RENT ROLL. The original application for the loan contained an economic feasibility study, which showed an anticipated yearly rental of $280,000 if all available rental space were leased. It also indicated that the project would be able to meet all probable expenses with an occupancy of just over 80%, that is, if the anticipated yearly income were not $280,000 but only $226,000. In paragraph 20 (Figure 1.28) the mortgage lender is now holding the borrower to that declaration, because the lender made his commitment on the basis of the borrower's figures. Obviously the borrower had to study the market to determine that the proposed rental schedule would produce a successful project.

1.1.5.51. The developer is not simply constructing an apartment building; he is actually creating a business which is adding to the economic wealth of the country. The business, as a business, has a value which is far in excess of the cost of the buildings. As an example, a barber shop contains only a small amount of equipment, but because of its location and the skill and personality of the barber,

---

18. AGREEMENT WITH CONSTRUCTION LENDER. At the time of execution of the construction loan documents, the construction lender shall agree to sell the Loan to you and you shall agree, subject to all the terms, including the satisfaction of each of the conditions, of this Commitment, to buy the Loan from the construction lender and both the Borrower and you shall consent to such agreement.

19. COMBINED CONSTRUCTION - PERMANENT LOAN. The terms of the construction loan documents shall be such as to meet all the requirements in this Commitment which are to be complied with on the date of our purchase of the Loan. Prior to the commencement of construction, the combined construction and permanent mortgage shall be recorded or filed for record.

Fig. 1.27

it has a value far in excess of the cost of the equipment. Similarly, this business of apartment rentals will have a large value because of the rentability of the units and the skill of the manager. After the project is constructed, it will add to the economic wealth of the country as an economic asset. There will be a cash flow of dollars in and dollars out. On the basis of these dollars, the mortgage becomes $1,450,000. On the basis of the value of the buildings as buildings, only a very small mortgage, if any, would be placed, because purely as buildings they are almost useless. It is only when they are put to use, producing a cash flow of money spin-off every year, that they begin to have value. Similarly the land, as land, although always worth something, is worth a great deal more when it is used as farmland on which to raise pigs, for example, or as a base upon which to raise buildings. In this case the buildings have been grown on the land, in a manner of speaking, and the land and buildings are now productive in that they act as a means of producing income.

1.1.5.52 FLOOR AND CEILING OF MORTGAGE.   Let us suppose that the business is not successful. In that case, the land and buildings will still be worth something, though not as much. It is hoped that in the future the business can be successful. The lender considers that in such a case the property is worth only $1,200,000 instead of $1,450,000 in terms of a mortgage. Therefore, if no apartments whatsoever are rented, the bank will still lend $1,200,000. This minimum is called the *floor of the mortgage* or, simply, *the floor*. Should the required rental of $226,000 per year be achieved (this is called the *rent roll achievement*), the bank will lend the full amount of $1,450,000. The full amount is called *the ceiling.* In summary, for the case under consideration, the maximum amount that will be lent is $1,450,000, and the minimum amount is $1,200,000.

1.1.5.53.   As was pointed out previously in the commitment, the developer has about 1½ years to complete construction and to achieve the rent roll. If at the date of expiration of the commitment the required rent roll has not been achieved, only the floor will be funded. The borrower will then be required to pay interest only on the amount of money actually received, that is, on $1,200,000, but he will have an additional 3 months to raise the occupancy rate to the desired level, at which time he would receive the balance of the loan ($250,000), bringing the total loan up to $1,450,000.

20. RENT ROLL. The annual rental (including rental for parking) from not more than 81 percent of the apartments in the buildings on an unfurnished basis with the landlord paying for cold water only, shall be not less than $226,000, and the space rented shall be rented on a basis so that if the buildings were 100% rented, the annual rental would be at least $280,000. Such apartments shall be occupied by tenants on a current, rent-paying basis under written leases or rental agreements of at least 1 year terms. The Borrower shall have given to you a rent roll certified to be correct indicating the apartments and annual rentals therefrom relied upon to satisfy this condition. You shall send the rent roll to us and certify to us that you have examined the rent roll and the leases or rental agreements and have checked the occupancy of the Real Property to establish the accuracy of the rent roll statement. No rental concessions to tenants shall have been made and your certificate should so state.

If on the date of our purchase of the Loan said annual rental has not been achieved on the foregoing basis, the maximum amount of the Loan will be $1,200,000 and there shall be appropriate adjustments in the instalment payments, cash fee and net interest rate.

Fig. 1.28

1.1.5.54 CONCESSIONS. The bank is insisting (Figure 1.28) that the rental achievement be obtained with legitimate 1-year leases. They will not tolerate any leases whereby the tenant gets free rent for 3 months if he signs for 1 year, or the owner pays all moving expenses and all utilities without increasing the rent, or any other such gimmicks. Indeed, in order to meet the required rent roll, some developers have submitted fake or dummy leases, but this is a fraudulent practice that can lead to a jail sentence if it is discovered.

1.1.5.55. The inclusion of the word "you" may make paragraph 20 somewhat confusing, but it is easily explained. The commitment supplement was written by the Metropolitan Life Insurance Company and sent as a directive to the broker, which is the Jacksonville National Bank. Thus the word "you" refers to the broker.

1.1.5.56 TERMS OF THE FLOOR. Notice the sentence that is set off by itself just before paragraph 21: ". . . there shall be appropriate adjustments in the instalment payments, cash fee and net interest rate." This means that, if the permanent financing is issued at the floor level of $1,200,000 instead of at the ceiling level of $1,450,000, the payments will not be $11,177 per month but rather will be $9250 per month *if* the same constant of $9\frac{1}{4}$ is maintained. However, if only the floor can be funded, then the rent roll has not been achieved and the project is not a money maker, so that any mortgage is issued with a larger risk involvement. Therefore the lender reserves the right to adjust the interest rate. But in such a circumstance the cash fee or discount would be reduced from $14,500 (1% of $1,450,000) to $12,000, which is 1% of $1,200,000. The gain to the borrower which accrues from paying a smaller discount is more than offset by the problems that evolve from getting a much smaller mortgage. Thus the extreme importance to the developer of achieving the 81% rent roll is evident. This means that a very detailed and thorough market analysis should be made before the project is started, so as to arrive at the proper type and size of building with the best rental schedule for what is being offered. Such an analysis will be discussed in Chapter 3 on land purchasing.

1.1.5.57 STREET DEDICATION.   The sentence which constitutes paragraph 21 (Figure 1.29) will be included in a commitment only when the developer is putting in his own streets or when the streets are shown on a map but have not yet been cut through and paved, or in some similar circumstance. The meaning and intent of this sentence are self-evident.

1.1.5.58 COMPLETION.   Paragraph 22 (Figure 1.30) is interesting. Once a lender has decided to lend money to a certain project, he is anxious to get his cash into it so that the dollars can be put to work earning interest. Furthermore, while it is sometimes to the borrower's advantage to pay interest only on the construction loan for as long as possible, the permanent lender wants to help the short-term lender by buying his loan, thus returning his capital to him. The short-term lender is in the business of making loans for short periods of time, getting in and out of a project as fast as he can. He makes more money in that way because of the discount and by keeping his money moving in more projects. Thus the permanent lender

21. STREET DEDICATION. Evidence shall be submitted that all streets adjoining the Real Property have been completed, dedicated and accepted for maintenance and public use by the appropriate governmental authorities.

Fig. 1.29

22. If, at any time, during the term of this commitment, the property, in our judgment, has been sufficiently completed and has otherwise complied with the terms of our commitment, including rental achievements if any, the loan is to be tendered to us for purchase within 60 days of such completion and compliance, and amortization is to commence in accordance with the terms of our commitment.

Fig. 1.30

wants to help his fraternal banking brother by relieving him of the loan as fast as possible. Therefore paragraph 22 of the commitment requires the borrower to convert the construction loan into the permanent loan as soon as practicable.

1.1.5.59 CONSTRUCTION LOAN AVAILABILITY. The sentence which constitutes paragraph 23 (Figure 1.31) simply states that the owner has 1 month from the date of the commitment (i.e., from March 13, 1968, to April 12, 1968, for the case in hand) in which to find a bank that is willing to make him a construction loan. It is best to find such a lender before signing the commitment, because if one cannot be found after signing, the developer will have forfeited his $14,500 deposit.

1.1.5.60 START-UP TIME. Paragraph 24 (Figure 1.32) gives the developer an additional 90 days to complete preliminary work before construction must start. This period from April 12 to the second week in July would be used to complete the architectural work, get the survey made, and line up subcontractors.

If the total period of time allowed before construction must start is not long enough—and sometimes it just is not adequate—construction must be started somehow or other, or the commitment is voided and the deposit is forfeited. One expedient that has been used in such a case is to deliver a load of concrete blocks to the site. When concrete blocks have been placed on the site, then legally or technically construction has started. There is a lien on the job, based on materials rather than labor, which is perfectly legitimate. This satisfies the requirements of the lender without

23. At our option, this commitment may be terminated unless within 30 days from the date of your acceptance hereof, we receive a letter, in form and substance satisfactory to us, from a bank that it will furnish sufficient funds so that the building or buildings will be completed in accordance with the terms and conditions of this commitment.

Fig. 1.31

24. At our option, this commitment may be terminated unless actual construction is started within 90 days from the date of the above required letter from the construction lender, and is diligently pursued thereafter, except for circumstances beyond the borrower's control.

Fig. 1.32

aggravating a building inspector to the point where a building permit will not be issued, as would be the case if footings had been dug and poured without a permit in· hand. This point should be checked locally, however, since practises may vary from state to state and from locale to locale.

1.1.5.61. Paragraph 25 (Figure 1.33) contains a condition that covers the draperies mentioned earlier. The developer will still be able to place a second mortgage on such items, but when they are finally paid for, they will belong to the project and not to the borrower. This is rather disheartening if one considers, for example, the income from laundry machines or other auxiliary income from vending machines. To circumvent the lender, it is a good idea to have a separate company own such items. Perhaps the children of the builder might be the owners, and they could then lease these items to the project. Although this arrangement may sound evasive, it is both legal and ethical, and it has been known to put many a builder's children through college. Auxiliary income from such things as laundry machines may amount to $1.50 per tenant per week or more. In this example of a project of 140 units, the laundry income could be $200 to $250 per week, which is indeed a tidy sum. When the machines are completely paid for, they will thus be the property of others, not belonging to the project, and they can be financed separately if they need replacing. Even in the unfortunate case of default in mortgage payment, the income from the laundry would continue unabated.

A scheme of operation such as the one just outlined requires preplanning. On the preliminary application for the loan, all this type of equipment would have to be shown as leased to the project, so as to remove it from the stipulation of paragraph 25.

1.1.5.62. An interest equalization tax (Figure 1.34) is not universal but is peculiar to projects which involve international finance.

---

25.   ADDITION TO CONDITION #2 - CHATTEL MORTGAGE. In addition to the first lien which we require on items of equipment specified on Page 1 of this commitment, we require a lien upon the borrower's equity in all other personal property at any time located on the mortgaged premises or used in connection with the operation of said premises.

Fig. 1.33

26. INTEREST EQUALIZATION TAX. We shall not be obligated to purchase the loan unless
we are furnished with evidence, satisfactory to our Law Department that the
transaction is not subject to the Interest Equalization Tax.

Fig. 1.34

1.1.5.63 INFLATION KICKER.   Paragraph 27 (Figure 1.35) contains what is called an *inflation kicker*. Although the interest rate of the mortgage is fixed, the lender wants to insure his participation in any future inflation so as to increase his yield. Therefore paragraph 27 stipulates that if the total annual rent roll exceeds $280,000, which is the projected gross income at 100% occupancy, the lender will get 10% of the excess. Thus, if the rent is raised so that the gross income for 1 year becomes $300,000, the lender will get ($300,000 − $280,000) × 0.10 = $20,000 × 0.10 = $2000 for that year, in addition to the usual mortgage payment.

On the surface, this sounds like a reasonable sort of request. Some companies ask for as much as 25% of the excess. However, it does not take into account increased costs in the operational expenses of maintenance, utilities, and taxes. Usually, if rents go up the reason is that costs of operation have increased. The net result might even be that the project would lose money if such a stipulation were agreed upon. Even if the additional $20,000 of income were completely used up in meeting added costs, the borrower would still be obligated to pay an additional $2000 to the lender.

1.1.5.64 PARTICIPATION.   Another method of inflation protection employed by some lending institutions is called *participation*. In this case the borrower pays a small percentage, say 2%, of all rents collected directly to the lender before making any other payments. The argument here is that the one who is putting in most of the cash is entitled to at least a small piece of the ownership. If the project anticipates 20% profit at 100% occupancy, then it is giving away only 2/20, or 10%, of the profit. In other words the lender would

27   The Borrower shall submit to the Metropolitan an annual statement of the gross
rents collected. The statement shall be certified by a C.P.A. and the Borrower
shall submit to the Metropolitan 10% of the gross rents collected in excess of
$280,000. The statement and payment shall be submitted annually within 90 days
from the closing of the books.

Fig. 1.35

be a 10% partner. The difficulty is that there may not be 100% occupancy, but the borrower must still pay 2% of the rent roll. This could result in very little, if any, profit to the borrower. Furthermore, the usual mortgage payment is approximately 40% of the rent roll. Although the additional 2% does not sound like much, it increases the lender's yield by 2/40, or 5%. Thus his effective interest rate has shot up from $7\frac{1}{2}$% to almost 13% without violating usury laws. A deal like this is about as beneficial to the borrower as the bubonic plague and should be avoided with the same determination.

1.1.5.65 OWNERSHIP CHANGE.   In effect, the contents of paragraph 28 (Figure 1.36) refer back to the application for the loan. When the application for the loan was made, the developer listed the various members of his group or company, together with their net worth statements. The lender relied on this aggregate credit rating when making the loan. As stated previously, the loan was made not to the land or to the buildings, solely to the business; it was made also to the reputation and financial responsibility of the borrowers. To protect itself against the inclusion of a dummy member of the borrowing company who let his name be used simply to bolster the total credit rating of the company, the bank demands in paragraph 28 that the sum of $100,000 be paid on the mortgage principal before any member can drop out of the corporation, or when the property is sold. In the case of a legitimate sale to a legitimate third party, the bank would probably waive this requirement.

Paragraph 28 refers to a corporate structure. It is entirely possible to have several companies involved in the project. In fact, to take advantage of present tax laws, it might be best to have the buildings constructed by a corporation for a limited partnership organization. In other words, although exactly the same men are involved throughout, liability is protected during construction, and the final ownership has the tax advantages of a limited partnership.

28   In the event of any conveyance or transfer of any of the property covered by the lien of our mortgage or in event of any internal change in the members of the Borrower corporation, Borrower shall, at the option of the lender, make an addition al payment of principal in accor' with the amortization schedule within 30 days thereafter, so as to reduce the unpaid principal balance of the loan to an amount not in excess of $1,350,000.

Fig. 1.36

In any event, some sort of company structure is necessary because most banks will not lend large sums of money to individuals, one reason being that in case of foreclosure it is much easier in a legal sense to deal with a company than with an individual, who might be entangled in community property rights and so forth. Also, usury laws permit higher rates of interest to be charged to corporations or limited partnerships than to individuals. Therefore most banks require a company structure so that they can charge a higher interest rate. Company structures will be discussed more fully in Chapter 2.

1.1.5.66 ARCHITECTURAL REQUIREMENTS. Finally, paragraph 29 (Figure 1.37) deals with some pecularities applicable only to this job. First, there apparently were some possibilities of sound transmission between bathrooms of adjacent units, or from bathroom to dining room in some of the units presented in the preliminary proposal, and the bank's architect noticed that potential source of trouble and is rightfully requiring that the annoyance be eliminated by soundproofing. Second, it would seem that nothing was shown on the design concerning the window sills, so the lending institution is requiring some kind of permanent material for these. It may be that wood was originally called for, but the lender wants a harder, more durable surface. The third item mentioned concerns the finish in the bathrooms. Perhaps the builder hoped he could get away with painted walls, but the lender believes that the apartments will not rent well unless a more attractive finish is used. The fourth item is incomprehensible. Why cast iron tubs? Nobody knows. Perhaps the lender believes that the enamel on cast iron tubs will not chip,

29. In addition to any requirements of our Architect we shall require:

1. Reversal of the fixture wall or adequate sound proofing of the interior bath/dining area wall in the F, K, & L units.

2. Marble or ceramic tile window sills.

3. Vinyl wallpaper or ceramic tile on bath fixture walls and ceramic tile base moulding.

4. Cast iron tubs.

Fig. 1.37

but that the finish on steel tubs will peel off. Regardless of the reasoning involved, the fact remains that if Prime Meridian Corporation wants the loan at the terms preferred, then Prime Meridian Corporation must agree to all the terms and paragraphs of the commitment, including all of the changes requested in paragraph 29. The alternative is for the borrower to present a counterproposal. For example, he might say, "I agree to everything except item 4 of paragraph 29, where I would use Fiberglas tubs instead of cast iron." The bank will either agree to the substitution or remain firm on its demands. If the bank stands firm, the borrower must either acquiesce or refuse the commitment and ask his broker to find some other lender.

1.2 Construction Loan

As was pointed out at the very beginning of this chapter, every part of construction funding hinges on obtaining a commitment for a permanent loan. Once a commitment for a long-term mortgage is obtained, all the other pieces of the financial puzzle will fall into place. On the assurance that money will be forthcoming from a mortgage lender, it is possible to obtain a construction loan and any other financing that is necessary. Let us now consider the construction loan.

1.2.1 Sources of Construction Loans

From a study of the commitment form, it became apparent that the final mortgage money would be made available only after construction was completed. The permanent lender places his money solely in finished projects. Other funding must be obtained to pay the bills during the construction process. With a firm commitment in hand, however, this is not difficult to obtain. In fact, the mortgage broker will direct the borrower to at least one commercial bank that makes such loans, and the broker will not charge a fee for this service.

Although construction loans sometimes come from savings and loan institutions, on larger projects the usual source is either a commercial bank or an REIT. For an FHA-insured job the permanent loan and the construction money are often issued by the same bank.

1.2.2 Commercial Loans

The construction loan is generally placed by a commercial bank because it is a short-term business loan. For the purposes of this book, a short-term loan is one which is completely repaid in 3 years or less, and that is the maximum time limit of most commercial bank construction loans. It is a business loan because the money is to be used to create a business of rentals, be they office, warehouse, or motel rentals. It can also be considered a business loan because it is in essence loaned to a builder so that he can profitably operate his business. As an example, consider the case of a man who wants to establish a clothing business. He has a lease on a store, which is just empty space, analogously to a developer who has a piece of land. The merchant must have stock in order to have a business, just as the developer must have buildings in order to have a business. Now the merchant wants to buy, say, $100,000 worth of suits, but does not have that much cash. Accordingly, he approaches a bank and obtains a loan with which he can buy the merchandise. Once he sells the suits, he will have enough money to pay off the bank loan and other expenses and then buy more suits. Similarly the developer wants to put up buildings, and once the buildings are rented he can pay off the construction loan with the proceeds of the mortgage loan. The commercial bank does not want to be the owner of either the suits or the buildings. It has no desire to go into either the merchandising business or the real estate business. The bank is in the money business. It wants to rent its money at a reasonable rental rate called interest, and then it wants to get its money back and rent it out again.

In order for a merchant to get money from a bank he must meet two requirements:

1. He must show a *need*.
2. He must have a *plan* for repayment.

His need lies in the necessity of having a stock; furthermore, by borrowing he can buy a larger quantity of suits at a lower price, thus giving him an opportunity to make more money. His plan of repayment is to sell the suits at a profit large enough to repay the debt and have cash for himself.

The builder's need is to erect the buildings, and he plans to repay the loan with the permanent loan.

1.2.3 Conformity of Commitments

The commercial bank has a guarantee that its construction loan will be paid back in the fact that the developer has a commitment from the permanent lender. In order to make the guarantee stick, the two loans must have the same terms involved. Therefore, paragraphs 1 through 29 of the commitment must apply with equal force to both the construction loan and the mortgage loan. Therefore the construction lender insists that these paragraphs apply also to his loan, as noted in paragraph 19.

1.2.4 Entrepreneur

Even though there is a guarantee, the lender in a construction loan still incurs some risk. This risk lies mostly in the character and the experience, or the lack thereof, of the entrepreneur, or developer. An entrepreneur is one who puts together the entire package and acts as a sort of president of a supercorporation. The vice presidents of the pseudo-corporation would be the architect, the attorney, the owner of the land, the banker, the builder, and so on. In other words, an entire new company is put together, consisting of many departments that embrace the facets of land acquisition, design, financing, construction, and management. The entrepreneur must be of such character that he will handle large sums of money wisely, will actually repay the loan, and will not get into financial difficulties.

In this connection remember paragraph 3 of the commitment, which concerns adverse change. It is entirely possible that, during the time involved from the beginning of construction until the rent roll requirement is achieved, an inexperienced or unethical entrepreneur might go bankrupt or at least get into grave financial difficulties, so that he would start using the lender's money for the payment of his other debts and obligations even though he is not supposed to. It is rare that a builder will go under because of the job he is currently working on; financial disaster usually occurs because of two preceding jobs. If there were two bad ones just before the present job, or if the builder did not pay his bills on the past two jobs but instead took the cash for himself, he will use the money from the present job to pay off past debts. Then the current project will not be completed, and the construction loan will founder on rocky shores. To salvage its loan, the bank will then have to take over the job and complete it.

1.2.5 Effect of Discount

Therefore, even though the construction loan is covered by the security blanket of the mortgage loan, some risk is involved in a short-term building loan. Because of this risk the construction lender asks for a discount of about 2 points. This discount is deducted from the loan before any money is disbursed and in a sense becomes prepaid interest. Consider an example: Suppose that the bank makes a loan of $100 at 6% interest. At the end of the year the borrower will have to pay the bank $106. If he holds the money for only 6 months, he will have to pay $103, the interest on $100 for 6 months being half the interest for 1 year. If at the time the loan was made the borrower paid the bank a $2 fee, that fee would be income for the bank. The bank has received $2 from the borrower. At the end of 6 months the bank will receive another $3 in interest from the borrower in addition to the repayment of the $100 loan. Thus, for letting the borrower use its $100 for 6 months, the bank has received a total income of $5, made up of the first $2 and the last $3. Therefore, in truth, the bank has received $5 in interest over the 6-month period on the $100 loan. If the bank makes the same arrangement with the next borrower for the next 6 months, it will have received a total of $10 for the use of $100 for 1 year, so that the bank will actually be earning 10% on its money and not 6%. As will be shown later in Chapter 7, the true interest is even higher. The 2-point discounts paid in the example just given amount to more than 4% interest.

1.2.5.1. The nominal interest rate on the construction loan is usually about the same as the interest rate on the permanent loan, but the discount increases the true interest. Thus a $7\frac{1}{2}$% nominal interest rate with a 2-point discount will produce a yield of perhaps 10% or more for the bank, depending on the length of the job and the manner in which the money is doled out.

1.2.6 Amount of Construction Loan

To minimize its risk, a commercial bank will not lend as much as the ceiling of the mortgage loan in the construction loan. In the commitment just studied, the construction loan would not be for $1,450,000 because it is possible that the rent roll will not be achieved. The permanent lender is guaranteeing only $1,200,000 as the amount it will put out; therefore the construction loan will be based on this floor of $1,200,000. Even so, the construction lender will not lend this amount, because quite a bit of that money will have to be used for fees, interest, and closing costs. Therefore the construction lender will probably lend only about 75 or 80% of the floor.

1.2.7   Stand-by Commitment on the Gap

All costs should be added up at this point. Will the construction loan be sufficient to get the project built? If it is enough to do the job, well and good. If not, where can additional funds be obtained? If the construction loan is going to be for only $960,000 and the actual construction cost will be $1,100,000, including construction loan interest and all other costs, there remains a difference of $140,000 that has to be obtained if the project is to be completed. The money might be borrowed from the construction lender provided that he is given some kind of guarantee that he will be repaid. Banks insist on security, and rightly so since they are public institutions. A bank acts as an agent holding the money of all or part of a community, and it has an obligation to safeguard its deposits. Hence the initial construction loan commitment was based on the floor of the mortgage, since the floor amount is a certainty.

But there exists a gap between the floor and the ceiling. In this case the gap is equal to $1,450,000 − $1,200,000 = $250,000. There are lenders who will issue a stand-by commitment covering the gap. They are willing to back up a builder's firm conviction that his project will be successful and will indeed achieve its required rent roll within the allotted time. However, if the rent roll achievement is not met, the mortgage lender will fund only the floor of $1,200,000. At that time the stand-by lender must come in with the other $250,000—the gap. The stand-by lender will then have a second mortgage with no specific security. Since this is a very risky business, the cost of a stand-by commitment is relatively high. Often the requirement is a fee of 5 points on the amount of the gap, cash in advance at the time the stand-by commitment is made, and the stand-by commitment must be made before the construction loan commitment is obtained. On a matter of $250,000, 5 points would amount to 5% of $250,000 or $12,500. This $12,500 is not refundable and is paid only as an inducement to the lender to issue a stand-by commitment. Even if the rent roll is achieved and the lender never has to take $1 out of his wallet, he can keep the entire sum of $12,500. The reason for paying such a large fee is to obtain security for an increase in the construction loan, thus inducing the construction lender to increase his loan by 75 or 80% of the gap, which, in this case, would be an increase of, say, $0.8 \times \$250,000 =$ $200,000. The borrower's payment of $12,500 has increased the construction loan from $960,000 to $1,160,000, and he now has enough money to do the job.

This fee of $12,500 cannot be dealt with lightly. It is a large sum. But sometimes it is a necessary expenditure if there is no other way to get the job done. There is a vast difference between coming up with $12,500 and providing the necessary $200,000. If a builder does not have $200,000 but does have $12,500, he pays the $12,500 in order to get somebody else's money to work for him.

1.2.8 Cost of Gap Financing

After the job is finished and all construction is complete, the permanent loan will be funded. Suppose that only 50% of the rent roll is leased instead of the required 81%. In that case the permanent loan will be $1,200,000, and the stand-by lender will provide an additional $250,000.

Interest must be paid on all borrowed money. The gap financing will carry an interest rate that is higher by about $2\frac{1}{2}\%$ than the rate on the permanent loan and may be even higher. If the permanent lender has an interest rate of $7\frac{1}{2}\%$, the gap loan will be at 10% or more.

If during the month or two immediately after completion of construction the rental achievement is met, the permanent lender will bring his loan up to the ceiling, and the borrower can use that money to pay off the gap financer. Thus the gap lender would get back his $250,000, in addition to the $12,500 he was paid before a construction loan was obtained and in addition to any interest he was paid for the use of his $250,000 during the month or two that the borrower actually held it.

1.2.9 Construction Loan Application

To review briefly, the entrepreneur has obtained a commitment for a mortgage loan. He has added up all of his costs and determined that he will need a stand-by commitment to fund the gap between the floor and the ceiling in order to get the project completed. After obtaining the standby commitment, the developer approaches a construction lender and gets a construction loan commitment for the maximum amount possible.

The process of obtaining a construction loan is not difficult. The builder deals directly with the loan officer of the bank. He presents to the loan officer the commitment from an acceptable permanent lender and, if need be, a commitment from an acceptable gap financer. He will also have to present a correct estimate of actual construction cost and evidence that there is no first mortgage on the land. In actuality he presents an application containing not only all of these various documents but also, perhaps, a financial statement of his company and personal financial statements. The loan officer of the bank will also want to know how all the contingencies are going to be met. In other words, he wants to know how the whole project is going to be finished. He wants to be absolutely certain that if he lends the money it will be enough to do the job when added to the resources of the borrower. The bank has no desire to be stuck with a partially finished project. The loan officer does not want to have a builder come back some time later and say, "I'm sorry, but I underestimated my costs and need more money." In such a situation the bank almost has to lend more money to protect the substantial investment it already has in the project. It will never get its money out of the permanent loan unless the whole project is finished, and it is the permanent loan that pays off the construction loan. Therefore, the loan officer will demand that the entrepreneur add up all of his costs to begin with and show exactly how they are going to be met.

1.2.9.1. If it can be demonstrated that the money from the desired construction loan will be enough to complete the job, the construction lender will issue a commitment, and this commitment can then be sent to the permanent lender so as to satisfy the requirement of paragraph 23.

1.2.10 Single-Home Loans

The entire procedure is greatly simplified for a smaller project, such as a single house. Here there is no need to get three different commitments before construction can start. One commitment will do the job. In fact, the construction loan and the mortgage loan are both made by the same bank. The initial discount is the only fee paid to the bank.

1.2.10.1 DRAWS. Money is paid out to the builder from time to time, upon completion of various stages of construction, as will be discussed in Chapter 5. These timely payments are called *draws*. The bank has a formula as to what percentage of the loan will be forthcoming for each stage of completion, and the definitions of the stages of completion are also enumerated. For example, when the foundation is finished, a certain amount of the loan is issued; after the house is dried in, another amount is issued; and so on.

1.2.10.2. Interest must be paid on any money actually borrowed. Interest starts accumulating immediately after each draw. In other words, the very day that money comes from the bank to the borrower, interest begins to be reckoned on that money. No interest is due or payable until money is actually received; but the very day that it is received, interest begins to accumulate for the draw, and each draw will have its own interest assigned to it. The full amount of interest due is the sum of all the interest obligations on all of the draws. This will be explained in more detail later.

1.2.10.3. When construction is completed to the satisfaction of the loan officer, the last draw is issued, bringing the total lent up to the total amount of the construction loan. The bank will hold out any interest due on the loan up to that point. For example, suppose that the commitment was for $30,000 and the total interest owed to the bank at that point is $700. Then the last draw will bring the total amount received from the bank up to $29,300

($= \$30,000 - \$700$). However, although the builder has received in cash only $29,300, he has actually borrowed $30,000 and has "paid" the bank $700 in interest. If it is assumed further that the house was built on contract for a specific owner, each of the draws would go from the bank to the owner and then to the builder. It is the owner who would be obliged to repay the loan to the bank, and the construction loan would become the permanent mortgage without any further paperwork. In fact, at the conclusion of construction, the owner would start repaying the loan by making to the bank uniform monthly payments based on the interest rate and duration of the loan, until the entire $30,000 was repaid. The construction interest is part of the cost of construction, and was paid to the bank out of the last draw. The bank got paid what was due it, just as the surveyor and the carpenter were paid.

1.2.10.4 SPECULATIVE HOUSING.   In the case of a speculative house, that is, a house erected in the hope of selling it to some customer, after completion, the bank will generally accept payments of interest only until such time as the house is sold by the builder. There is a time limit on this grace period (generally about 1 year), and the construction loan will be considerably less than the final mortgage that will be granted to a qualified buyer. The monthly interest payments made by the builder will be only on the actual construction loan. One bank, though, does everything. The construction loan is part of the final mortgage loan, all issued by the same bank. There is no floor, no ceiling, no gap, no rental achievements. It is a very simple process.

1.2.11 FHA Loans

The process of obtaining construction money is also simplified when the Federal Housing Administration (FHA), which is now a part of the Department of Housing and Urban Development (HUD), is involved. When the loan is to be insured by the FHA, the entire process is about as complex as obtaining a small home loan, even though it may involve $1,000,000 or more. The insurance has the sole purpose of guaranteeing that the loan will be paid to the bank in the eventuality of a default. The guarantee is backed by the full faith and credit of the government of the United States. This insurance is not a protection against damage or fire; it is simply insurance against nonpayment of the mortgage. The bank thus knows that its loan is going to be repaid, and its risk factor is virtually eliminated. The government will actually make the mortgage payments only until it finds a private buyer for the property, but the money will flow to the bank from some source. Because of the governmental guarantee of payment in case of default, the final lender can make progress payments during construction in the same way that a savings and loan bank does for a house. In other words, even for a substantial project, the construction lender and the final lender can be the same bank.

1.2.11.1 FHA DIFFICULTIES. Of course, the borrower has to pay a small premium for this insurance, usually about $\frac{1}{2}$ of 1% of the amount of the mortgage, and the FHA design requirements are much stricter than those of a conventional lender. They call for certain distances between buildings, certain minimal sizes for rooms, certain amounts of storage, and so on, that can prove restrictive. These are all spelled out in the Minimum Property Standards (MPS) of the FHA, both for single-family and multiple-family housing. Another difficulty with FHA financing of apartment complexes is rent control. One would expect such a restriction of subsidized rental programs, but it applies also to nonassisted programs which place no limit on the income of the tenants. Rents in such projects can be raised only after receiving written permission. Approval is usually forthcoming quite rapidly, provided the owner can prove that the increase is needed because costs have gone up since the rent schedule was established. However, an owner often cannot obtain permission for as high a rent as is charged in a project next door to his, which has units of exactly the same size and exactly the same amenities. This means that his profits are restricted to a level determined by the government. The FHA does not insure ventures that are totally commercial in nature, such as office buildings or motels, but a project that is mostly residential, with a small amount of auxiliary commercial rental space, can qualify for an FHA loan. Nursing homes and related facilities can also qualify.

1.2.11.2 FHA LOAN BENEFITS. The two obstacles of (*a*) the small premium paid for the insurance and (*b*) the design requirements are almost trivial in comparison to the benefits derived from an FHA loan. To begin with, the interest rate is lower with an FHA loan than with a conventional mortgage. The discount is higher because the bank wants a higher yield on its loan than the maximum interest it is permitted to charge on an FHA loan. Theoretically the bank should be satisfied with a lower interest rate when the risk factor has been removed through the medium of insurance, but the banks consider that the interest rate established by the government for FHA loans is just too low. However, the true interest rate, even considering the effect of a higher discount, is lower than that for a conventional mortgage, and the period of time for repayment is much longer, leading to lower monthly payments for an FHA loan.

1.2.11.3.   Second, whereas a conventional lender will give only 65 to 80% of the value of a completed project, an FHA-backed loan may be as high as 90 to 97%, depending on the project and its sponsor (i.e., whether or not the project is built for profit, whether or not the rental is subsidized, and so forth). The FHA was established to encourage capitalism, and it does an excellent job in that role. Anyone who qualifies can have a successful project with a minimal investment if FHA rules are followed. Details of various FHA programs are given in Figures A.10 through A.18 of the Appendix.

1.2.11.4 CONVENTIONAL MORTGAGE INSURANCE.   The FHA also insures small home loans, but the loan procedure is so much like that of a savings and loan bank that it will not be discussed here, the major difference being in the amount of the loan. To avoid governmental standards and regulations, and yet secure a 90% loan on a single house, it is possible to obtain conventional mortgage insurance directly through the bank that is making the loan. The bank acts only as an agent on the insurance, the issuing company being probably in some other city, but the insurance is easily obtainable by any qualified buyer.

1.3 Front Money

Suppose, then, that the commitments for the permanent loan and for the construction loan have been obtained. Before construction can start, a great deal of money will have to be paid out, and during the first month of construction still more money will have to be expended. Money will be needed to make a good faith deposit on the loan; to pay legal, architectual, and surveying fees; to meet various other closing costs; to pay for the building permit and for the bonding fee if one is required; and to move onto the job and actually start construction. During the first month money will be needed to meet weekly payrolls and perhaps to pay for certain materials. All of this is in addition to any expenditures on the land. All this cash used before the first draw is obtained is called *front money*.

1.3.1 Sources of Front Money

Like every other fiscal requirement of the project, front money either can come from the developer's own capital or can be borrowed. Various methods of raising company capital will be discussed in Chapter 2. There are sources that will advance front money as a loan to the developer, provided that he has a firm commitment from a mortgage lender and another commitment from a construction lender. Since the risk for a bank that lends front money is not as great as that for a gap lender, the interest rate will not be as great. The cash of a front money loan will be forthcoming at the time of initial closing, but it must be arranged well in advance of that date. On the day of closing it is not possible to run around and suddenly borrow the needed money.

1.3.2 Cost of Front Money

The borrower will pay interest on a front money loan only for the time that the actual cash is held. (There will also be a small discount involved, but that will not be very extensive.) If the interest rate is, for example, 10%, and the amount borrowed is $100,000, at the end of 2 months the borrower will have to pay back $2/12 \times 0.10 \times \$100,000 = \$1,666.67$ in interest in addition to the principal amount, because the rate, in this case 0.10, is always on a yearly basis and the money was held for 2/12 of a year.

1.3.3. FHA Obviates Front Money

No front money is needed when the FHA is involved in a large residential project. The first draw of the construction loan is made at the time of the initial closing, and amounts to a substantial percentage of the builder's costs up to that date. This is a much more sensible way of doing business because it involves fewer lenders. Furthermore, it presumes that the entrepreneur is a professional and treats him accordingly. However, in the conventional case no money is forthcoming from the construction loan until about 1 month has ensued since the start of construction, which may be more than a month after the initial closing.

1.4 Retainage on Construction Draw

Now the front money has been advanced, and construction has started. During the first month of activity no further money will be forthcoming from sources outside the contractor's coffers. At the end of the first month the construction lender will let the developer have a certain number of dollars, the amount depending on the value of the work put in place. Suppose, for example, that $100,000 worth of work has been put in place during the first month. The builder will then submit a request for a draw of $100,000 against the total that was committed as a construction loan. The request will have to be approved by the bank's representative, perhaps an architect appointed by the bank. The bank will then let the builder have the money. However, the bank will not lend full value, but will retain a certain percentage of the request. This percentage will generally be either 10 or 20%. The retainage will be spelled out in the construction lender's commitment. The reasons for a retainage are not very clear. Perhaps the bank considers that 10 or 20% is the amount of the builder's profit, and he is not entitled to a profit until the job is completed. Whatever the reasoning, there is going to be a retainage.

1.4.1 Last Draw

Suppose again that the first draw request was for $100,000 and that the retainage is going to be 10%. In that case the builder will receive only $100,000 less 0.10 × $100,000, or $100,000 − $10,000 = $90,000. If at the end of the second month an additional $150,000 worth of work has been put in place, bringing the total value of work in place up to $250,000, the builder will receive an additional amount equal to 90% of $150,000 or an additional $135,000. At the end of the first month he received $90,000, and at the end of the second month he received $135,000, so that at the end of the second month he has received a total of $90,000 + $135,000 = $225,000, but he has put in place $250,000 worth of value. When the entire job is completed, at the time of the last draw, all the retainage will be added to the last request, so that the builder will finally get all the money that was committed to the loan on the project. The bank will not pay the builder any interest on the money that was held out, nor does the builder have to pay the bank any interest on the money he did not receive.

1.4.2 Required Capital

During the course of the first month the front money is used to meet all obligations. At the end of the first month, when $90,000 is received, the front money loan can be paid off, but because of the retainage there will be no extra money to meet the obligations of the second month. This means that the builder has to find money to pay labor, overhead, and materials suppliers. If the net construction draw is not sufficient, the builder must use his own cash or be able to borrow it. Contractors who perfer to use their own money find that they need about $1 in the bank for every $10 in the contract. With this reserve they do not have to borrow anything during the course of construction except for the construction loan.

1.4.3 Borrowing on the Contract

The additional required funds above and beyond the construction loan can be borrowed, possibly from a commercial bank as a business loan. The security for the loan will be the contract itself. The contract between the builder and the owner stipulates that a certain sum of money will be paid provided a certain service is performed, that is, provided the project is built in accordance with the owner's plans and specifications. From the bank's point of view, it can lend the builder money so that he can perform that service. This is a satisfactory arrangement. The contract in a sense guarantees payment, in a manner similar to that in which the permanent loan commitment guarantees payment of a construction loan. Since a profit is anticipated on the construction contract, the commercial bank believes that it will be paid back from the proceeds of some future draw.

1.4.3.1.   When the entrepreneur and the contractor are the same person, it may seem strange that he can borrow additional funds, but actually two different operations performed by two different companies should be involved. The business of the entrepreneur's company is to create the entire project, involving the purchase of land, arranging for design, and so forth. The business of the contractor's company is solely building, which constitutes only one part of the entire project. Although a man cannot sign a contract with himself, it is possible for one company to sign a contract with another company. The contractor might have a corporation for building, while as an individual he is one of the limited partners in a development company. Therefore the builder would have a valid contract with the developer and could use that contract to obtain interim financing during construction.

1.4.3.2.   The interim financing goes on from month to month during the course of the job. It may be paid back each month, or it may be arranged to be in the form of an open note which is renewed at the end of each month, when accrued interest is paid on the principal until the end of the job. For instance suppose that $10,000 is borrowed to meet the labor payroll during the second month. This has nothing to do, really, with the amount of the holdback; it is simply the amount that the contractor needs to meet ongoing expenses. If there had been no holdback, the contractor would have been richer by the amount held back, and would have had that much more operating capital. He might still have borrowed the money in preference to using his own capital, holding on to his money for other purposes. The decision to borrow or to spend is a management decision that involves many factors. Suppose that the contractor elects to borrow. At the end of the second month the note becomes due. He can pay back the $10,000 plus the interest, or he can pay the interest only. If he pays back principal and interest, it is quite likely that he will immediately have to borrow the same amount again in order to meet similar bills during the third month. If the loan is left in place, he will have enough money in the bank from the construction draw to meet his obligations during the third month. The two methods are about the same, except that in some states each time money is borrowed certain small taxes must be paid on the transaction. At the end of the project the loan should be paid so as to maintain good credit standing. Bankers recommended that all open notes be cleared up once each year. This is simply good banking policy.

1.5 Holdback on Subcontractors

Any money that is borrowed from a bank must be paid back with interest. To avoid the cost of interest some contractors employ the practice of "borrowing" from their subcontractors. An unscrupulous builder will do this by not paying his bills when they are due, but stalling to some future date. If a bill is not paid, then money is owed on that bill. If money is owed, then it has in a sense been borrowed. If a subcontractor has performed a certain amount of work for which he is entitled to payment, he is counting on being paid. If he does not get paid, he has in a sense lent the money in question to the general contractor, and will be so short of capital that he may have to borrow in turn from a bank. His financial difficulty, if it becomes great enough, might put the completion of the job in jeopardy when he becomes unable to pay his men. The entire practice is unethical and unfair and should be harshly condemned.

1.5.1 Fairness of Holdback on Subs

However, if the bank is going to withhold 10% of each draw, then every reasonable subcontractor will also agree to a 10% holdback. He expects it. It would not be fair for him to expect to get paid completely when the bank is not disbursing completely. Therefore, if his bill is $100, he expects to be paid $90. At the end of the job, he expects to be paid everything that is owed to him, and this is the usual practice.

1.5.2 Extra Holdback on Subs

It may be possible to get a subcontractor to agree to a 20% retainage by the general contractor upon the promise that the remaining 80% of each of his draws will be paid within a stipulated number of days after the first of each month. If a plumber, for instance, has put $1000 worth of labor, materials, overhead, and profit into a project during its first month of construction, he may agree to wait until the 20th of the second month to be paid, not $1000, but $0.80 \times \$1000 = \$800$ at that time. The other $200 is owed to him and will be paid to him at the end of the job. Such an agreement should be put down in writing before any work starts and should be scrupulously adhered to. Every bill should be paid no later than the agreed upon date at the agreed percentage.

1.5.2.1.   Obviously there is a differential between the 10% withheld by the bank and the 20% withheld by the general contractor. In this case, the $1000 of plumbing work will be a part of the total request that the general contractor submits to the bank. The bank will let the general contractor have $900 of that $1000, and the general contractor will then pay the plumber $800 of the $900, leaving the general contractor with $100 of working capital. This spread can be used to help pay the general contractor's labor and overhead.

1.5.2.2.   There is nothing immoral or illegal in the retainage just described, provided that both parties agree to it before any work starts.

1.5.3 Numerical Example

Consider the numbers that have been used in the discussion above. The amount of the mortgage loan ceiling was to be $1,450,000, and the final mortgage floor was to be $1,200,000. The construction loan would probably be about $960,000, which is 80% of the floor. If a gap commitment had been obtained, the construction loan would then be, say, $1,160,000, but without gap financing the construction loan would not exceed $960,000. Now suppose that the actual cost of construction, including a builder's fee is $1,160,000. Of this we can assume the builder's fee to be perhaps $50,000, leaving an actual out-of-pocket builder's construction cost of $1,110,000. Because the construction loan is for only $960,000, there remains a differential of $1,110,000 − $960,000 = $150,000 between the construction loan and the actual construction cost. Where is this money to come from?

It is reasonable to believe that the general contractor will do about 20% to 30% of the work, and the rest will be done by sub-contractors. Suppose in this case that the general contractor will do $250,000 worth of work, and that the subcontractors will do $860,000 worth. In other words, the total of all the subcontractors is $860,000, including the total overhead and profit of each of them. If 20% is held back on each of the subcontractors, then 20% of $860,000 or a total of $172,000 will be held back until the end of the job. This is more than adequate to cover the differential of $150,000 that existed between the construction loan and the total cost of construction. Remember that the total cost of construction does not include legal fees, closing costs, and so on. It is solely the *brick and mortar* cost, as it is called, of the building alone, exclusive of land and landscaping costs. Summarizing briefly, we have:

Final mortgage ceiling	= $1,450,000
Final mortgage floor	= $1,200,000
Actual construction cost	= $1,160,000 (brick and mortar cost)
Construction cost without builder's fee	= $1,110,000
Subcontracted portion	= $ 860,000
Holdback on subcontrac-tors (0.2 × $860,000)	= $ 172,000
$1,110,000 − $172,000	= $ 938,000 (from builder)
Construction loan	= $ 960,000 (from bank)

Therefore the construction loan is greater than the amount of money needed to complete construction. The differential would be used to pay interest on the construction loan.

1.5.3.1. The general contractor and, in turn, his subcontractors will all be paid in full when the final mortgage is funded at the floor or ceiling as the case may be, hopefully at the ceiling.

[1.6 Summary *very good*

The financing of a real estate project begins with obtaining a commitment for a mortgage loan. After this is in hand, a commercial bank can be induced to give a commitment to make a construction loan. Both of these contain the same requirements and stipulations, and the borrower will have to pay a fee or discount of 1 or 2 points (1 point is 1% of the total loan) in addition to any money borrowed on each. This discount is actually prepaid interest.

The mortgage commitment will have a floor, or minimum loan, and a ceiling, or maximum amount which will be forthcoming only if the rent roll indicates a required level of achievement. The amount of the construction loan is based on the floor. The difference between the floor and the ceiling is the gap. To increase the amount of the construction loan, a stand-by commitment that covers the gap can be obtained.

During the course of construction, the construction loan will be issued from time to time in amounts based on the value of work completed—monthly on large projects, but as the work progresses on single homes. Because the lender holds back a percentage of each draw, the builder should retain at least that same percentage from the draws made on him by his subcontractors. If between draws the builder does not have the funds to meet his payroll, he can borrow on his contract.

Before any construction starts, a substantial sum of money is needed for initial closing costs and other fees. This front money can also be borrowed if a commitment for the permanent loan has been secured.

2

Capitalization and the Importance of Money

2.0 Corporate Thinking

There is a tendency on the part of many a builder to think of his company as belonging to him when in fact the exact opposite is the case. A builder is a part of the company. He is a very important part, but his role must be clearly understood—management is a company tool. General Motors would continue to exist even if the chief executive officer retired without notice. His management decisions are extremely important to the company, and he is richly rewarded for taking the responsibility of those decisions, but he remains an employee. As an employee, he is a tool of the company, one of the many that make the company successful in producing its products at a profit. The other tools include the other levels of management, the superintendents, the mechanics, the laborers, and the buildings and machinery used by the company. Of course the chief executive officer is much more important than a welding torch, but he is nonetheless a tool of the company in that the company operates through him; he does not operate through the company. In a similar vein, although a builder has at his disposal other levels of management, other men, and other tools, he remains subsidiary to the company, even though he "owns" the company outright.

2.1 Money as a Company Tool

Once this concept is clearly understood, the role of money as a company tool falls into place. If the company were to rent a tower crane for a certain job, it would be a management decision to determine the proper size, type, and speed of crane to use. An effort would then be made to lease the most appropriate crane at the lowest cost. Should the cost of leasing prove to be too high, the company would buy the necessary equipment. In either event, the crane requires an expenditure of cash. The cash can either be rented (borrowed), or it can come from the company coffers.

2.1.1 The Use of Money

The decision that is then made between the alternatives of renting dollars and using company capital is a management decision based on advantages and disadvantages to the company. It is not a personal decision. The builder is not dealing with his own money—it is the company's money. Pride of ownership of a tower crane must remain secondary to the company objective of amassing all the money in the world. Perhaps that is too grandiose an objective; nevertheless, the goal of business is profit, and unless the profit objective is maximized, the business will probably fail. The amount or percentage of profit to be made on any one job is not under discussion; we are considering only the use of money as it applies toward that objective.

2.1.2 Liquid Assets

The most important point is that a company must have capital in order to operate. Cash in the bank is called a *liquid asset*, because it can be converted into cash in the hand within 24 hours. Other liquid assets include stocks, bonds, and receivable notes. Banks are more favorably disposed toward lending money to companies with sizable liquid assets. In fact, they will lend much more than the value of those assets. Therefore liquid assets allow for leverage, because a smaller amount can move a much larger amount, in a manner reminiscent of the boast of Archimedes, who claimed he could move the world if he had the proper lever. Thus, with a reasonable amount of capital, a company can take on a rather large job. Generally, in construction, liquid assets should be about 10% of the dollar value of the job. Hence the company's capital should be jealously guarded, and expenditure, although sometimes the best course, should be undertaken with great caution. One of the major objectives of a company, then, is to start with a reasonable operating capital and to add to that sum as much as possible as time goes on.

2.2 Capitalization

There are four types of organizations which can produce the capital necessary to start a construction company:

1. Individual.
2. Partnership.
3. Limited partnership.
4. Corporation.

Each of these has certain advantages and disadvantages with regard to funding. The methods of borrowing shown in Chapter 1 are about the same for each, except that with the latter two forms of organization the chief executive officer of the company, or perhaps the owner with the most liquid assets, will, in most cases, be required to sign personally for any notes up until the time construction is completed. Thereafter the permanent loan is in force, and the mortgage lender has the property as security, and does not need personal liability from an individual.

2.2.1 Individual Ownership

Any man who wants to make a fortune can still do it on his own in construction. The starting capital need not be too large, say $5000 or $6000. It can be accumulated in the old-fashioned way, combining hard work, morality, and self-denial. The hard work produces cash, the morality holds on to the cash, and the self-denial leads to savings. Two alternatives are to have a rich father or to marry a wealthy girl, but these courses are not usually available. A steady savings plan will yield the necessary dollars in a reasonable amount of time.

2.2.1.1. With only $5000 a neophyte builder can expect to erect about $50,000 worth of houses. If he follows the criteria of Chapter 3 and chooses the right location, builds for the proper market, and gives fair value, he should sell the houses about 4 months after he starts, with a net profit of perhaps 5%, or $2500. Net profit is taken after all costs have been considered, including the builder's wages. Remember that the boss is working for his company, and he is therefore entitled to a reasonable salary. The salary is part of the company's cost of doing business and must be assigned to overhead on the jobs. Notice that the profit of $2500 is 50% of the initial capital, but only 5% of the volume of business that was accomplished.

2.2.1.2. If the houses can indeed be sold within 4 months after starting, then in 1 year's time the fledgling builder will have turned over his money three times and made a total profit of $7500, in addition to wages. If the original capital has not been dissipated, the total capitalization will now stand at $7500 + $5000 = $12,500. With liquid assets of $12,500 the volume of business can be increased to 10 × $12,500 = $125,000 in each business cycle. The anticipated profit will now be 0.05 × $125,000 = $6250 at the end of each 4-month period, leading to a gain of $18,750 for the second year. Now the bank account stands at $12,500 + $18,750 = $31,250. So in 2 short years the original $5000 has grown to $31,250, in addition to any salary taken from the business. And with capitalization of $31,250 the builder is ready to start on some larger projects.

2.2.1.3. The largest advantage to individual operation is the feeling of pride and accomplishment that comes when the company proves to be a success. The total operation has hinged on the expertise and decisions of the man who started it, and success of the company means success of the individual. No reward can be richer. Additional advantages include the ability to manipulate the company funds for the financial gain of the owner. For example, the company should pay for some life insurance on its owner, since he is the key man, and if he is lost to the company, the business might fail. In the event of the owner's death the insurance could be used to help pay off current debts. It might even be possible to salvage the business with the use of the insurance money. Furthermore, the company can easily employ members of the owner's family to gain tax advantages on income sharing. Any imaginative accountant can list several other advantages of individual ownership.

2.2.1.4.   But with responsibility there also comes liability. First, if instead of making money the company should lose money, the loss would be a personal one. Second, any borrowing done by the company would actually be personal borrowing, constituting a personal indebtedness, even though there exists a company structure. For example, if Raymond Cornpone is doing business as Cornpone Building Company, and he signs all notes R. Cornpone, d.b.a. Cornpone Company, he will still be personally liable for the notes. If the company declares bankruptcy, he himself will have to make good on the notes or else undergo personal bankruptcy, which does not always get rid of all debts. Furthermore, his personal liability probably extends to all company operations. If a child is severely injured while playing on his job after working hours, the company might be found liable. If there is not adequate insurance coverage, Raymond will have to come up with the cash, besides feeling personally responsible for the injury to the child for the rest of his life.

2.2.2 Partnership

An impatient man will not want to wait several years before he can start on some large projects. If he has experience and knowledge, but no cash, he must borrow capital if he wants to start with big things. It is not likely that a bank or other financial institution will lend the money on the sole basis of a dream, so he must borrow it from individuals. At times it is possible to find a sponsor who will lend several thousand dollars at a reasonable rate of interest just because he has confidence in the builder's eventual success, but most intelligent people will demand a piece of the action. In other words, they will want to be an integral part of the business and to share in the future profits and capital growth of the company. Under such conditions, the company structure will be either a partnership or a corporation.

2.2.2.1 GENERAL PARTNERSHIP.   A partnership can consist of any number of people. At times every one of the partners performs some function in the business of the company, in which case they are all *active partners*, whereas in some companies one or more of the partners are partners in name only, in which case they are *silent partners*. Often a man who contributes nothing but cash will be a silent partner—it will certainly be to the advantage of the company if this is the case, since the financier probably knows nothing of construction and could only prove to be a hindrance to operations. Yet his money will be essential to the success of financing operations, at least while the company is young and growing and has not yet built up its own liquid assets to any substantial degree. If nothing is written down to the contrary and filed in proper form by an attorney, the partnership will be a general partnership, wherein every partner has a share in the rewards, losses, and liabilities of the company, in a manner similar to that of the individual ownership. It can be stipulated that all partners are not equal, even though the partnership remains a general one. For example, one person might be a 10% partner, while each of two others has a 45% share of the business. But, in any case, each and every partner remains liable for all debts of the company. The advantages and disadvantages of a partnership operation are therefore quite similar to those of an individual operation, with ease of capitalization being a plus factor for the partnership. One example of a very large partnership is the Van Sweringen Brothers Company, which owned a railroad, a large metropolitan office building, and a limited access interurban streetcar line, and which originally also owned and developed the entire city of Shaker Heights, a suburb of Cleveland, Ohio.

2.2.2.2 LIMITED PARTNERSHIP. A limited partnership is somewhat similar to a general partnership in that at least two people are involved in the formation of the company. However, in a limited partnership each partner, except for one general partner, is financially liable only to the extent of his fiscal contribution to the founding of the company. Thus, for example, if a company is started with seven men, and each of them contributes $10,000, then in case of failure or bankruptcy of the company, or some court suit which is settled against the company, the total loss will be limited to the original $70,000 plus whatever assets the company owns. In other words, no one of the seven individuals will have to dig into his personal bank account or his other personal liquid assets, such as stocks or bonds, to cover the indebtedness of the company. His only loss will be his original cash investment of $10,000. Of course if the company had been successful up to the time the catastrophe occurred, and had accumulated $1,000,000 in cash on hand, it could lose all of that, but each individual would lose no more than his original contribution.

2.2.2.3 THE GENERAL PARTNER. In a limited partnership there must be one man who is the general partner. The general partner does not have limited liability. He has, in fact, unlimited liability, in a manner similar to a man owning a company by himself. If an individual who is to be the general partner wants to protect himself against unlimited liability, he must do it with a corporate shield; that is, he must have a corporation which assumes the role of the general partner, and then the corporation rather than the individual is the general partner. All the other limited partners can be individuals. There are certain special laws applying to this arrangement, and a good tax attorney should be consulted before the company structure is established.

2.2.2.4. The shares in a limited partnership can be divided in any way that seems reasonable, just as the shares in a general partnership can be divided. For example, with seven partners, the six limited partners might each have a 7% share, while the general partner has a 58% share. In that way the general partner can make all management decisions, including the sale of the company's assets. But the general partner does bear a vulnerable liability.

2.2.2.5. In the preceding example the shares could be split. Instead of $10,000 giving 7 shares of the total of 100 shares, $5000 would give $3\frac{1}{2}$ shares, so that instead of 7 partners there might be 13 partners. In that case each of 12 of them would have $3\frac{1}{2}$ shares, and 1 partner would retain 58 shares. Or there could be 8 partners with $3\frac{1}{2}$ shares each, 2 with 7 shares, and 1 with 58 shares. In other words, shares in a limited partnership are somewhat similar to shares of stock in a corporation.

2.2.2.6. The reason for selling shares, of course, is to raise initial capital. That is the whole point of it—to get capitalization. Before the first attempt is made at raising initial capital, the price of each share has to be decided upon, based on the anticipated operation and the amount of cash needed. If the price is too high, all the shares necessary will not be sold, and the initial capital will not be enough to go into the proposed business. On the other hand, if too many individual shares are sold at a very low price, there may be too many partners voicing opinions on the operation of the venture.

2.2.2.7 TAX LOSS.   One of the big advantages of limited partnerships, in addition to limited liability, involves the application of tax laws to real estate ventures. In a real estate operation the value of the buildings can be depreciated rather rapidly for tax purposes. During the first few years of ownership this rapid depreciation will be greater than the income, thus showing a theoretical net loss. The cash in the treasury can be disbursed directly to each of the partners in a pro rata form; a 7% partner would get 7% of the cash, and a 58% partner would receive 58%. All of this cash flow would be tax free. No income tax would be paid on it. In fact, the excess loss can also be distributed pro rata to each of the partners, so as to offset their own personal incomes from other sources. This makes for a very attractive proposition. Suppose, for example, that an individual has an income of $50,000 per year, and his share of the cash flow from a limited partnership is an additional $25,000. Now suppose that the net loss of the limited partnership is such that his share of the loss if $40,000. Then he would receive an income of $50,000 + $25,000 = $75,000, minus a loss of $40,000, giving a net taxable income of only $35,000. In other words, while actually taking in $75,000 in that year, he would pay taxes on only $35,000 of that income. Some men have enough tax loss to cover their entire incomes, thus paying no income taxes whatever.

2.2.2.8.   Any business venture should be set up by an attorney before it is started. It is essential to get the best possible legal advice on how to set up the company and its operation. Preplanning always pays off. Legal advice is especially necessary because in many repects a limited partnership is similar to a corporation, and there are stringent laws governing the sale of shares in each. These laws must be investigated thoroughly before any public offerings are made. Continuing competent legal advice is essential to any properly conducted business.

2.2.3 Corporation

Another way of raising initial starting capital is through a corporate structure. A corporation, like a limited partnership, must be set up by an attorney before any shares are sold. The laws regarding corporations are quite explicit, and offerings for sale of shares must be handled in a way that does not offend the Securities and Exchange Commission. Before starting a corporation, it is wise to consult with an accountant as well as an attorney as to all pertinent rules and laws. However, once the decision to proceed is made, it will be found that a corporate structure offers some attractive financing advantages.

2.2.3.1 SECOND OFFERINGS. Not all the stock has to be sold at the initial offering. If, for example, the price per share is pegged in such a way that 24% of the total shares will produce the required initial capital, the company can retain the remaining 76% of the stock in its treasury, or the originator of the company can keep these shares in his name. After a time, if the company has prospered, another 24% can be sold on a second offering but at a higher price, leading to a substantial amount of cash for the company or for the man who has built the company, if it is handled properly. Yet the individual who started the company can still retain control of it with his remaining 52% of the stock. In fact, it is possible to have control of a company with less than a majority of the outstanding stock, provided all the other shares are distributed in even smaller lots. But having a majority of the stock leads to absolute control of the company, and the individual having such a majority can make all management decisions, including the sale of the assets of the company. However, the rights of minority shareholders cannot be overlooked, and their interests should be kept in mind.

2.2.3.2 BONDS. Bonds represent another means whereby a corporation can raise the capital needed for some venture. A *bond* is like a note, in that it describes a secured loan and the method by which the loan will be repaid. Rather than borrowing one large sum from a bank, a corporation can borrow many smaller amounts from a number of individuals, and issue bonds to them as evidence of indebtedness. A bonded debt is usually paid off at the expiration of a stipulated number of years; meanwhile interest is paid only at stated intervals, usually every half year or every year. Some bonds do not pay anything at all until the date at which they become due, called the *date of maturity*, at which time the principal and all accumulated interest are paid in one lump sum.

2.2.3.3.   It is not the intention here to describe company management or company operation; this book is concerned only with construction funding. Therefore all the discussions of this chapter are devoted to the methods of raising capital, and perhaps to the advantages and disadvantages of these various methods of getting together initial funds, and then to methods of borrowing money and of doing business.

2.2.3.4.   Another advantage to a corporate structure is due to usury laws. In most states the maximum interest rate that can be legally charged to an individual for a business loan is less than that which can be charged to a corporation. For example, disregarding small loan companies and time payments on merchandise, the maximum interest rate that can be charged to an individual might be, say, 10%, whereas for a corporation it might be 15%, depending on local or state laws. Since the discount will bring the true rate of interest on a construction loan up to 11 or 12% or higher, which is more than 10% but less than 15%, a commercial bank could not make such a loan to an individual without dropping its interest rate. Because the bank wants the full 11 or 12% or whatever, it will demand that the developer have a corporate structure. Only in that way can the bank legitimately make such a loan at full interest.

2.2.3.5.   The main advantage of a corporation, though, lies in its limits on liability. Every stockholder of a corporation is shielded, or protected, against unlimited financial loss. The only loss that can come to any part owner of a corporation is limited to his initial financial investment in the company, together with his pro rata share of its assets. Again, if the corporation grows to the point where it has $1,000,000 in assets after a small beginning, in the event that all those assets disappeared, no one could come after any individual of the company because of the corporate debts, provided that everything has been done legally at all times. In some small corporations, those with rather limited financial backing, one or more members of the company might have to sign notes personally in the event of borrowing from a bank. In this case they would be personally liable for the amount of the indebtedness and any other borrowings on which they had extended their personal guarantees, but they would not be liable for other debts incurred through the daily operations of the corporation.

2.2.4 Combinations

It is possible to form companies and raise capital by making various combinations of the four types just described. For example, several individual construction companies could band together into a partnership on a joint venture when a particular job would be too large for any one of them to handle alone. The company so formed could be a partnership, limited partnership, or corporation, with each of the individual companies having a mutually agreed upon share. Each of the individual concerns would retain its own company characteristics, so that the joint venture company might be composed of two corporations and one limited partnership, and those three together would form a new limited partnership. Instead, the final partnership could be composed of four corporations, each one acting as one of the partners, not all necessarily equal. Or the combined corporation could be made up of three separate partnerships, or any other combination. The entire organization would probably be disbanded and dissolved at the end of the job, when each of the member companies would again go about its own business. The purpose of a joint venture is simply to have enough operating capital and enough company strength to take on a large job without diluting the strength of any individual member. Legal advice should be obtained before contemplating this.

2.2.4.1. Sometimes a single company will contain within itself multiple distinct companies, without being a joint venture. This is often the case in a design-build operation, which provides engineering service, architectural service, and construction service to any outside owner. In other words, the company can completely design and build a project for some owner. The construction arm of that company might well be a corporation, acting as a limited partner with the architect, while the design team is in actuality an integral part of the total company structure. The reason for doing this stems from the possibility of failure in a building. If there were to be, for example, a collapse of a building, who would be responsible, the designer or the builder? Each of them would be somewhat protected in a limited partnership type of operation. Furthermore, if the builder should go bankrupt, the architect would not be hurt too badly, because he would not be liable for the debts of the corporate arm of the partnership. This arrangement is slightly complicated and should be established by a competent attorney.

2.2.5 Subsequent Capitalization

Sometimes a company (or an individual) wants to put together a project which apparently is a little too large for it to handle; that is, a preliminary financial study of the proposed project indicates that the amount of cash that will be needed in addition to the construction loan is more than the company has in its treasury. The company must then raise more money. Suppose that the owners of the company do not want to take on any more partners, nor do they wish to sell some stock from the company treasury, for either course of action would mean that each of the present owners would own a proportionately smaller share of the company. In this case each of the existing owners can contribute some of his own funds to the company coffers, or the company can utilize some of its assets to raise money, for example, by refinancing.

2.2.5.1 REFINANCING.   As each mortgage payment is made, part of the payment goes toward interest, and the rest is applied on the principal. Over a period of years quite a sum will be paid on the principal, thus reducing the amount of indebtedness. Meanwhile, if the rents have held steady, or if they have increased, the economic value of the property has certainly not been reduced. Therefore the same value of property would then have a much lower indebtedness, and the lender of the mortgage would probably be amenable to lending the borrower an amount equal to that which he has paid off, thus bringing the mortgage back up to its original level. To the borrower this would mean a lump sum of fresh capital in a sizable amount. The process just described is called *refinancing*, and an existing company can apply it to some property that it has held for 5 or 10 years.

2.2.5.2. The best thing about refinancing is that all the cash derived from such a transaction is tax free, because it is borrowed money. It is not money derived from earnings or from profit; therefore there is no tax on it, because no one pays income tax on borrowed money. If a company obtained a first mortgage for $1,450,000 10 years ago, then today it could perhaps obtain over $400,000 in refinancing, and every one of those beautiful dollars would flow in tax free.

2.3 Summary *Good*

To start a company requires a certain amount of initial capital. In order to undertake any construction, some money has to be available at the start of it, and the company has to have a good financial statement, which indicates a certain amount of cash in capitalization. The amount of money needed depends on the size of the project that is contemplated.

There are four types of company struuctures within which this money can be raised:

1. An individual can raise it on his own.
2. A group can get together in a partnership, each contributing cash or talent.
3. A limited partnership can be formed, in which only one of the partners is the general partner who accepts all fiscal responsibility, while each of the other partners has his loss limited to his actual cash investment at the time the company was formed.
4. A corporation can be formed, which raises its needed capital through the sale of stock and limits any stockholder's liability to his initial investment.

In every case the owner or president should not think of himself as owning a company, but rather as working for a company. This type of thinking is called corporate thinking.

Each of the four types of companies—individual ownership, partnership, limited partnership, and corporation—has advantages and disadvantages with regard to obtaining money. The methods of borrowing discussed in Chapter 1 are about the same for each. In most cases, the chief executive officer of the company, or perhaps the member with the most liquid assets, will be required to sign personally on any company note, up until the time when construction is completed. He is the one that will be looked to, rather than the company itself, until the permanent mortgage has taken effect. During the course of construction large sums of money are changing hands, and the bank wants to make sure that the company will not use these funds for some other purpose. If such should be the case, then one financially responsible individual would be personally liable for seeing that the bank got its money back. This individual would therefore "ride herd" on the company, making sure that all money was properly spent, all loans were promptly repaid, and the affairs of the company were properly managed.

The personal liability discussed above applies to front money, construction loans, borrowing on the contract to meet payroll, and gap financing. After construction is completed, the mortgage lender will have property as security and will not need or want individual liability.

In every instance the company structure should be established only with the counsel of a good business lawyer. The value of competent legal advice cannot be overemphasized. The details of organization should always be put down in writing, particularly when two or more people are involved, as would be the case with a partnership, a limited partnership, or a corporation. Early use of a lawyer's expertise in the planning of a company structure can avoid much future difficulty and may even save future tax dollars, for example, through the use of Subchapter S in the tax regulations.

3

Site Selection and Development

3.0 Importance of Location

Real estate men all agree that the three most important criteria for the success of a project are: (1) location, (2) location, and (3) location. Actually there is a germ of truth in this exaggeration, for the "location" includes within it most other factors of importance in selecting a suitable site for a proposed project, and unless the mortgage broker is convinced of the suitability of the site, no funding will be forthcoming.

3.1 Site Selection

The problem becomes one of choosing the best possible piece of land for the type of development to be erected. The following discussion is based on the supposition that an apartment project is being considered, but with slight modifications the approach is equally applicable to a housing subdivision, an office building complex, a shopping center, a warehouse, or a motel.

3.1.1 Market

An aggressive developer must assume that he is perfectly capable of erecting a project anywhere in the world, if he is going to build

77

a number of successful projects. The first general aspect of location is finding the proper town in which to build. Every municipality needs some kind of construction, but whether or not it needs apartments depends on the existing occupancy ratio, construction activity, and a forecast of demand. If the number of vacancies in all apartments in the area constitutes less than 5% of all available units, there may be a demonstrated need for additional units unless a major amount of apartment building is already in progress. Furthermore, all rentals must be firm, without landlords giving a free trip to Las Vegas as a bonus for signing a lease, 2 months' free rental included in a 1-year lease, or any other gimmicks. The condition of all rentals being firm and without give-aways is called a *hard market*. Given a 95% or better occupancy ratio and a hard market as described, it is still necessary to determine the type of unit to build. In an industrial town the factory workers could afford approximately 1 week's pay per month for housing. The project should therefore be geared to a lower rental than it would be in a prosperous suburb, and these lower-cost units should be built on lower-cost land. Similarly middle-income and luxury units each have special requirements, but should be undertaken only where the area economics warrant their erection. Furthermore, if all the units in the area are luxury units and *no* lower-rent units are available, there is an obvious market for the latter, even if there is a good occupancy ratio on the former. The mortgage broker must be informed of the type of project that is proposed, and he must sometimes be convinced of the validity of the reasoning leading to the proposal.

3.1.2 Factors

The various factors that make one site superior to a second site within the same municipality are all relative to the selected market, be it prestige, white collar, or blue collar. They include the following:

1. Location.
2. Adaptability.
3. Accessibility.
4. Transportation.
5. Commuting time.

6. Shopping.
7. Schools.
8. Recreation.

Not all of these factors will apply to all projects, and they will all have relatively different importance, depending on the market selected. In addition to the above list, plus factors to be considered are public improvements and environmental amenities. Public improvements include paving, sewers, municipal water, and gas or electric lines to the property. Environmental amenities include scenic views and proximity to ocean, lake, mountains, desert, or even some man-made point of great interest, such as a cathedral, any of which constitutes a subliminal influence in the general frame of location. But the public improvements have a profound influence on the value of a location.

3.1.2.1. Although the *location* may be fantastic in that it is 400 yards from an expressway and along a mountain, with a clear trout stream running through it, while overlooking an 18-hole championship golf course with the ocean beyond, it will still be worthless if it is not adaptable to the project. *Adaptability* includes covenants, laws, and geography. *Covenants* or *restrictions* are included in the abstract of title or in the deed, and are recorded. If, for example, the land is restricted by deed to the building of single-family homes, then no one can build apartments, even if the zoning is favorable. Covenants against race or religion are no longer valid, but minumum areas of dwelling units can be prescribed. The *laws* governing adaptability are found in local ordinances and include building codes and zoning regulations. Various laws could prohibit an economically successful development. For example, a very expensive piece of land should have a high-rise building erected on it, but local ordinances might limit the height or density (number of units to the acre). Or building within a fire zone might require methods and materials of construction that are prohibitively expensive. Or requirements governing setbacks, side yards, and off-street parking might combine to make a proposed walk-up project unfeasible. Similarly, land should not be purchased with the vague hope that the zoning restriction against the expected use can be changed—if the zoning is not proper, the site should be eliminated from consideration. Even if the zoning can be changed, the process of getting it amended is extremely time consuming and usually not worth the effort. Finally, the term *geography* embraces both topography and subsoil, both of which are significant influences on construction costs. If a visual inspection of the site shows swampy or marshy land, steep ravines, rock out-croppings, or poor surface drainage, obviously a large amount of work will have to go into site preparation, before any buildings can be started, thus in effect increasing the cost of the land. Similarly, if there is a high water table, or if there are pockets of muck under-neath the topsoil, the construction cost will be increased, and the value of the land proportionally decreased. Excavation costs should not come as a surprise after financing is arranged. A large project warrants the taking of test borings before purchase of the land is consummated. Test borings are not expensive and can be done by any competent testing laboratory.

3.1.2.2.   An otherwise fine piece of land is worthless if there is no way of getting to it. Probably the best location has frontage on a side street, a short distance from a main thoroughfare. Of course successful apartment projects have been built alongside a six-lane expressway, but in every case it must be easy for automobiles to drive right into the property. *Accessibility* does not preclude building out in the country, provided that a major highway goes nearby. People in all strata of society rely heavily on the automobile as their major mode of transportation, and access by means of a long stretch of dirt roads should be shunned. However, if the project is within a very short, easy walk to work and shopping, it could prove just as successful as one located in an idyllic surrounding. Accessibility is particularly relevant to the selected market.

3.1.2.3.   *Public transportation* may soon replace automobile traffic to a great extent. Even if that time never arrives, this factor will remain a strong consideration in locating an apartment. The high density in land usage inherent in apartments leads to a demand that good public transportation be available for the tenants. If the project is large enough, it will lead to the extension of such facilities from the central municipality to the development, but it is better not to rely on such an extension and to select a site located within a short walk of existing bus or train lines. Furthermore, the routing should be direct if possible. For example, it is best if executives do not have to make any transfers on their way to or from the office.

3.1.2.4. Public transportation availability is equally as important as accessibility, and both factors are considered in computing *commuting time* from the apartment to work. Either private or public means of travel may be used, or the two may be adjoined, but the time from dwelling to work should not be excessive. Because of other important factors such as environmental amenities, it does not necessarily follow that the shortest time is best. In fact, it may be desirable to live some distance from a factory, but the time of travel is more important than the distance. To drive 10 miles on an expressway probably takes less time than to ride 2 miles on a local bus, and may be preferable.

3.1.2.5. The availability of *community facilities* should also be a consideration. These include shopping, schools, churches, and recreation such as parks, playgrounds, and entertainment centers. With good transportation available, and easy access to automobiles, all of these become secondary considerations, but they should be included in evaluating one site over another. It is preferable to be within walking distance of such community facilities, but this is not mandatory.

3.1.2.6. Each of the factors so far presented can be given a weighted value according to its order of importance. Each weighted value is a percentage, and the total of all the percentages should be 100%. A suggested list is as follows:

1. Location   20%
2. Adaptability   20%
3. Accessibility   15%
4. Transportation   15%
5. Commuting Time   10%
6. Shopping   10%
7. Schools, recreation 10%

                       100%

Every site being considered would be given an overall grade on each of the factors. That grade would then be multiplied by the appropriate percentage, leading to a number of points for that site, for that factor. For example, if at site 1 the location was given a grade of 85, that site would earn 85 × 0.20 = 17 points for location. If site 1 had a grade of 80 for transportation, it would earn 80 × 0.15 = 12 points additional. Adding up all the points for each site would lead to an unbiased selection of the best location, and do away with selection based on the fact that someone's mother "just loves that darling oak tree." An example follows:

		Site		
Factor	Value	1	2	3
1. Location	0.20	18	18	15
2. Adaptability	0.20	16	14	14
3. Accessibility	0.15	12	12	14
4. Transportation	0.15	12	10	9
5. Commuting time	0.10	9	5	8
6. Shopping	0.10	7	8	7
7. Schools, recreation	0.10	8	7	6
Total	1.00	82	72	73

Obviously site 1 is the clear-cut winner. But if site 1 is not available for some reason, the choice between sites 2 and 3 is not evident. Even though site 3 scores 1 point more than site 2, the location superiority of site 2 (18 points vs. 15 points) would tip the balance in its favor, and site 2 would be selected in preference to site 3.

3.1.2.7. The grade points based on values that are given to each of the seven different factors constitute an approach called *matrix analysis*. The various points should not be based on hunches or gut reactions or even emotional preference, but should be coldly determined by serious consideration of precise data. The data can be put in any form that seems suitable, but they must be based on inspection reports. A check list for site appraisal is given in Figure 3.1 merely as one suggested way of obtaining all relevant data. In addition to filling out such a seven-page form, it is advisable to prepare a location map showing the topography, and to photograph the site and its neighborhood amenities, so as to corroborate visual impressions. Additional check lists for commercial projects are given in Figures A.1 through A.9 of the Appendix.

CHECK LIST FOR SITE APPRAISAL

Site _____

Date Visited _____ ; By _____

Comments: _____

_____

OWNERSHIP AND DESCRIPTION

Owner _____

Agent _____ (address) _____ (phone)

Address of Tract _____ (address) _____ (phone)

Legal Description ___ (street) _____ (city) ___ (country)

_____

Tract Size: Dimensions _____ X _____ Acres _____

Adjacent Land Ownerd _____

Comments: _____

_____

LAND USE AND VALUES

Asking Price: Per Acre _____ Total _____

Debts Against Tract _____

   Held by _____

Special Assessments _____

Buildings on Tract _____

   Est. Value _____

Land Use Now _____

Tax Assessor's Value _____ Tax Rate Used _____

Your Estimate of Value: For Use Pending Development _____

   For Development _____ Per Acre _____ Per Lot _____ Total _____

Comments: _____

_____

Fig. 3.1

83

TOTAL LOCATION

Miles From City _____ Direction _____

Nearby Communities: _____

Distance From Central Business District: Miles _____ Minutes by Car _____

   Minutes by Public Transportation _____ Fare _____

Comments on Highways _____

Type of Public Transportation _____ Good ☐ Fair ☐ Poor ☐

Local Streets and Roads _____ Good ☐ Fair ☐ Poor ☐

Approach to Tract _____ Good ☐ Fair ☐ Poor ☐

Surrounding Development: Class; High _____ Medium _____ Low _____

   Price Range of Homes _____

Employment Centers: _____

   Type _____ Miles _____ Minutes _____ Fare _____

   Type _____ Miles _____ Minutes _____ Fare _____

   Type _____ Miles _____ Minutes _____ Fare _____

Remarks: _____

_____

_____

ENVIRONMENT AND CONTROLS

Zoning of Tract _____ Nearby Lands _____

_____

Protective Convenants for Tract _____

   For Nearby Lands _____

Subdivision Regulations _____

Any Easements on Land? _____

Subdivision Plan Recorded? Yes ☐ No ☐ ; Area Master Plan? Yes ☐ No ☐

Comments: _____

_____

Fig. 3.1   (*Continued*)

HAZARDS AND NUISANCES

Is the Tract Free From Existing or Likely?

	Yes	No	Remarks
Heavy and Frequent Rail Traffic	☐	☐	_____
Heavy Highway or Street Traffic?	☐	☐	_____
Airport Noise and Hazards?	☐	☐	_____
Aircraft Approach Patterns?	☐	☐	_____
Other Unusual Noise, Vibration?	☐	☐	_____
Unusual Crowds, Heavy Parking?	☐	☐	_____

Is There Adequate Distance and a Buffer Between the Tract and: _____

	Yes	No	Remarks
Likely Sites of Fire?	☐	☐	_____
Smoke Sources?	☐	☐	_____
Chemical Odors?	☐	☐	_____
Other Odors?	☐	☐	_____
Dust or Dirt Sources?	☐	☐	_____
Unsightly Views?	☐	☐	_____
Floods?	☐	☐	_____
Polluted Bodies of Water?	☐	☐	_____
Dilapidated Structures?	☐	☐	_____

Observations: _____

_____

_____

_____

_____

_____

_____

_____

_____

Fig. 3.1 (*Continued*)

TOPOGRAPHY

Is the Tract Characterized by or Are There Large Acres of:

Yes No   Remarks

Swamp or Marsh? ☐ ☐ _____

Steep Ravines or Grades? ☐ ☐ _____

Rock Outcroppings: ☐ ☐ _____

Soil Erosion? ☐ ☐ _____

Rocky or Sandy Soil? ☐ ☐ _____

High Water Table? ☐ ☐ _____

Poor Surface Drainage? ☐ ☐ _____

About how much of the tract is: Hilly? _____ % Rolling? _____ % Level _____%

What is the average elevation of the land? _____High Point____Low Point____

Are existing roads or streets above grade or below? _____

Heavy Cutting Needed: For Streets _____For Homesites_____

 For Other Purposes_____

Heavy Filling Needed: For Streets _____ For Homesites_____

For swampy Areas _____ For Other_____

In Gneral, is the tract adequately drained? _____

Special Drainage Provisions Needed: _____

Type of Soil_____

Trees: Woods _____ Sparse Woods _____ Scrub _____ Open _____

Comments: _____

_____

_____

_____

_____

_____

_____

_____

Fig. 3.1 *(Continued)*

86

UTILITIES AND SERVICES

Are These Present of Readily Available? _____

                                Yes No

Public Water Supply?   ☐ ☐ Distance to Main _____ Size of Main _____

Private Water Needed   ☐ ☐ Individual System _____ Private Wells _____

    Remarks _____

_____

Public Sewage Disposal? ☐ ☐ Distance to Main _____ Size, Invert _____

Private System Needed? ☐ ☐ Subdivision Plant _____ Septic Tanks _____

    Remarks _____

_____

Storm Sewers?   ☐ ☐ _____

Paved Access Streets?   ☐ ☐ _____

Public Street Upkeep?   ☐ ☐ _____

Snow Removal & Sanding? ☐ ☐ _____

Police Protection?   ☐ ☐ _____

Fire Protection?   ☐ ☐ _____

Garbage Removal?   ☐ ☐ _____

Electrical Utility   ☐ ☐ _____

Telephone?   ☐ ☐ _____

Gas?   ☐ ☐ _____

Street Lighting?   ☐ ☐ _____

Observations: _____

_____

_____

_____

_____

_____

_____

Fig. 3.1 (*Continued*)

TYPE OF DEVELOPMENT SUGGESTED

Price Range of Homes: Average _____ High _____ Low _____

Number and Nature of Unsold New Houses in Area: _____

_____

Sizes of Lots Required: _____

Estimated Lot Yield: _____ Per Acre _____ Total _____
COMMUNITY FACILITIES NEEEDED:
   Shops, Schools, Churches, Other Structures: _____

_____

   Parks, Swimming Pool, Playgrounds, Etc.: _____

_____

Summary of Observations on Worth of Tract Against Market Survey Results: ___

_____

_____

_____

_____

_____

_____

_____

_____

_____

_____

_____

_____

_____

_____

_____

_____

Fig. 3.1   (*Continued*)

COMMUNITY FACILITIES

Name, Address	Distance—Center of Tract	Transportation Time Minutes Walk	Car	Public	REMARKS: Crowded, Age, Condition, Other Factors
SCHOOLS					
Nursery					
Kindergarten					
Elementary					
High School					
Other					
SHOPPING					
Main Centers					
Neighborhood Stores					
CHURCHES					
Denominations					
PARKS					
PLAYGROUNDS					
SWIMMING POOL					
LAKES, STREANS					
OTHER OUTDOOR SPORTS AREAS					
ORGANIZED SPORTS AREAS					
Golf					
Riding					
Other					
ENTERTAINMENT CENTERS					

Fig. 3.1 *(Continued)*

3.2 Land Purchasing

Once the decision is made to purchase a particular site, the site should be tied up so that no one else can buy it while the financing is being arranged. The owner of the land should be given a small sum of money which binds him to selling or leasing it to the buyer, depending on which way the agreement reads, and prevents him from letting any one else having it. In other words, the builder gets an *option* to buy or lease. The option agreement should be drawn up by the buyer's attorney, and the buyer must be prepared to drop the option should the need arise. In other words, if sufficient financing is not available at a reasonable rate, or if construction costs should suddenly increase, or if any other valid reason should arise, he must be mentally prepared to lose all the option money. That money must then be considered as an unavoidable ordinary business expense.

3.3 Land Financing

If the proposed development is large enough, it could be possible to borrow a considerable amount of the money necessary both for land acquisition and for land development, thus retaining operating capital as a liquid asset, rather than burying it in the ground. The minimum size site that the FHA can consider for financing is 10 acres, but conventional sources have no such restriction and may require either more or less land.

3.3.1 Appraisal

Once the binder has been made and the option to buy or lease is in hand, the next step is to make an application for a loan. At this stage, the FHA will consider only a purchase option, but an REIT, which is perhaps the most frequently used conventional source for sizable land financing, will also consider a subordinated lease agreement. In both cases the land must be appraised to determine a fair market value on which to base the loan. The appraisal can be made by a member of the organization that is going to make the loan or by a member of the Appraisers Institute (an MAI), and will probably not result in the same dollar value as the purchase price. In fact, in the case of the FHA, the valuation of the land will be based on the market value that will exist after development is completed, which is much greater than the value of raw land.

3.3.2 Loan Application Requirements

In addition to an appraisal, an application for a land acquisition loan will contain several other items, the first of these being a survey made by a registered surveyor. Second, it is necessary to prove that the zoning is proper for the proposed project. This can be accomplished by either a current zoning map or a letter from the building inspector. If utilities are not in place up to the property line, it is necessary to obtain a letter of intent from the governing municipality or from the appropriate utility company, stating that the necessary utilities will be brought to the property if the development is culminated. Finally, in some marginal cases, it will be necessary to furnish soil borings, designs for retaining walls or seawalls, or anything else that special conditions require. In all cases, the lender will demand evidence of good title. Since at this stage the buyer has only an option on the land, the title will not be in his name, but the abstract must show that there will be no trouble in getting title insurance.

3.3.3 Good Faith Deposits

At the time of application, a bank such as an REIT will ask for a refundable good faith deposit, which is exactly the same in concept as the similar deposit made with a mortgage loan application. If the loan is approved but the borrower reneges, the lender keeps the deposit to pay for his time and effort in processing the application. The true purpose of a good faith deposit is to keep prospective borrowers from shopping around and wasting everyone's time. It acts as evidence of sincerity.

3.3.3.1.   The loan officer of an REIT will issue a loan memorandum after he has the loan application and all necessary supporting documents, together with the good faith deposit. The memorandum can actually be issued before the documents are in hand, in which case it is made subject to a survey, an appraisal, and so forth. In either case, it is simply a descriptive story that spells out, in some detail, what the loan is all about and who the borrower is. The memorandum is given to a loan committee that will either approve, disapprove, or ask for additional information. If approval is forthcoming, a commitment will be issued, which states that documents are additionally required. The attorneys of the lender will then write a letter to the borrower telling him what he must submit. After the borrower complies with all the requirements, the closing of the loan can take place.

3.3.3.2.   The amount of a land acquisition loan made by an REIT typically will be at least 60% of the appraised value of the site, and can go as high as 75% or even 80%. The credit rating of the borrower, together with the type of securities pledged against the loan, will determine the amount as well as the rate of interest. If a borrower pledges liquid assets in an amount equal to the face value of the loan, he will get much more favorable terms than a borrower who offers only slightly more than the land itself as security. The true rate of interest that is charged will be not less than $4\frac{1}{2}\%$ over the prime rate. (The prime rate is that which is charged by the biggest banks to their best customers on short-term loans. For example, if a very large corporation pays the Chase Manhattan Bank at the rate of 7% per year on a 90-day note, the interest charged by an REIT on a land loan will be $11\frac{1}{2}\%$ per year minimum.) The true rate of interest is the effective yield to the lender and includes both interest and fee or discount, because the discount is nothing more or less than prepaid interest. The maximum true rate of interest that can be charged is determined by state usury laws, as previously explained.

3.3.3.3.   A land acquisition loan is in reality a short-term first mortgage, and as such carries with it a note and a mortgage. The mortgage is secured by the land, and the note is secured, at least in part, by liquid assets. Generally the time set for repayment of the principal of the loan is less than 24 months, with an option to renew, although it is sometimes possible to get a 5-year land loan. A rather short time limit is set for the purpose of insuring future construction. A land loan is not made to enable a speculator to warehouse a tract, and unload it at a hoped-for handsome profit at some future date. Speculation is far too risky a venture to be financed by a bank, but investment is a reasonable avenue for the lending of funds. Therefore the bank requires that the land be put to use as soon as practicable, in which case the bank will be repaid by the proceeds of other loans, when the project is completed.

3.4 Land Development Financing

Money can be borrowed to develop land from its raw state up to the time when construction of buildings commences. Such on-site improvements include not only streets, sidewalks, sewers, water, and electric lines but also site preparation. Site preparation consists of reshaping the land by changing existing grades through cutting and filling, and removing any trees that stand within the intended walls of the buildings. All of this work should be done in accordance with plans made by an architect working with a landscape architect and an engineer.

3.4.1 Land Development Loan Draws

On a large project site preparation will take several months. The first draw on a construction loan may not occur, therefore, for some time after the contractor moves onto the job. The purpose of a land development loan is to provide interim financing and to enable a speculative house builder, for example, to get a subdivision ready for building. The money on a site development loan will be paid out in draws, each of which has been certified by an engineer at the end of each month, that is, the engineer verifies that the value of the amount of work stated in the draw request is proper and correct, and that the work has been performed satisfactorily in accordance with the plans. After the on-site improvements have been completed, the borrower will be obliged to repay the loan in monthly installments, in a manner similar to that for a first mortgage loan on a building. The interest rate is about the same as that for a land acquisition loan.

3.4.2 Title X

The minimum size tract that was eligible for a Title X loan under FHA financing was 10 acres, and the maximum was set at 1000 acres. The principal amount of the loan amounted to 50% of the raw land value, plus 90% of the cost of developing the land, up to a maximum combined total of $20,000,000. In addition to the outlay for streets, curbs, gutters, walks, and sewer and water lines, the cost of developing could include such amenities as a recreation center, a golf course, tennis courts, and perhaps public buildings. Furthermore, the total replacement cost contained professional fees, utility costs, and interest on the loan while it was being paid back, and all of these items were also included in the development cost when computing the principal amount to be lent.

3.4.2.1. The terms of a Title X loan seemed quite favorable to the developer. The interest rate included a 2-point discount, plus a basic rate of 7% per year, plus an additional $\frac{1}{2}$ of 1% payment to the FHA for mortgage insurance. No payments were to be made for 3 years after the initial closing. The developer was supposed to complete his work within the first 2 of those 3 years, and then take the third year to begin to sell off lots and parcels of the complete tract. Monthly payments began at the end of the third year, and were scheduled so as to amortize the loan by the end of the tenth year. Thus all the payments were to be made within a total of 7 years, beginning three years after the initial closing, but there was no penalty if the loan was paid off sooner.

3.4.2.2. In fact, a proportionate part of the principal was to be paid as soon as some part of the land was sold to a third party. When such a sale took place, the proceeds from the sale were given to the lender, who then released the appropriate parcel of land from the mortgage. The release clause of the mortgage stipulated that the land must be sold for at least 110% of the pro rata mortgage amount. In that way, when 90% of the land was sold, the loan would have been paid off in full. But the terms of the mortgage permitted subordination to a construction loan.

3.4.2.3. An example of the potential of Title X is given in the following case. A developer obtained an option to purchase 465 acres of land by paying the owner $5000 and promising to pay the balance on closing the loan. He then hired an architect to design the land for a fee of $1000 paid initially, the balance to be paid if FHA approval were forthcoming. The design envisioned 90 acres used for a regional shopping center (the site was near a large metro-politan area), 120 acres developed with multiple-family buildings, 120 acres devoted to town houses, and the remaining 135 acres reserved for single-family homes. All lots were laid out along well-planned streets. With the aid of a mortgage broker, the FHA was persuaded that the design, if carried out, would raise the value of the land to $4,000,000.

Therefore, at the initial closing, the developer got 50% of the land value, that is, $2,000,000. He then paid $1,000,000 for the land, and pocketed $1,000,000 tax free! (The second million was borrowed money, and thus neither income nor capital gains, so it was not taxable.) Part of the second million was used to pay the 10% of the cost of development not covered by the loan, but as the land was sold, that money was returned.

The developer then built a sewage treatment plant on land adjacent to the 465 acres, using some Title X money. He paid for the sewage plant with tie-in charges levied on individual owners who had bought plots from him on the 465 acres. During the course of operation of the sewer system he took a profit, which was covered for tax purposes by depreciation; 10 years later, when he could no longer gain by depreciation, he deeded back the system to the public.

This public-spirited citizen was thus richly rewarded for adding something of wealth to the economy, and at the same time perform-ing a public service.

4

Preparing the Request for Funds

4.0 *Importance of the Application*

Although the purchase of the correct piece of land is important, as is the method of buying it, and although initial capital is absolutely essential when it is desired to start a business, everything in a real estate venture hinges upon successfully obtaining a substantial permanent mortgage loan. The amount of a permanent loan on any given project can be increased by a really well thought out and well documented presentation on the part of the borrower. The application becomes extremely important, therefore, in obtaining this keystone—the permanent mortgage loan—to the whole operation.

When the application has a professional quality to it, the lender will assume that the developer is a professional. He will be favorably disposed toward lending more money than otherwise on the belief that the entire project has been very well planned and will undoubtedly be a success. The form of presentation can influence a lender, if not in a rational manner, at least subliminally. Subconsciously he will think that the man who is presenting it really knows what he is doing, and that he will do a much better job than the average borrower—he will manage things well and make a profit.

96

4.1 Equity

The differential between a strong presentation and a weak request might be as much as 5% on a loan. On a $1,000,000 project a well documented proposal could mean a loan of $50,000 more than would be issued on an unsubstantiated request, such as "How much will you lend me if I build a 100-room motel on this land?" Obviously, if the developer can obtain a loan that is larger by $50,000 than he would otherwise get, his company will not have to invest that $50,000 out of its own capital funds. The more money that is borrowed, the less capital utilization that is needed. The differential between the total cost of a project and the total amount that is borrowed can be provided only by capital investment, and this capital is called *equity*. The larger the loan, the less equity is required. If the loan is large enough, it is sometimes possible to eliminate the cash equity requirement completely. Sound financing principles, however, require a substantial cash equity.

4.2 Requirements

An application for a loan will require a financial statement of the developer, or a financial statement of each one of the partners in some instances. In addition, the lender will need a "pretty picture and a price," that is, an indication of what the project will look like, including some preliminary plans, and an estimate of what it will cost to build. But one of the essential parts of an application is a computation of the economic value of the proposed development.

4.3 Income Approach to Value

On a single home the loan value will be based on a probable sales price, or at least on an appraisal made by a lending officer of the bank, that is, on the value of the proposed house as a piece of merchandise. The size of the house, its amenities and materials of construcrion, the size of the lot, and the quality of the neighborhood are all taken into consideration in arriving at an appraisal of value of the completed building, and a mortgage is issued in an amount equal to a certain percentage of that value. But on a commercial venture the loan will be based on the economic worth of the project, that is, not on the buildings or on the land, but on the project as a business. This requires a bit of explanation.

4.3.1 An Analogy

Consider, for example, the case of a man who has a clothing store. An empty store is not worth anything to a bank. The bank will not lend money to a man who simply has a lease on an empty shell, and no plans of doing anything with the space. But it might lend money to a leaseholder who says to the bank, "I have experience in the clothing business, and I want to buy $60,000 worth of suits that I can sell for $100,000. Furthermore, I believe that I can buy and sell this stock within a period of 4 months, so that I can repeat the process three times in 1 year. Thus I plan to gross $3 \times \$100,000 = \$300,000$, with a margin of $3 \times \$40,000 = \$120,000$ in 1 year. Out of that money I can pay all business expenses, keep a reasonable salary, and repay a loan of $60,000 plus interest. I have already paid the rent for 1 year, I have paid my attorney and my accountant, and I have enough money for advertising, but now I need money for merchandise."

4.3.2 The Value of a Business

The bank is not interested in the merchandise. If the man fails in his business, the bank will be the owner of the suits. But the bank does not want the suits; it wants the return of its loan plus interest. Therefore the bank judges the character and financial reputation of the man; and if it thinks that he will be able to sell the suits, it concludes that he will be a success, and the loan will be repaid. Accordingly, the bank will lend him the money with the belief that he will make a sufficient gross profit to pay back the loan and have enough cash left over to stay in business.

The situation is similar with regard to an apartment, a motel, or a shopping center. The buildings as buildings, and the land as land, are not worth much to the bank. The bank does not want to own buildings or land. The whole project has a value only when it is considered as a business. The business will produce money, because ultimately the cash flowing in will exceed the cash flowing out. After all the money is collected from rentals and all expenses have been paid, there will be cash left over to pay on the loan and to give the investors a reasonable profit. It is only the money evolved from the business that can pay off the loan—an empty building cannot generate cash flow simply as an empty shell, just as 1000 suits packed in cartons in a warehouse do not generate cash until they are taken out and sold.

4.3.3 The Bank's Attitude

The loan, then, is to be paid back from the proceeds of a business venture, and the bank will lend money when it can see how it is going to be paid back. The bank will not lend money solely because the landscaping for the project is beautiful and the design of the buildings is excellent.

4.3.4 Numerical Example

Therefore the applicant must demonstrate to the bank the economic worth of the business he is about to create. He accomplishes this by working up an *income approach to value*, which shows how much money will be coming in each year, how much will be spent on expenses, and what the economic value of the residual cash will be. The amount of money that is left after all expenses have been paid can be used to pay off the loan and yield a profit, and this has an economic worth. The example shown in Table 4.1 will explain this idea a little more fully. The example involves a hypothetical apartment project, but the form of the presentation would be quite similar for any real estate venture, such as a motel, a warehouse, or an office building, provided that certain modifications were made here and there as applicable. An explanation follows the example.

Explanation

4.3.4.1 "NUMBER OF UNITS." The number and mix of the units should be maximized to obtain the most return from the project. The "mix" means the type of units that will be built, that is, the relative percentage of three-bedroom units, the percentage of two-

Table 4.1 Income Approach to Value: Picanos Villa Apartments, Urbane City, USA

INCOME

Number of Units	Type	Area (sq. Ft.)	Rental each × 12 = per Month	Rental Each per Year	Extension
25	Studio	500 × 22¢ = $110	$1320 × 25 =	$33,000
35	1 BR	680 × 21¢ = $142	$1704 × 35 =	$59,640
18	2 BR	800 × 21¢ = $168	$2016 × 18 =	$36,288
22	3 BR	850 × 20¢ = $170	$2040 × 22 =	$44,880
10	2 BR	950 × 20¢ = $190	$2280 × 10 =	$22,800
110 units	Total = 78,900 sq. ft. rental area			Gross annual income	$196,608

Less vacancy and collection loss @ 7%	−13,762
Gross income	$182,846
Auxiliary income	2,700
	$185,546

OPERATING EXPENSES

Electricity (common areas only @ $0.70/unit/month)		
12 × 0.70 × 110	say	$ 930
Waste and sewage @ $2.50/unit/month		3,300
Garbage, including dumpster rental @ $1.80/unit/month		2,380
Janitor and yardman		
1 full time @ $90/week		4,680
1 part time @ $45/week		2,340
Painting @ $60/unit/year		6,600
General repairs @ $30/unit/year		3,300
Supplies @ $10/unit/year		1,100
Replacement reserve		
Mechanical equipment		4,400
Carpeting		5,500
Management @ 5% of effective gross income		9,280
Taxes		
Payroll		1,200
Real Estate		23,600
Insurance		1,300
Advertising and accounting		1,200
Total		$71,110

(Continued)

Table 4.1 (*Continued*)

GROSS INCOME	$185,546
Less Expenses	−71,110
Net income	$114,436
Less interest on $94,000 land @ $7\frac{1}{2}\%$	−7,050
Annual net income available for interest on and recapture of value of improvements	$107,386
Building value capitalized @ 9.4% = $107,386/0.094 =	$1,142,404
Add land value	94,000
VALUE BY INCOME APPROACH	$1,236,404
First mortgage loan @ 75% of value = 0.75 × $1,236,404	$927,303
Loan Requested	$927,000

bedroom units, and so forth. In this example, perhaps the builder asked his architect to produce a design containing 50% two-bedroom units and 33% one-bedroom units, the rest being no-bedroom or "studio" apartments. The builder decided on this balance after studying his market, looking at trends in the area, and considering national trends. It is a ratio which must be carefully considered, and constitutes the first management decision that the developer makes in his project.

4.3.4.2 THE ARCHITECT'S JOB. As soon as the site has been selected and an option to buy has been placed on it, an architect should be employed. Of course an architect cannot work in a vacuum, so he must be given a topographic survey showing the size of the plot, the relative elevations of the land, the location of the street and all pertinent utilities, and so on. But the entrepreneur decides what type of project he wants to build and what amenities he will put into it, such as a swimming pool, laundry building, utility building, clubhouse, tennis courts, or whatever; he also must tell his architect the approximate size of each apartment unit that he wants to build. This is part of the original decision-making process of the developer. The architect then puts all these parts of the program together and attempts to satisfy his client while designing a handsome building. In this example the architect came quite close to the owner's request for 50% two-bedroom, 33% one-bedroom, and the rest studio units, while placing as many units as possible on the land. Maximizing the number of units decreases the proportional cost of land per unit, and actually increases the relative amount of mortgage per unit. At times, however, it may be desirable to disregard such a goal by purposely cutting down on the number of units that could be built. That will lead to large open spaces and perhaps to a more attractive and more rentable complex. The final decision depends on the cost of the land and the type of competition in the area. Existing zoning regulations, off-street parking requirements, building height restrictions, and side yard and setback rules will also play a part in determining the number of units possible. In fact, local laws and regulations might be such as to make the entire project unfeasible, by restricting the possible units to so small a number that the land cost would be disproportionately large.

4.3.4.3 RENTAL. The rate of rent charges is the next major decision that must be made by a developer. A survey of the local market must be made before any project is begun to determine what amenities should be included, what rent per square foot is being charged against those amenities and the raw rentable space, and how the local rental trends compare with regional and national trends. If, for example, all existing apartments in Urbane City have two bathrooms, then either any projected apartments will have to provide two bathrooms or else the proposed apartments must have a reduced rent if they are to have only one bathroom. On the other hand, any additional features that are not provided by the competition will call for a higher rent than that charged by others. If the competition offers simply living space but the proposed project will have a swimming pool and a clubhouse, the projected rental can be higher than that of the competition. Other amenities could well include fireplaces, dishwashers, and sauna baths, but it is well to remember that additional mechanical gadgetry demands increased maintenance, and that the increased rental might not prove to be worthwhile with these higher maintenance costs. There is also replacement of equipment, which can prove expensive and troublesome, to consider for the future. Amenities do not always pay for themselves. Their inclusion depends entirely on the market for which the project is being built.

Table 4.2 Competition Comparison Analysis

Amenities	Project Identification Number							
	1	2	3	4	5	6	7	8
1. Rent ($)								
1 BR								
2 BR								
3 BR								
2. Space								
1 BR								
2 BR								
3 BR								
3. Monthly rent per square foot								
1 BR								
2 BR								
3 BR								
4. Balconies and Patios								
5. Kitchen Equipment								
a. Disposal								
b. Dishwasher								
c. Refrigerator Size								
6. Eat-in space in kitchen								
7. Number of Bathrooms								
2 BR								
3 BR								
8. Air conditioning								
9. Other equipment								
a. Washer and dryer								
b.								
c.								
10. Flooring								
a. Parquet								
b. Carpet								
c. Other								
11. Draperies								
12. Swimming pool								
13. Others								
a. Playground								
b. Recreation lodge								
c. Nursery school								
d. Extra Landscaping								

4.3.4.4 HIGH-RISE RENTALS. In a multistory building the costs of construction increase as the building gets higher. Therefore the rental must be more in a high-rise building than for comparable space in a one- or two-story walk-up structure. The difference will probably be at least 10% more on the average. In the final analysis, rent can be determined only by local market conditions, regardless of what the national averages show.

4.3.4.5 VARIATIONS IN RENT. Notice that in the example of Table 4.1 the rent per square foot per month is not uniform for all the different apartment units. The reason for this spread is due to the cost of construction. It costs more to build a studio apartment than a two-bedroom apartment because a studio apartment still has to have a bathroom and a kitchen, which are very, very expensive, and the cost of these two rooms cannot be spread out over a large area of living space. The square-foot cost of a bathroom is probably more than ten times the square-foot cost of a bedroom. Thus, when a 500-square-foot apartment unit has a 35-square-foot bathroom, and when a 1000-square-foot apartment likewise contains one 35-square-foot bathroom, the total cost of the 500-square-foot unit will be considerably more per square foot than the comparable square-foot cost of the larger unit.

In a similar vein, mainly because of materials handling, the top floor of a multistory building costs more to construct than a lower floor, and therefore must have a higher rental. It is also more desirable to be higher up—the view is better, it is quieter, and there is less disturbance from people going by. For these reasons also, a higher floor commands a higher rental.

Location within a project may also affect the rent schedule. In an office building a corner office is more desirable than an interior space, and in an apartment a unit with a better view or a unit in a prestige location will carry a higher dollar value. Thus balcony units bring more rent than ground-floor units, and those overlooking a valley are worth more than those facing a parking lot.

4.3.4.6 TODAY'S DOLLARS. There is no need to consider future rentals at a higher rate. It may be that, by the time the job is finished and the doors are opened to tenants, either inflation or demand for space will have made a higher rental feasible, but all computations must be based on today's costs and today's rental rates. This gives a uniform basis on which to compute value, and value is always based on present worth. (The concept and meaning of present worth will be discussed in Chapter 7). All dollars are related to today's costs and today's dollars, including the dollars used in construction, the cost of borrowing, and the amount of rental that will be forthcoming. Such a procedure eliminates as much guess work as possible, and puts all computations on the same footing and the same time basis. Although rents and interest rates could go up, they could also go down, and one might go up while the other went down. Everything will be on a uniform basis if estimated in terms of today's dollars, using today's rental and interest rates.

This steady-state concept, however, does not consider the effects of inflation. If, because of inflation only, the interest rate is high, it should be acceptable to establish the rent schedule at the rental rates that will be in force after construction is completed, that is, the rents that will prevail about $1\frac{1}{2}$ to 2 years after the application is first submitted.

4.3.4.7 "VACANCY LOSS." The next item shown in Table 4.1 after "Gross annual income" is "Vacancy and collection loss." This is included to account for the fact that the possible gross annual income is based on 100% occupancy for an entire year. It would be very nice if this were actually the case, but in all likelihood there will be some vacancies, and at least some income will be lost between the time one tenant moves out and the next one moves in. Furthermore, a very small percentage of tenants will leave without paying a current bill, and there may be some bad checks that cannot be collected when certain tenants leave town.

When the two factors, that is, the vacancy ratio and the bad debts, are added together 7% seems like a reasonable figure to use for vacancy and collection loss. Many mortgage lenders will accept a 5% figure; in the case that we are now studying, this will lead to an increase in projected income of $3932, that is, 5% of $196,608 = $9830 instead of the $13,762 shown, so that the gross income with a 5% vacancy loss would become $186,778. Eventually, if the new figure is followed all the way through the table of income approach to value, the first mortgage will increase by $31,370. Thus, if a 5% vacancy ratio is used instead of 7%, a higher first mortgage loan can be obtained. The 7% figure was used here to be on the pessimistic side, but a 5% figure is more common.

4.3.4.8 "AUXILIARY INCOME." The main business of a real estate project is the rental of space. However, there are opportunities for obtaining income from other sources, for example, from laundry machines, vending machines, enclosed parking spaces, or fees for swimming club memberships in the case of a motel in a city. It is not necessary for the project to actually own any vending machines. They could be owned by some other company that pays a royalty or fee to the projects; this royalty or fee would become auxiliary income. It is well to note that every additional $1 of income will mean an additional $8 in the amount of the mortgage, and this, in turn means that the owner will not have to put in as much of his own capital—his equity will be reduced by those $8 of borrowed money. It is therefore a good idea to get as many dollars as possible into the income column, but at the same time every dollar shown there must be realistic.

In fact the entire rental schedule must be realistic. As shown in Chapter 1, once the mortgage broker and the lender accept the rental schedule, and the lender makes a commitment based on that schedule, the borrower will be held to it. He will have to produce the stipulated amount of income before the floor or ceiling of the the mortgage is funded in cash. If the rents are too high, the apartments will remain empty, and the floor of 81% of dollar occupancy will never be realized. The developer will perhaps then lose the project and his equity in it, and he may lose much more. If he has signed personally for any loans, he will be held responsible for their payment. Therefore the management decision of a rental schedule must be very carefully considered, as it is a most important one. Lower rents mean a lower mortgage, and a lower mortgage means that the owner must provide more equity cash. That is to be avoided if possible. On the other hand, higher rents, which lead to a higher mortgage, might lead to so many vacancies that the owner could not meet his financial obligations, and the entire project might be lost. In summary, the leverage of $8 of mortgage for every $1 of income produces a large swing in both directions and must be very studiously balanced. The rent must be at just the right level to maximize the profit with the greatest possible occupancy, and this rental rate will produce the maximum possible mortgage.

4.3.4.9 "OPERATING EXPENSES." After a realistic total income is computed, the net operating expenses for the year must be determined. The cost of operation of a real estate project can be divided into seven broad categories:

1. Utilities.
2. Payroll.
3. Maintenance and repairs.
4. Replacement reserve.
5. Management.
6. Taxes.
7. Miscellaneous.

1. The *utilities* to be listed are those which must be paid by the project. These include public lights, public water and sewer, and any other utilities included in the rental. Some places pay all electric and gas bills of tenants, and others include heat and air conditioning in the rental, all of which are utility costs.

2. The *payroll* of the project covers the yardmen, maids, janitors, and maintenance help who are employed on a regular basis and are not a part of the management of the project. The payroll often includes payroll taxes, insurance, and any fringe benefits offered by the company.

3. *Maintenance and repairs* include all items that are the responsibility of the owner. In some cases, such as shopping centers, the owner takes care of the exterior and the tenant is responsible for everything inside the building shell. In apartments or motels the owner must take care of everything that would be included in normal wear and tear, such as repairing a faulty toilet.

4. A successful business always has enough cash on hand to cover emergencies. Real estate operation is no exception to the rule, but too many owners neglect to put money aside, preferring to operate on a hand-to-mouth basis while hoping for the best. They drain as many dollars as possible from the project in the mistaken belief that difficulties will never catch up with them, but sooner or later the day of reckoning comes. At that time the money must be found to replace thousands of yards of carpeting, or to buy 100 new refrigera-

tors, or whatever the case might be. Therefore a *replacement reserve* should be set aside every year into a separate bank account, so that the necessary money will be on hand when it is needed to pay for a large expense of capital equipment. Such a fund should also include something for repairing or replacing the roof, for exterior painting, and so on. In any event, the mortgage lender knows that the expenditure will occur at some future date, and he can easily equate that future expense to a uniform yearly cost, as will be shown in Chapter 7. The yearly cost (or savings set aside toward the future cost) must therefore be shown on an income approach to value as an operating expense.

5. *Management* expenses are those strictly associated with the costs of management. These include the costs of collecting rents and making out checks to pay the bills, as well as the salaries of a resident agent, if there is one, and of his assistant, if he has one, plus any home office expense associated with the project.

6. *Taxes* include licenses, fees, and ad valorem (according to value) real estate taxes, in addition to any income taxes paid by the company before any money is transferred into the hands of the owners. Some prefer to include payroll taxes in this category, but it seems more logical to put payroll taxes into item 2, since they are a direct cost.

7. *Miscellaneous* covers everything else, and is a bad term to use. It is a catch-all for anything that does not fall into the first six categories of expense items. It might include, for examples, advertising, accounting, and legal costs.

In Table 4.1 these seven headings have been subdivided into more specific divisions so as to gain a greater degree of accuracy in predicting expenses. Expenses should actually be estimated as accurately as possible, and they should be based on existing costs and conditions in so far as they can be determined at the time the project is proposed, for much the same reasons as given for income prediction. If the expenses are set too high, the mortgage will not be as large as it should be, and the owner will have to invest an undue amount of cash. Every dollar that can be saved on expenses will add a dollar to the net income, because expenses are subtracted from gross income to obtain net income, and every $1 added to net income means about $8 more on the mortgage. On the other hand, if the expenses have been underestimated, the mortgage will be so large that the payments on the inflated amount may prove to be an impossible burden. Once the development is a reality, it will become necessary to meet all bills. If all the money has gone to make mortgage payments, so that none is available for maintenance, for example, then either the tenants will move out of the resulting slum or the creditors may force the owner into bankruptcy. There must be enough income to pay both the expenses and the mortgage, and the income cannot be increased without destroying a very carefully balanced rental schedule.

The total of all operating expenses, then, does not include payments on the mortgage. And this total of all operating expenses should be in the neighborhood of 40% of the gross rental income. In the case of Table 4.1, 0.40 × $182,846 is approximately $73,100, which is not too far above $71,110, the figure shown for the total expenses. Therefore the figures presented would be acceptable to a mortgage broker, since the total of all expenses is 71,110/182,846 = 0.389 or 38.9% of the gross rental, which is very close to 40% and looks realistic.

4.3.4.10. The operating expenses do not include payments on the mortgage for two reasons. First of all, every payment on the mortgage includes some portion which is a payment on the principal amount, and any payment on the principal is not an expense but is a reduction in debt and therefore an increase in equity. In other words, the more the principal is paid off, the larger the dollar amount of ownership becomes. If the mortgage loan was for $1,000,000, when the entire million is paid off the owners will have an additional $1,000,000 of equity in the project above any money they have put in initially. Money applied to equity is investment, and can come only from surplus cash or from profit. Equity represents capital, whether put in initially or at some later stage. It is not a cost of doing business, because it is a measure of the ownership or value that the owner has in the businesss.

The second reason that operating expenses do not include payments on the mortgage is that the lender will view the analysis of income approach to value as though he were the owner. He wants to visualize the project as though the entrepreneur defaulted or could not make payments, and the bank had to take over and become the owner in fact. If the bank were the owner, it wants to know what kind of annual income it could anticipate. That annual income would be the gross income less the operating expenses, which would be out of pocket to the bank. Obviously, if the bank is the owner, it does not have to make mortgage payments to itself. Thus the expenses do not include mortgage payments.

The bank wants to know what the net annual income will be so that it can determine the value of the business as a business, and decide how much to lend on such a basis. The bank has no desire to become the owner; it wants nothing less than to own real estate ventures. It wants only to know the true economic value of the proposed business, and this should be measured solely in terms of cash during the planning stage.

4.3.4.11 PRESENT COST. All of the dollar amounts shown in Table 4.1 are hypothetical, and no particular accuracy is claimed for them. The costs of utilities should be verified with the governing municipality and with the electric company that will service the property. The figures given are only crude approximations and could vary widely in different parts of the country. Janitorial wages can be obtained by inquiry in the area. It is of no importance as to what the costs will be next year or at any time in the future. If costs go up, rents will also rise to cover such increases. The only realistic approach, as stated previously, is to put everything in terms of today's dollars, so that expenses and rentals are both based on the situation that currently exists.

4.3.4.12 LAND COST AND VALUE. Land, say the American Indians, is eternal. No one can really own land, since we mortals only come and go and pass over it, but the land remains. Thus the value of a project is to some extent independent of the value of the land in this respect.

Another way of looking at the same proposition is that land has a value equal only to what someone is willing to pay for it. It can be appraised and reappraised; it can be thought of as being extremely valuable or not worth very much; but if a developer pays $94,000 for a certain tract, then that parcel is worth $94,000 at the time he buys it. It takes two people to make a sale, a buyer and a seller, and it takes the same two to establish the value. The seller alone cannot establish value.

However, when a developer buys land and spends his money, he has given up the right to receive interest on that money, because money has a timely value. If it is agreed that the interest rate on the permanent loan is to be $7\frac{1}{2}\%$, then any money connected with the project should get a return of $7\frac{1}{2}\%$. Therefore it must be assumed that money invested in the project could earn at least $7\frac{1}{2}\%$ if invested elsewhere, because the going rate of return has been established by the mortgage rate. In other words, money put into the land is thought of as losing $7\frac{1}{2}\%$ interest that could have been obtained if the same money had invested in some business. Land is not a business, and in that sense cannot generate wealth. Land can generate wealth only to a miner or a farmer. The project under consideration is not a farm, so the interest on \$94,000 at $7\frac{1}{2}\%$, which comes to \$7050 per year, is deducted from the net income of \$114,436, leaving \$107,386 available for interest on, and recapture of the value of the improvements.

The foregoing procedure is not usually followed by many mortgage brokers when computing the income approach to value. It is done here because it is theoretically correct and is used by some brokers. The concept of subtracting interest from the income amounts to a statement that lost interest is a cost of doing business. The developer has, in a sense, buried his money in land, which is nonproductive in a business sense, and he must therefore charge off the return that he would otherwise have received if he had invested the same money in some other way.

4.3.4.13 CAP RATE. The question now is, What is the value of a business that produces a net yearly cash increment of \$107,386? It is assumed that this amount will be forthcoming forever, that is to say, that in each and every year from now on, the business will have a cash flow of \$107,386 after expenses are deducted from gross income. There is no concern about inflation or deflation, because we are considering only present dollars and present worth. Since this is a perpetual yearly income, it is a cash flow at a given rate. In other words, what lump sum today is equivalent to \$107,386 per year forever? That lump sum is the value of the project.

The value of the project is now found by dividing the yearly return by a capitalization rate, or *cap rate*. The value thus found is an economic value, and is the worth of the project as a business. It is not the value of the buildings or of the land or of any combination thereof, but is the value of the project as a business in terms of dollars today.

4.3.4.14.   There is no scientific basis for establishing a cap rate, since it fluctuates in the same way that interest rates fluctuate. During a period of inflation or at times when the demand for money is quite strong, the cap rate will rise, and this will decrease the apparent value of the project, which is equal to the uniform annual payment divided by the cap rate. The larger the denominator, the smaller will be the value:

$$\text{Value} = \frac{\text{Payout}}{\text{Cap Rate}}$$

A smaller denominator will produce a larger value. The cap rate is set by the lender. A high cap rate means that the lender is not very eager to lend money at that time, because a lower value will mean a lower mortgage, and this will demand a higher equity. The lender is thus asking for more security, and less risk for his loan. Conversely, when the demand for funds is weak and the supply of money is plentiful, the cap rate will drop, thus giving a larger value to the business, so that a lender can lend out more money and entice an entrepreneur to borrow funds then instead of waiting.

4.3.4.15.   In the case under consideration the thinking of the lender might have been something like this: "The loan will be for 75% of the value of the project (see Section 4.3.4.18). Therefore the borrower has an equity position of 25% of the value of the project, the equity being the difference between the loan and the total value. As a lender, I want to get $7\frac{1}{2}\%$ interest, plus something for a risk factor, say another 1%, for a total of $8\frac{1}{2}\%$ or 0.085. My share, then, is 75% of 0.085 or 0.0635. The borrower should get a return of about 12% (or 0.12) on any real estate investment, so his share would be 25% of 0.12 or 0.0300. The total of the two value factors is 0.0635 + 0.0300 = 0.0935, which rounds off to 0.094 or, say, 9.4%, the cap rate."

Notice that the interest rate, the risk factor, and the borrower's rate of return are all established at the discretion of the lender, but are based on the money market existing at the time that the loan application is made. In other words, the lender can either increase or decrease the interest rate as he chooses, and he can do the same with the risk factor or the investor's rate of return. All of these are completely arbitrary and are set solely at the lender's discretion. Every time any one of these factors is changed, the change effects the total cap rate. For example, if the interest rate were increased from $7\frac{1}{2}\%$ to 10%, the increase in the cap rate would have been $(0.75 \times 0.10) - (0.75 \times 0.075) = 0.075 - 0.0562 = 0.0188$, and the cap rate would have been 11.2% instead of 9.4%, corresponding to a decrease in economic value of almost $184,000. The land has not changed; the buildings have not changed; the neighborhood has not changed; nevertheless the project has a much lower value to the lender only because he is not as eager to lend money, and has arbitrarily set a higher cap rate.

4.3.4.16. A formula for the cap rate that is based solely on interest, time, and the net yearly cash increment, without regard to risk factor or equity, will be developed in Chapter 7, where it is called the *rate of capitalizaton*. However, this is only theoretical and is of no use whatsoever in predicting a cap rate for any given time. Only a mortgage broker can say what banks are using as a cap rate at any specific time.

The total cap rate is completely at the lender's discretion. There is no argument about it. If the cap rate is undesirable, the only alternative is to postpone the project, or to find a banker who uses a lower figure—an unlikely prospect.

4.3.4.17 VALUE OF INCOME APPROACH. In any event, with a cap rate of 0.094, the building value becomes $107,286/0.094 = $1,142,404. This is not the value of the buildings, but rather the value of the business. It is considered to be the value of the buildings only for the purpose of computing the amount of the mortgage. The buildings themselves, it should be remembered, are not worth anything to the lender. The lender is putting his money into the business. The actual cost of the buildings could well be less than $1,100,000. But even if the buildings were completely leveled by fire, earthquake, or bomb blast, the land will still have a value of $94,000 because we are considering only present worth. Then the total value by the income approach is the sum of the business value of $1,142,404 plus the land value of $94,000, giving a grand total of $1,236,404.

As stated previously, many mortgage brokers do not bother to deduct interest on land. If in this case those computations had been eliminated, we would have used the original figure of $114,438 and divided it by the cap rate. Then the economic value would become $114,436/0.094 = $1,217,404, which is very close to the $1,236,404 obtained from the complicated computations. The simpler approach thus seems to be eminently satisfactory.

4.3.4.18 "75% OF VALUE." As indicated in the discussion of the cap rate, a lender will generally provide a mortgage equal to about 75% of the business value of a proposed project. A mortgage is never equal to the total economic value of a new project because every bank wants the investor to have a strong interest in making it a success. The 25% differential between the mortgage of 75% of value and the total value must be contributed by the investor. Equity should always be present in any loan. In the case of an automobile loan, for example, equity might be composed of part cash and part trade-in, or perhaps it would consist entirely of the trade-in. In other words, equity does not have to be cash. It can be contributed by providing something of value. In a real estate venture, equity might take the form of work, or perhaps even of land that was inherited.

The only time that a bank will lend an amount equal to the total value of a security is when the security is cash. Otherwise, a borrower must have some equity in a project so that he will be interested in getting a good return, in making timely payments on his debt, and in keeping up the value of the property.

4.4 Cost Approach

As stated above, the equity position of 25% of value does not represent the actual cash involved. From the lender's point of view, an owner should have some hard cash in a project and should receive a reasonably attractive return on that cash. Therefore the lender wants to know the actual dollar cost of the project, from which the developer's investment can be estimated. From this, in turn, the percentage of return on his investment can be computed. It is not necessary to furnish a builder's estimate which shows a complete analysis of construction costs, but summaries should be presented somewhat as in Table 4.3.

4.4.1 *"Construction Cost"*

The approximate construction cost is often called the *brick and mortar cost*. It includes site work and on-site and off-site development, in addition to the actual costs of materials and labor on the buildings themselves. Thus paving, sidewalks, landscaping, and all utilities are included, but not the builder's profit if the builder is also the developer. If the entire construction job is to be done by a third party, one who is not also the entrepreneur, then of course it is the third party's price to the owner that becomes the brick and mortar cost, and his price will include his overhead and profit. Notice that in the example of Table 4.3 the construction cost amounts to $945,000 out of a total of $1,124,990, which is only 84% of the total cost. Quite often it will be only 80% of the total.

Table 4.3 Construction Cost Summary:
Picanos Villa Apartments, Urbane City, U.S.A.

USE OF CASH

Land	$ 94,000
Approximate construction cost	945,000
Loan brokerage @ 2% (of $927,000)	18,540
Bank discount @ 1% (of $927,000)	9,270
Construction interest, including discount	49,680
Closing costs, including title insurance	6,000
Taxes during construction	2,500
Total cash outlay	$1,124,990

SOURCES OF CASH

First mortgage	$927,000	
3 months' cash flow, $\frac{1}{4}$ occupancy	12,290	
Total income		$939,290

ESTIMATED CASH REQUIRED
(use − sources)	$185,700

4.4.2 Replacement Cost

The total cost is the true *replacement cost* of the project. All the expenditures beyond actual construction cost are unavoidable and hence necessary. In other words, if anyone in the world were to go out and build this project, and employ everyone necessary to get the job done without doing any other work himself, it would cost him $1,124,990. Everyone would have to pay interest, taxes, and so forth.

4.4.2.1. The fact that the replacement cost is less than the value by the income approach is of no particular concern, especially since $1,124,990 is within 10% of $1,236,404. It is extremely rare for the two values to be exactly the same. A lender will be well satisfied if they are within 10% of each other. From the lender's viewpoint, replacement cost is less important than the economic worth of the business, because the lender must rely on the business to repay the loan, not on the bricks and mortar; nevertheless he does expect the value of the property, as property, to be somewhat close to its value as a business in a real estate venture. Furthermore, if the economic worth does not exceed the replacement cost, the project should be dropped.

4.4.3 Financing Fees

The "loan brokerage" (Table 4.3) was discussed in Chapter 1. The "bank discount" refers to the discount that is charged by the lender of the first mortgage. It is sometimes called an origination fee, and sometimes has other names. It could be omitted as a cost and deducted from the income calculation which follows the cost, but the first mortgage would nonetheless be recorded as $927,000 even though the discount had been deducted by the bank, so that the borrower had actually received only $927,000 − $9,270 = $917,730. Therefore, since the borrower has "spent" $9,270 and is obliged to pay back $927,000, the 1-point fee is shown under "Use of Cash," and the full mortgage is included under "Sources of Cash."

4.4.3.1. The construction interest can be estimated with a fair degree of accuracy if it is based on projected draw schedules, as will be shown in the following chapters. However, for a preliminary analysis a crude approximation will suffice. The amount of construction interest shown in Table 4.3 was based on several assumptions. It was assumed, first, that the job would take 12 months to complete, and then that all eleven of the construction draws would be equal. Actually, they will not be equal, but the assumption was made for the sake of simplicity. If a construction loan of $900,000 is assumed, each draw would be about 1/11 of $900,000 of $80,000. This is far from the truth, but is satisfactory for the approximate computation of construction interest. If the interest rate is $7\frac{1}{2}\%$ for 1 year, then it is 1/12 of $7\frac{1}{2}\%$, or about 6/10 of 1% per month. The interest on any one draw becomes $80,000 \times 0.006 = \$480$ for each month that it is held without paying it back to the bank. The first draw will be made at the end of the first month, and will therefore be held for 11 months, based on the assumption that the final mortgage will be obtained at the end of the twelfth month, when the job is completed. The interest on the first draw will be 480×11. Similarly, the interest on the second draw will be 480×10, the interest on the third draw will be 480×9, and so forth. The total construction interest will be $\$480 \times 11 + \$480 \times 10 + \$480 \times 9 + \cdots + \$480 \times 2 + \$480 \times 1 = \$480 (11 + 10 + 9 + \cdots + 2 + 1) = \$480 \times 66 = \$31,680$. Now, if it is assumed that the construction loan discount will be $18,000, the total construction loan cost becomes $49,680.

4.4.4 "Source of Cash": First Mortgage

It is hoped that the ceiling of the mortgage will be funded rather than the floor, so the full mortgage amount of $927,000 is shown in Table 4.3 as flowing into the project. There is just no point in presenting a pessimistic picture to the bank, for that will only tend to make the loan officer less enthusiastic about the request and more likely to turn it down completely. A bank is much likelier to lend money to the entrepreneur who exhudes confidence and seems quite sure of himself and his project. Therefore the full amount of $927,000 is shown.

4.4.5 "Sources of Cash": Cash Flow

A part of every building will be completed and ready for occupancy before the rest of it is. It is physically impossible to put the finishing touches on an entire building project at one instant of time. If a portion of it is completed some time before the rest of it, it is reasonable to assume that that portion can and will be rented before construction of the total building is finished. In the case being considered, it is assumed that an average of one quarter of the project will be occupied for 3 months' time before the end of the year, producing a cash flow of $1/4 \times 3/12 \times \$196,608 = \$12,290$, where \$166,608 is the gross potential rental income at 100% occupancy for a full year. Since the amount of \$12,290 is taken in before construction is complete, it is available to pay some of the costs incurred during construction, and is added to the cash obtained from the mortgage when computing the money available to pay for the project.

4.5 Income Feasibility

If an owner does not receive a sufficient return from a project, he will be tempted to take out cash that should be used for maintenance and put that cash in his pocket. If, on the other hand, the ratio of return to investment is satisfactory, the owner will maintain the project to a high standard in order that the cash flow will continue at the same rate. The latter course of action will protect the investment of the lender, and he will more readily make a loan if he knows that the borrower is going to receive a good return. The third phase of an income approach documentation is a feasibility analysis (Table 4.4), made on the basis of previous calculations.

4.5.1 Debt Service

Notice that up until this point no mention was made of payments on the mortgage. Now they are put into the computations as "debt service." The constant of 9.25 is arbitrary. Like the cap rate, it is set by the money market and must be obtained from a mortgage broker at the time application is being made. At one time most builders felt that a constant of 9.00 was the upper limit for a successful project. However, recently loans have been placed with a constant of 10.00 and even higher.

Table 4.4 Feasibility Analysis:
Picanos Villa Apartments, Urbane City, U.S.A.

Projected net income (effective gross)		$185,546
Expenses	$ 71,100	
Debt service @ 9.25 constant		
$927,000 × 0.0925	85,748	
Total	$156,848	
		$185,546
		−156,848
NET CASH FLOW PER YEAR		$ 28,698
Replacement cost	$1,124,990	
Mortgage + other income	939,290	
CASH EQUITY	$ 185,700	

$$\frac{\text{Return}}{\text{Equity}} = \frac{28,698}{185,700} = 15.5\%$$

4.5.2 Cash Flow

The total cash actually paid out by a project during a year will include all running expenses (in this case $71,100) plus payments of interest and principal on the mortgage ($85,748), for a grand total of $156,848 per year. Subtracting this figure from the projected income of $185,546 leaves $28,698 to go to the owner as cash profit each year, again based on present-day dollars. The cash profit is called the *cash flow*.

4.5.3 Rate of Return

Dividing the cash flow of $28,698 by the cash equity of $185,700 yields a rate of return of $15\frac{1}{2}\%$, which is considered satisfactory, and the proposal is a good one. The rate of return should be between 12% and 20%. Some investors demand 20%, but a substantial number are satisfied with the lower figure of 12%. The 15% shown here is a realistic goal, especially when the benefits of depreciation are thrown in.

4.5.4 Making the Equity

There are ways of producing the necessary equity without actually using dollars out of pocket. For example, if the land is purchased with a small down payment and the balance is in a subordinated second mortgage, the total appraised value of the land can be put into the package, even though the land will not be paid for until some time later. Furthermore, the land may have been purchased at a lesser value than the one shown as a cost, but the total appraised value is still applicable. Here the differential between cost and value represents a realized profit, because the land is, in a sense, "sold" to the project, so that profit on the "sale" becomes cash equity. Similarly, if the cost of construction should actually be less than the amount shown on the cost approach to value, the differential between true cost and indicated cost becomes a profit, and again this profit is part of the equity picture. In fact, it is not at all uncommon for a mortgage to cover all true costs, in which case it is said that the developer *mortgaged out*—his total cash equity lies in his profits on land and construction. But since profit represents cash, he does indeed have a true equity in the project.

4.5.5 Builder's Fee

Sometimes the indicated replacement cost is not close enough to the value obtained from an income approach, that is, there might be a 15% or 20% differential instead of the 10% in the example given here. In such a case the replacement cost can be legitimately increased through the inclusion of two fees, a builder's fee and an entrepreneur's fee. The builder's fee, or profit, will be accepted as about 5% of the brick and mortar cost. In the example of Table 4.3, it could be 0.05 × $945,000 = $47,220, say $47,000.

4.5.6 Developer's Fee

The entrepreneur's fee, or developer's fee, could well be taken as 2% of the total replacement cost. In the case under discussion, it would be 0.02 × $1,125,000 = $22,500, approximately. Certainly the developer is entitled to a fee. It is he who has put the entire package together and produced an economic good, where it did not exist before. He has coordinated raw materials and the labor and talents of many diverse individuals, and caused them to create a thing of value. He has, in effect, organized and managed an entire company whose purpose was the manufacture of these buildings. If it were not for his managerial skill, the whole project would never have materialized. Therefore a 2% fee seems quite reasonable.

4.5.7 Other Professional Fees

The architect's fee and those of all other design professionals are included in the construction cost in the example of Table 4.3. The fees could be listed separately and quite often are done so, in which case the construction cost would be not $945,000, but a lesser amount.

4.6 Building Budget Feasibility

Even though the figure may work out satisfactorily on an income approach to value, it is essential to determine the feasibility of a proposed project before spending large sums of money on architectural services and on accurate estimates of construction cost. A budget feasibility study is shown in Figure 4.1. It is a short, quick analysis that can be done in just a few minutes. It will indicate to a client whether or not he should proceed with a proposed project.

4.6.1 Example

A good builder knows what the approximate square-foot construction costs are for each general type of building in a given geographical area. By using a modified income approach, it is possible to compute the amount of money available for brick and mortar costs. A comparison of the cash per square foot available with the probable costs per square foot will immediately produce an indication of feasibility. The procedure shown in Figure 4.1 will now be explained in detail.

4.6.2 Preliminary Considerations

Again using the hypothetical Picanos Villa Apartments project of this chapter, numbers will now be introduced into the flow chart of Figure 4.1. Notice that the procedure is valid for any type of real estate venture and is not limited to apartments. The same diagram

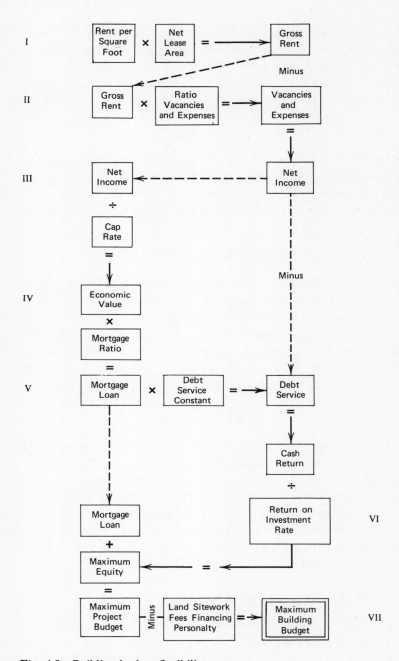

Fig. 4.1   Building budget flexibility.

122

could be used, but with different numbers, for a hotel, an office building, or a warehouse.

A rough idea of proposed area and rental is necessary before starting computations. Approximate numbers will suffice, since this is a preliminary study whose sole purpose is to indicate to an owner whether or not he should proceed.

4.6.3 Ground Rent

Assume an average rental of 21 cents per square foot per month, $0.21 \times 12 = 2.52 per year, say $2.50 per square foot per year. Suppose that, based on a rough sketch, it is believed that the total rentable area will be about 79,000 square feet. Then the gross rent will be

$$\$2.50 \times 79,000 = \$197,500 \text{ (Line 1)}$$

Auxiliary income is not included in Line I computations because this is a quick analysis, which is of sufficient accuracy for decision purposes.

4.6.4 Losses

Vacancies and expenses are lumped together in Line II. Vacancy and collection loss will be taken at 5%, while expenses will probably be in the neighborhood of 38%, giving a total of 43% of the gross rent. Then

$$\$197,500 \times 0.43 = \$84,925, \text{ say } \$85,000 \text{ (Line II)}$$

4.6.5 Net Income

Then the net income will be the gross rent minus the expenses, or

$$\$197,500 - \$85,000 = \$112,500 \text{ (Line III)}$$

4.6.6 Economic Value of Example

The cap rate must be current, as explained previously, and is obtained by inquiry from a mortgage broker. Let us suppose that the cap rate is 9.4%. Then the economic value is obtained as

$$\frac{\$112,500}{0.094} = \text{approximately } \$1,200,000 \text{ (Line IV)}$$

4.6.7 Amount of Mortgage

The first mortgage will usually be about 75% of the economic value, that is, the value found from the income approach. Therefore the mortgage loan will be about

$$\$1,200,000 \times 0.75 = \$900,000 \text{ (Line V)}$$

The mortgage will be a little higher than that figure when the land value is considered, but $900,000 is a safe figure to use. Anything more will be a pleasant bonus.

4.6.8 Debt Service of Example

Now the mortgage payments are taken into the calculations. The constant, that is, the percentage used in computing the yearly level constant payments to be made over the life of the mortgage, is also obtained from a mortgage broker, so as to be valid for the date at which the computations are made. If a constant of 9.25% is assumed, the debt service will be

$$\$900,000 \times 0.0925 = \text{about } \$83,300 \text{ (Line V)}$$

4.6.9 Profit

The net cash flow available to the owner will be the net income minus the payments on principal and interest. In other words, the answer on Line III minus the answer on Line V, or $112,500 − $83,300 = $29,200, gives the cash return to the owner, or the yearly cash flow or profit.

4.6.10 Return on Investment

Now the owner must determine for himself what sort of rate of return he wants on any cash investment he places in this project. This will be based on actual cash equity, not on anything hypothetical, such as a builder's profit. Generally, real estate should bring a return of about 20% on such a basis, but some owners want a higher return, while others are content with less, say 15% or thereabouts. Suppose that in this case the *ROI* (rate of *R*eturn *O*n *I*nvestment) desired is 20%. Since the ROI will be cash equity divided by cash return, the maximum cash that can be invested must be the cash return divided by the ROI. The maximum cash equity becomes

$$\frac{\$29,200}{0.20} = \$146,000 \text{ (Line VI)}$$

4.6.11 Cash Needed

The total cash available for completing the entire project can only be the money from the mortgage lender plus the money from the owner. There will be some cash from rental during construction, but it is best not to count on this. Any other borrowing is temporary and has to be repaid from one or both of these sources: mortgage and equity. The total cash available is thus estimated as

$$\$900,000 + \$146,000 = \$1,046,000 \text{ (Line VII)}$$

and the figure of $1,046,000 is the maximum project budget, if the owner puts in no more than $146,000.

4.6.12 Building Budget

The total project budget includes the brick and mortar cost, plus all other costs. The other costs include those of land, site work, professional fees, financing fees, and personalty. These five items of additional cost are either known, as in the case of land, or can be estimated from past experience. The cost of financing will generally be from 10 to 12% of the project cost, and includes brokerage, discounts, and interest during construction. Suppose that in this case the figures are as follows:

Land	$ 94,000
Site work	50,000
Fees	40,000
Financing	100,000
Personalty	36,000
Total	$320,000

Then the maximum building budget will be

$$\$1,046,000 - \$320,000 = \$726,000 \text{ (Line VII)}$$

Remember that the net rentable area is to be 79,000 square feet. If the building budget is known, the construction cost cannot exceed

$$\frac{\$726,000}{79,000} = \text{about } \$9.20 \text{ per square foot}$$

for the *net* area, or less than $8 per square foot for the gross area. In addition to rentable area, there will be public areas such as stairs and walkways that do not bring in revenues, but are part of the gross area and must be built and paid for.

4.6.13 Increased Equity

The bottom line gives the final answer. The building must be constructed for no more than $8 per square foot. There is no sense in being overly optimistic, or in hoping somehow to bring the project in, if it cannot be done for that figure. Unless the rents are too low and can be raised, the only alternative is for the owner to increase his cash equity, which would mean that he is willing to accept a lower ROI. If the owner will accept a 12% return on his cash investment, his equity must be

$$\frac{\$29,200}{0.12} = \$243,333$$

and the total cash available for the project will be

$$\$900,000 \times \$243,333 = \$1,143,333$$

leading to a maximum building budget of

$$\$1,143,333 - \$320,000 = \$832,333$$

or a cost per net square foot of

$$\frac{\$923,333}{79,000} = \$10.42$$

The budget would then become about $9 per gross square foot. If this figure is still not high enough, the project should be abandoned.

5

Draw Schedules

5.0 The Builder's Goal

In regard to the process of funding for construction, the method of obtaining construction financing, among other factors, has been considered. In this chapter assume that all financing has been arranged and construction has started. It is now the builder's job to get the money from the bank to cover his expenses completely, if at all possible.

5.1 Residential Draws

When building a house it is extremely difficult to cover all costs with the money obtained from the bank. The reason lies in the method by which banks disburse funds. Payments are made according to an arbitrary schedule set forth by the bank. A typical example is shown in Figure 5.1.

5.1.1 Amount of Each Draw

Notice that the money is not advanced in equal amounts, nor is it paid out monthly. Rather, the four payments are made according to the work performed, regardless of how long it takes to accomplish that work. In the schedule shown, the first draw of 15% of the total

THE CHARTER COMPANY

CONSTRUCTION LOAN PAYMENT SCHEDULE

Builder (Mortgagor):

TOTAL AMOUNT OF LOAN TO BE ADVANCED $_____

1st Advancement (15%) $_____
When ( ) 1st Intermediate FHA VA Compliance
Inspection Report received; or, ( ) some
person designated by the Mortgagee certifies
in writing that Items 1 through 3 are completed

      Lot   Block   Amount

CMC CONSTRUCTION LOAN NO._____

LEGAL DESCRIPTION:

1. Prefoundation work and footing poured.
2. Foundation walls and piers, including garage.
3. Termite shields, if required, and rough plumbing.

2nd Advancement (35%) $_____
When ( ) 2nd FHA VA Compliance Inspection
Report received; or, ( ) some person
designated by the Mortgagee certifies in
writing that Items 4 through 7 are
completed.

      Lot   Block   Amount

4. Subfloor laid or concrete slab poured.
5. Framed and dried in (including garage), exterior wall and sheathing or wood siding and felt or concrete blocks, exterior window and door frames, interior framing and ceiling joist, rough hardware.
6. Plumbing complete, including tub.
7. Rough electric complete.

3rd Advancement (30%) $_____
When ( ) some person designated by the
Mortgagee certifies in writing that
Items 8 through 16 are completed.

      Lot   Block   Amount

8. Fireplace and chimney (if applicable)
9. Lathing, rough plaster and finish plaster, or sheet rock installed.
10. Exterior wall covering complete (brick veneer or stucco).
11. Paint priming, exterior.
12. Sash and glazing.
13. Tile wainscoting and flooring.
14. Finish roofing.
15. Interior trimming, including doors and kitchen cabinets on site.
16. Duct-work (if applicable) and basic heating unit in.

Final Distribution (20%) $_____
When ( ) Final FHA VA Compliance Inspection
Report received; or, ( ) some person designated
by the Mortgagee certifies in writing that
Items 17 through 22 are completed.

      Lot   Block   Amount

17. Exterior trim, screens and garage complete.
18. Painting and caulking complete.
19. Floor sanding and finishing and linoleum.
20. Electric fixtures installed, plumbing fixtures installed, including septic tank.
21. Walks, drives, and finish grading and clean up all work, inside and outside complete, and house and garage ready for occupancy.
22. All releases required by Counsel of Mortgagee.

Fig. 5.1 The Charter Company construction loan payment schedule.

128

to be lent will be made when the foundations are complete, which can occur within 1 week after the initial closing. Since site clearing, layout, construction of footings, and rough plumbing may have a total cost of considerably less than 15% of the cost of the house, the builder has a chance at this point to recoup some of his expenses on land, design, and closing costs. Alternatively, he can use the extra money to meet his payroll during the next phase of construction. In any event, it should not be assumed at this point that a large profit is being made. Nothing is further from the truth. Too many builders make this mistake and use the extra money for some other job, only to meet with financial disaster later on.

5.1.2 Certification

Figure 5.1 shows that, even though no architect is involved, the bank requires certification of completion of each stage of work. In the case of an FHA or Veterans Administration (VA) loan, the government agency involved makes its own inspections and reports. If the government is not involved, the loan officer of the bank or his representative makes his own inspections.

5.1.3 Location Description

The words "Lot" and "Block" (Figure 5.1) describe the location in the subdivision. A block is usually surrounded by streets, while a lot is a single parcel within the block. It has happened that a house has been built on the wrong lot, a fact which might explain the bank's caution in requiring the land description to be put down for each draw. It is more likely, however, that several houses are being built simultaneously by the same builder, and the bank wants to make sure that the individual house being funded by this draw is getting the money assigned to it, rather than drawing funds from some other house, which might be a more expensive job.

5.1.4 Ambiguity of the Example

The second draw of 35%, when added to the first draw of 15%, brings the total funding up to one-half of the total loan. At this stage the house is ready for drywall or plaster, as the case may be. The form shown in Figure 5.1 is a general one, and has been prepared in such a way that it can cover almost any house that is built. Therefore it is somewhat ambiguous and must be used as it is applicable. For example, the first floor might be either a slab-on grade, or wood framing over basement or crawl space. Line 4 on the right-hand side considers both methods of building.

5.1.5 Variations

The third draw of 30% brings the total funding up to 80%. Notice that item 16 (duct work) would probably have been completed before any drywall was applied. Some banks therefore include this item in the second draw. In other words, the form shown is typical, but the actual form will vary from lender to lender.

5.1.6 Lien Release Form

The last part of the funding of the combined construction-permanent loan is made when the house is complete. An example of a form used to satisfy the requirements of item 22 is shown in Figure 5.2. It is advisable to get every signature required just as soon as full payment is made to any particular subcontractor, to avoid undue delay when the entire job is completed. He might be hard to find just when you need him.

5.1.7 Value of Efficiency

Obviously the most important single factor in house construction financing is organization and efficiency, because the draws are made on a basis of accomplishment rather than time. If the entire job can be finished in less than 2 months (this is not an impossible dream), the builder will be able to meet all of his labor and material bills without undue hardship. But if the job drags on, the contractor will be in trouble. When any subcontractor finishes his work, he expects to be paid, if not immediately, certainly by the tenth of the next month. If the rest of the work included in the same grouping within that draw is not completed, the contractor will not get any money from the bank and will not be able to pay the subcontractor as he should. For instance, the tile work may be complete, but if the roofing is not installed, the third draw will not be made, and the tile sub-contractor will not be paid. The word will get around, the other subcontractors will be hesitant to work for fear they will not be paid either, and the job will slow down even more. Furthermore, the contractor will lose discounts applicable to timely payments on materials, and the construction interest will increase.

5.2 Monthly Draws

On larger jobs a construction loan is disbursed monthly. Each month the contractor makes out his request and gives it to the supervising architect or engineer for his approval. Approved copies are then sent to the owner, and the bank issues a check for the approved amount. All requests are based on a schedule of values which were prepared by the builder before he started any work. The schedule of values can be either straightforward or front-end-loaded (see section 5.2.7), but in either case it will be based on the contractor's estimate.

5.2.1 The Estimate

A contractor's estimate is made in the usual way, taking off labor and materials, then running the extensions, adding payroll tax and sales tax as applicable, and listing subcontractor bids. Finally, the several sheets involved are brought forward into a summary esti-mate of costs, as shown in Table 5.1. Notice that labor and materials are not separated herein, and that all applicable taxes have already been included. However, many other items have not been included, such as administrative expense (office overhead), general super-vision, temporary utilities, miscelleneous small tools, trucking, and clean-up. Nor has the cost of bonding been listed, if it is required. Finally, no mention is made of the builder's fee or profit. This sum-mary estimate is solely a worksheet, to be retained in the contractor's office, and not shown to anyone. It serves as a basis for a construction bid, or, if the builder is also the developer, as a basis for the draw schedules. In this example we assume that the builder is the developer.

Mtg. Acct. No..

We, the contractor, the following sub-contractors and materialmen hereby acknowledge receipt of payment in full for all work, labor and materials furnished on construction work on property located , in Alachua County, Florida, and more particularly described as follows:

and we release all of our respective rights of lien against said property. Said property belonging to......
.... located at..
in the City of Gainesville, County of Alachua, State of Florida.

Dated at Gainesville, Alachua County, Florida:

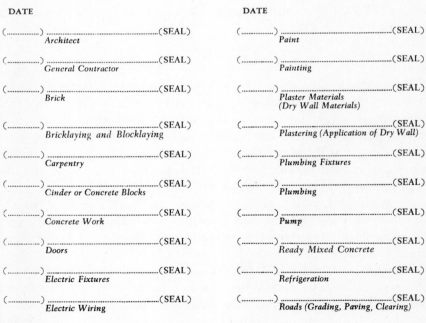

DATE

(................) ....(SEAL)
   Architect

(................) ....(SEAL)
   General Contractor

(................) ....(SEAL)
   Brick

(................) ....(SEAL)
   Bricklaying and Blocklaying

(................) ....(SEAL)
   Carpentry

(................) ....(SEAL)
   Cinder or Concrete Blocks

(................) ....(SEAL)
   Concrete Work

(................) ....(SEAL)
   Doors

(................) ....(SEAL)
   Electric Fixtures

(................) ....(SEAL)
   Electric Wiring

DATE

(................) ....(SEAL)
   Paint

(................) ....(SEAL)
   Painting

(................) ....(SEAL)
   Plaster Materials
   (Dry Wall Materials)

(................) ....(SEAL)
   Plastering (Application of Dry Wall)

(................) ....(SEAL)
   Plumbing Fixtures

(................) ....(SEAL)
   Plumbing

(................) ....(SEAL)
   Pump

(................) ....(SEAL)
   Ready Mixed Concrete

(................) ....(SEAL)
   Refrigeration

(................) ....(SEAL)
   Roads (Grading, Paving, Clearing)

Fig. 5.2

132

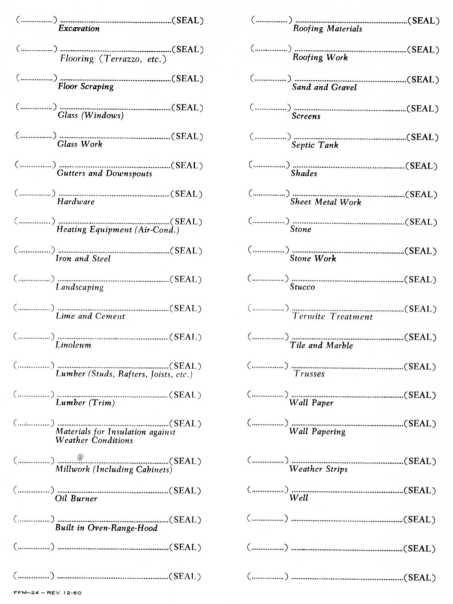

(................) ....(SEAL)
       Excavation

(................) ....(SEAL)
       Flooring (Terrazzo, etc.)

(................) ....(SEAL)
       Floor Scraping

(................) ....(SEAL)
       Glass (Windows)

(................) ....(SEAL)
       Glass Work

(................) ....(SEAL)
       Gutters and Downspouts

(................) ....(SEAL)
       Hardware

(................) ....(SEAL)
       Heating Equipment (Air-Cond.)

(................) ....(SEAL)
       Iron and Steel

(................) ....(SEAL)
       Landscaping

(................) ....(SEAL)
       Lime and Cement

(................) ....(SEAL)
       Linoleum

(................) ....(SEAL)
       Lumber (Studs, Rafters, Joists, etc.)

(................) ....(SEAL)
       Lumber (Trim)

(................) ....(SEAL)
       Materials for Insulation against
       Weather Conditions

(................) ....(SEAL)
       Millwork (Including Cabinets)

(................) ....(SEAL)
       Oil Burner

(................) ....(SEAL)
       Built in Oven-Range-Hood

(................) ....(SEAL)

(................) ....(SEAL)

(................) ....(SEAL)
       Roofing Materials

(................) ....(SEAL)
       Roofing Work

(................) ....(SEAL)
       Sand and Gravel

(................) ....(SEAL)
       Screens

(................) ....(SEAL)
       Septic Tank

(................) ....(SEAL)
       Shades

(................) ....(SEAL)
       Sheet Metal Work

(................) ....(SEAL)
       Stone

(................) ....(SEAL)
       Stone Work

(................) ....(SEAL)
       Stucco

(................) ....(SEAL)
       Termite Treatment

(................) ....(SEAL)
       Tile and Marble

(................) ....(SEAL)
       Trusses

(................) ....(SEAL)
       Wall Paper

(................) ....(SEAL)
       Wall Papering

(................) ....(SEAL)
       Weather Strips

(................) ....(SEAL)
       Well

(................) ....(SEAL)

(................) ....(SEAL)

(................) ....(SEAL)

FFM—24 – REV. 12-60

Fig. 5.2 *(Continued)*

Table 5.1 Estimate Summary: Picanos Villa, Urbane City, U.S.A.

1. SITE WORK

Site Preparation	$ 1,200	
Rough Grading	1,453	
Water Supply	9,051	
Sanitary Sewer	13,274	
Electric Service and Grounds Lighting	4,675	
Storm Sewer	5,243	
Curbs & Drainage	3,268	
Pavement	16,214	
Walks	10,230	
Swimming Pool	12,125	
Landscaping	4,867	
		$ 81,600

2. BUILDINGS

Excavation	$ 7,091	
[a]Footings, Concrete & Steel	7,375	
Masonry	55,162	
Waterproofing	686	
Concrete Floors & Cement Work	108,720	
Carpet	33,754	
Rough Carpentry	29,580	
[b]Millwork	10,422	
[b]Windows	18,615	
[b]Doors	22,463	
Metal Work	1,064	
Drywall	48,565	
[c]Insulation	8,164	
Roofing	11,205	
[c]Sheet Metal	3,010	
Painting	37,693	
[b]Finish Hardware	9,697	
Tile	48,283	
Kitchen Cabinets	23,629	
[b]Medicine Cabinets	1,210	
Plumbing	61,116	
Heat & Air Conditioning	76,292	
Electric	81,959	
Miscellaneous	6,892	
		$712,647

(Continued)

Table 5.1 (*Continued*)

3. PERSONALTY		
Ranges	$ 9,460	
Refrigerators	14,366	
		$ 23,826
TOTAL COST		$818,073

a To be included in Concrete Work.
b To be included in Finish Carpentry.
c To be included in Roofing.

5.2.2 Draw Schedules

There are, as previously stated, two ways of presenting the first draw schedule, which will be used in the same form for each succeeding draw. Consider the first way, which is quite straightforward. In Table 5.2 notice that the various items that were omitted in the estimate summary of Table 5.1 are now included. In addition, the costs of land, professional fees, and construction interest are also shown; but no mention is made of the builder's fee or the developer's (entrepeneur's) fee, although these, too, might be included if they were needed to make the total equal, or exceed, the construction loan.

5.2.3 Required Payments

In the example of Table 5.2 the total cost of $1,031,600 is greater than the mortgage of $927,000, and much greater than the construction loan, because the construction loan will be based on the floor of the mortgage, rather than on the ceiling. Suppose that the floor is 80% of $927,000, that is, $731,600. Then the construction loan will also be $731,600, unless a stand-by commitment has been obtained for the gap. If there is no stand-by commitment, there is a difference of $300,000 between the total cost of $1,031,600 and the construction loan of $731,600. In order to protect itself, the bank that is providing the construction loan will not give out any money on any draws until such time as the developer shows that he has already spent $300,000 on the project. In other words, after the first $300,000 worth of value has been paid for, and there remains a balance of $731,600 needed to finish the project, then and only then will the

Table 5.2 Draw Request: Picanos Villa, Urbane City, U.S.A.

DRAW REQUEST - PICANOS VILLA
Urbane City, USA

ITEM	VALUE	% COMPLETED	VALUE COMPLETED	BALANCE
Land	$ 94,000	100	$ 94,000	0
Professional Fees	39,810	72	28,540	11,270
Construction Loan Interest	49,680	0	0	49,680
Overhead & Bond	30,037	22	6,537	23,500
Site Work	38,164	0	0	38,164
Walks & Paving	26,444			26,444
Swim Pool	12,125			2,125
Landscaping	4,867			4,867
Excavation	7,091			7,091
Concrete	116,095			116,095
Masonry	55,162			55,162
Waterproofing	686			686
Rough Carpentry	29,580			29,580
Finish Carpentry	62,407			62,407
Metalwork	1,064			1,064
Drywall	48,565			48,565
Roofing	22,379			22,379
Painting	37,693			37,693
Tile	48,283			48,283
Carpet	33,754			33,754
Cabinets	23,629			23,629
Plumbing	61,116			61,116
Heat & A.C.	76,292			76,292
Electric	81,959			81,959
Miscellaneous	6,892			6,892
Ranges & Refrigs.	23,826	0	0	23,826
	$ 1,031,600	12.4%	$ 128,077	$ 903,523

Less payments to date   0

This draw $ 128,077

Less 10% retainage   12,808

Due this draw $ 115,269

construction loan begin to be funded. Draws will be made against the balance of $731,600, and that money will be used to finish the job.

Even if a stand-by commitment were obtained, there would still exist a difference between the total cost of $1,031,600 and the total construction loan available, which would then be $927,000, but this difference would be only $104,600 rather than $300,000. Once again, the bank would insist that this amount of $104,600 be spent by the developer before any construction money was disbursed, and, similarly, the bank would lend only toward the balance. Notice in Table 5.2 that actually $128,077 has been spent, as shown in the "Totals" row, under the column headed "Value Completed." All of this $128,077 was spent before any construction took place. The bank might therefore be induced to lend the difference between $128,077 and $104,600, that is $23,477, at the time of the initial closing, but in all likelihood it would refuse.

5.2.4 Reasons for Holdback

The bank would not lend this money for several reasons. First of all, a construction lender is not making a land-purchase loan; and if no work ever starts, the $23,477 will actually have been put into the land alone. Second, up to the time of the final draw, the lender withholds 10% of all value in place. Ostensibly, this is to prevent an unscrupulous contractor from absconding with the money because he has already made his profit and does not care to complete the job. Alternatively, it can be argued that the 10% withheld is a reserve fund to meet any bills that the contractor has incurred and failed to pay for some reason. Theoretically, the 10% represents the contractor's profit, and the banks apparently feel that a contractor is not entitled to his fee until the job is completed. However, if the builder holds a completion bond, that argument is at best specious. Bankers contend that the amount withheld also covers any disagreements that might arise. Thus, if a draw could be made upon initial closing, it would be for a maximum of $128,077 − $12,808 = $115,269. However, even if the bank lent money at that time, it would still insist that the developer provide the first $104,600, so that bank would lend only the difference between $115,269 and $104,600, which is $10,669. It does not seem worth the effort to request a draw that amounts to only about 1% of the total cost of the project. It would be much better to wait 1 month, meanwhile accomplishing a good bit of work on item 5: "Site Work," item 9: "Excavation," and perhaps item 10: "Concrete."

5.2.5 Avoiding Difficulties

To avoid all this difficulty, it would be advisable to have the "total" under the column headed "Value" read the same as the amount of the construction loan, If, for example, the construction loan is to be $927,000, then item 1: "Land" could be omitted completely, and item 2: "Professional Fees" could be reduced by $10,600, so that the total reduction would be $104,600, thus bringing the total of $1,031,600 down to $927,000. In that way there would be no arguments or misunderstandings when the draws are presented during the course of construction, and the first draw could be honored without any questions regarding equity. Obviously, if the "total" reads the same as the loan, the developer has already put up his cash equity. The bank will then be able to lend the rest, and the first draw will be honored in full, less the 10% withholding.

5.2.6 Alternative Draw Schedule

Some contractors prefer to show only the items directly related to construction, and then therefore omit all incidental or related items, such as profit or fee, overhead, and construction interest. Notice that Table 5.3 has only 22 items, whereas Table 5.2 shows 26 items, although both describe the same job. The difference lies in the fact that the first four items of Table 5.2, "Land," "Professional Fees," "Construction Loan Interest," and "Overhead & Bond," have been omitted from Table 5.3. These four items have the following values:

$$
\begin{array}{r}
\$ \ 94,000 \\
39,810 \\
49,680 \\
\underline{30,037} \\
\text{Subtotal} \quad \$213,527
\end{array}
$$

Table 5.3   Draw Request: Picanos Villa, Urbane City, U.S.A.

DRAW REQUEST - PICANOS VILLA
Urbane City, USA

ITEM	VALUE	% COMPLETED	VALUE COMPLETED	BALANCE TO DRAW
Site Work	$ 47,660	85	40,600	7,060
Walks & Paving	33,040	0	0	33,040
Swim Pool	12,730	0	0	12,730
Landscaping	5,110	0	0	5,110
Excavation	8,790	100	8,790	0
Concrete	145,100	20	29,020	116,080
Masonry	68,860	5	3,440	65,420
Waterproofing	720	0	0	720
Rough Carpentry	36,980			36,980
Finish Carpentry	78,110			78,110
Ironwork	1,120			1,120
Drywall	50,990			50,990
Roofing	23,500			23,500
Painting	39,580			39,580
Tile	49,700			49,700
Carpet	35,580			35,440
Cabinets	24,810			24,810
Plumbing	64,170			64,170
Heat & Air Condition	80,110			80,110
Electric	86,060			86,060
Miscellaneous	7,240			7,240
Ranges & Refrigs.	26,980	0	0	26,980
	$ 927,000		$ 81,850	$ 845,150

Less payments to date   0

This draw $ 81,850

Less 10% retainage   8,185

Due this draw $ 73,665

Subtracting this subtotal from $1,031,600 leaves a net of $818,073. But if the construction loan is for $927,000, it is necessary to add the difference of $927,000 − $818,073 = $108,927 to the items of Table 5.3 so that the "total" of this table will equal the construction loan amount.

5.2.7 Front End Loading

Before the contractor ever gets the first draw, he will have spent a large portion of his own money, not only on the construction itself, but also on such things as the estimate, which is time consuming and expensive, and on setting up the job in the office and in the field. It is reasonable, therefore, for the builder to attempt to recapture his cash outlay as rapidly as possible. It is also reasonable to conclude that a builder needs only a small profit margin on cost items that are fixed and definite, such as subcontractors' bids and the purchase of equipment, whereas he needs a larger profit on risk items, such as work done by his own forces, which might have a cost overrun. For all these reasons the items of Table 5.3 are *front-end-loaded*. The amount of $108,927 is not distributed uniformly among all 22 items, nor is it applied as a uniform percentage override. If it had been applied as a uniform percentage, it would have been necessary to add

$$\frac{108,927}{818,073} = 0.1452 = 14.52\%$$

to each one of the 22 items. For example, item 5: "Site Work" of Table 5.2 would have been increased by $38,164 \times 0.1452 = \$5541.41$ to give an item "cost" of $38,164 + \$5541.41 = \$43,705.41$. Instead, fixed cost items are increased by about 5 or 6%, while the contractor's own work is increased by about 20 or 25% in such a way that the "total" comes up to $927,000, the desired amount. None of the resulting dollar values is exact, and they have all been rounded out to show a zero as the last number.

It is not intended to present this as a rule or law, or to imply that this procedure must be followed. Table 5.3 is shown only as an illustration of one possible way to front-end-load a draw schedule. Many other combinations of numbers would be equally acceptable. It would be definitely wrong, though, to overdo the process in such a way as to make the entire list suspect to the architect. For example, it would be wrong to increase "site work" from $38,164 to $147,091 and leave everything else as is. The "total" would be $927,000, but the architect would never approve the first draw, and he would be extremely suspicious throughout the job because of what he would regard as deceit on the part of the builder, because of the bad draw schedule. Comparison of the items in Table 5.3 with those of Table 5.2 shows that the override in site work is

$$\frac{47,660 - 38,164}{34,164} = \frac{9496}{38,164} = 0.249, \text{ about } 25\%$$

whereas the override in plumbing is only

$$\frac{64,170 - 61,116}{61,116} = \frac{3054}{61,116} = 0.0498, \text{ about } 5\%$$

The figures under "Value Completed" in Table 5.3 are based on the assumption that this draw request was presented 1 month after construction started.

6

Cash Forecasting

6.0 Planning Expenditures

In Chapter 2 it was pointed out that a well managed company keeps its capital intact, and in fact tries to accumulate more capital so that it can do more work and larger jobs, and thus make more money. Sometimes, though, some money must be spent. Obviously it is necessary to plan each job carefully so as to avoid spending any more capital than is absolutely essential. The same careful thought and planning must go into the expenditure of money as go into the planning and coordination of the actual work of construction, which involves the scheduling of men, materials and specialty contractors. Thus, before the job starts, it is wise to try to forecast just how much cash will be needed each month, and to figure out how to obtain that money without utilizing any more capital than is necessary.

6.1 Bar Charts

Tentative draw schedules can be predicted before the job starts if enough time is devoted to planning. Most knowledgeable contractors make use of critical path method (CPM) diagrams to establish the length of the job and to speed up the process of construction. From a good CPM diagram it is not at all difficult to draw a Gantt diagram,

142

more often called a *bar chart*. The actual drawing of the bar chart takes very little time, and the chart itself makes it easy to see at a glance just what percentage of each item on the draw schedule will be completed each month.

6.1.1 Example

Of course it is not necessary to synthesize a CPM diagram into a bar chart, but this is a more accurate process than drawing one based on intuition or experience. In either course the final drawing will resemble Figure 6.1. The example shown is far from complete and is given merely for purpose of illustration. Notice that at the end of the first month all the excavation will have been com-

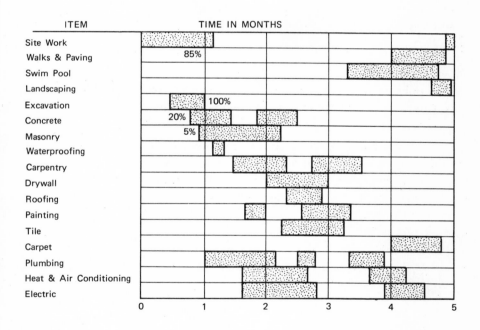

Means work in process

Fig. 6.1 Bar chart.

pleted, 85% of the site work will have been accomplished, and 20% of the concrete work will be finished; however, it is estimated that only 5% on the masonry will be in place, if all goes according to schedule.

6.1.2 Cost Per Month

The estimated percentages of completion can now be applied against the values shown in the draw schedule of Table 5.2 to obtain a good idea of the amount of cash required during the first month, as shown in Table 6.1. The values for "Land," "Fees," "Interest," and "Overhead" would be obtained from the estimate summary and not from the bar chart. These are the amounts that will actually have been spent on the job. A similar estimate could be made for each month of the job. All of these several estimates would then be combined into a summary of totals, as shown in Table 6.2.

6.1.3 Purpose of Bar Charts

The purpose of the bar charts, then, was to make it possible to easily compute the anticipated percentages of completion of each item

Table 6.1 $ Values Completed, First Month:
Picanos Villa, Urbane City, U.S.A.

Item	Beginning of Month	End of Month
Land	$ 94,000	$ 94,000
Fees	28,540	28,540
Interest	0	0
Overhead	6,537	11,237
Site Work	0	32,500
Excavation	0	7,091
Concrete	0	23,219
Masonry	0	2,758
.	.	.
.	.	.
.	.	.
Electric	0	0
Total	$129,077	$199,345

Table 6.2 Estimated
Summary of Total Costs:
Picanos Villa,
Urbane City, U.S.A.

Month	Value
0	$ 129,077
1	199,345
2	426,862
3	793,176
4	937,214
5	1,031,600

in the job for each month during the duration of the job. These percentages are applied against the dollar values of the items, so as to obtain an estimated total of the dollars required each month as the job progresses. Most of these dollars will come from the monthly draws. The rest will have to come from operating capital, or else the difference will have to be borrowed as front money at the beginning of the job, or as short-term loans as the job progresses, as described in Chapter 1. The differences can best be seen if the two totals (actual cost vs. draws) are plotted on a graph, as shown in Figure 6.2.

6.2 S-Curve

The graph has as an ordinate (vertical axis) dollar values, and it has as an abscissa (horizontal axis) the time in days, weeks, or, as shown here, months. When the predicted cash outlay is plotted on the graph, it will be a series of dots. The first dot will show the amount of money spent before construction starts, which would be $129,077 for the example of Picanos Villa, and will be placed above time zero. The prediction was that at the end of the first month of work $199,345 would have been spent, so that point is plotted, and so forth. When all six points of the predicted actual cost have been plotted in Figure 6.2, they can be connected either with straight lines or with a smooth curve. In either event, at this stage the shape of the drawing will

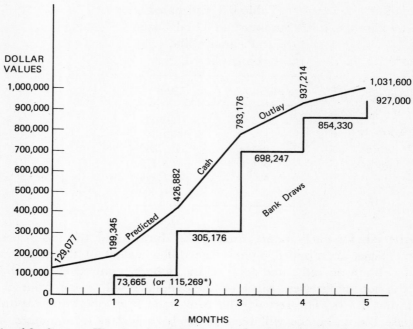

Fig. 6.2 S-curve. The time has been shortened to 5 months simply to make the explanation easier. The same principles apply if the job takes much longer. *See discussion in Sections 6.3.2 and 6.3.3.

look roughly like an elongated or tilted letter "S," and therefore this is called the S-curve of cost versus time.

6.2.1 Plotting Bank Draws

On the same graph it is not difficult to plot the predicted bank draws. Each one of these draws will have to be based on an estimated draw schedule, which has been made up by the technique shown in Section 6.1.2, as applied to the schedule of Table 5.2 as an example.

6.2.2 The First Draw

The first draw might occur at the initial closing, that is, at time 0, when construction is just about to start. Such would be the case in certain FHA loans, but in general the first draw does not occur until after the first month has gone by. In the example of Figure 6.2 it is assumed that conventional financing is used, so the estimated first draw of $115,269 is plotted just above the point that indicates the end of the first month.

6.2.3 Step Curves

The several dots of the bank draws cannot be connected with a curve because no additional money comes in until the end of the month. In the case of actual cost a curve was drawn because money is actually spent each day of the job, or at least work is done which cost money, so that the actual cost is constantly increasing until the job is completed. However, since the level of each bank draw does not change during any given month, a step curve is drawn to connect the five points shown in Figure 6.2.

6.3 Cash Forecasting

Now the additional cash necessary at the beginning of each month, and also the cash necessary on any given day of the month, can be predicted. At the start of the job $129,077 will have been spent. Perhaps "front money" can be borrowed to cover a good part of this expenditure; but in that case interest will have to be paid on that front money, and the principal will have to be paid back at the end of the first month.

6.3.1 Difference Between Curves

During the first month an additional sum of $199,345 − $129,077 = $70,268 will have been spent, and the builder must figure out some way of getting a good part of that money to meet his payroll during the month, since most of the work done during the first month will be done by the general contractor, as shown in Section 6.1.2. The various ways of meeting payroll are discussed in Chapter 1.

6.3.2 Net Actual Cost

At the end of the first month the first draw of $73,665 will be obtained from the bank (see Table 5.3) but it will not be enough to cover all costs up to that date. There will be a net difference of $199,345 − $73,665 = $125,680. Of course, if the costs of land and professional fees were omitted, the actual cost at the end of the first month would be reduced by $94,000 (land) + $28,540 (fees) = $122,540, leaving a net actual cost of only $199,345 − $122,540 = $76,805. (The starting figure of $129,077 shown on the graph in Figure 6.2 is more than $122,540 because it includes some allowance for building permits, estimating costs, and so forth.) In fact, the net actual cost of construction during the first month will be less than $76,805 because the draw schedule has been front-end-loaded. The true total costs to the general contractor from the time construction starts until the first draw is received should not be very much more than the first draw if the schedule has been arranged properly. The actual total cost of the complete package, which includes land and fees, will be considerably greater than the draw, however, and this differential will remain large throughout the job.

6.3.3 Developer's Cost

If the cost of land and fees had been included in the draw schedule, as would perhaps be the case when the builder is the developer, the first draw would have been $115,269, as shown in Table 5.2. In that case, there remains a spread of $199,345 − $155,269 = $84,076. Since the value of the land alone is greater than this spread, successful financing then depends on being able to buy the land without investing too much capital, as discussed in Chapter 3.

6.3.4 Effect of Time Lag

It should be noted now that the step curve of bank draws is an idealistic situation. If the draw requested is not submitted until the last day of the month, the money will probably not be received until the tenth day of the following month. Therefore the contractor should estimate the amount of work he will accomplish during the last few days of the month, and submit his bill 3 days before the end of the month. The owner's architect or engineer will then be able to check it, authorize it, and submit it to the bank by the first of the month, in which case the money will be forthcoming by the fifth.

There will still be a time lag, and costs will continue to mount up, but the time lag will have been shortened. The entire step curve of bank draws should therefore be shifted to the right, along the time scale, by about 5 days or 1/6 of 1 month. The gap between draws and actual cost will now become greater, and must be considered in financial planning.

6.3.5 Predicting Construction Interest

A second point that should be noted is that the predicted actual cost must include interest on the construction loan, particularly if the contractor is the developer. If the first draw is $115,269, and if the job duration is 5 months, then this money will have been held for 4 months. If the interest rate is $7\frac{1}{2}\%$ (per annum is understood), the interest during the 4 months will amount of $3647.44 on the first draw. At the end of the second month the interest on the first draw will be only $720.43, but it compounds during the ensuing months, as will be explained in Chapter 7. In fact, each draw will have interest charged to it for the time during which that draw is held. For the example shown in Figure 6.2 the second draw will be held for 3 months, the third draw will be held for 2 months, and the fourth draw will have interest charged to it for only 1 month. Theoretically, the fifth draw will not have any interest charge, because the permanent financing will take effect at that time. However, there is usually a time lag of 1 month before the permanent financing takes over the construction loan, so that every one of the interest computations for every one of the predicted draws should be increased proportionately. The first draw, therefore, will probably be held for a total of 5 months until the construction loan has been purchased by the permanent lender. In that case, the total interest due on the first draw of $115,269 will amount to $4390.66, and the total interest due on all the draws will add up to $20,227.35, which includes 1 month's interest on the last draw of $927,000 − $854,330 = $72,670. The total construction interest of over $20,000 is probably equal to half of the contractor's profit, if indeed he is fortunate enough to make a profit. But remember that the origination fee of 2 points must also be paid to the construction lender; this amounts to $0.02 \times$ $927,000 = $18,540 in the example of Figure 6.2. Thus the construction lender will be getting total true interest of $20,227.35 + $18,540 = $38,767.35, and this figure must be included in the computation of predicted actual cost.

6.4 Summary

All well-managed companies predict how much cash they will need at various times in the future, and then attempt to raise that amount before it is actually required. At the very least they make plans for securing the cash when they will need it. Construction companies can do the same. The S-curve can be based upon estimated *actual* costs to the contractor, and the draw schedule can then be fixed up by front-end-loading so that all the necessary cash will be available to cover all actual costs each month. This process is not illegal or immoral. The greatest percentage of the estimated surcharge of overhead and profit is placed quite properly on the contractor's own work, and smaller percentages are placed on the various subcontractors' work, all of them fixed up so that the numbers come out right each month. These percentages can be applied only one time, though: when the first schedule of values is presented to the owner's agent. After that they are fixed. This means that a little time should be spent in financial preplanning, using a CPM, a bar chart, and the S-curve and step-curve.

7

Time Value of Money

7.0 Money as a Company Tool

As explained in Chapter 2, money is a tool to be used to the best advantage of the company. At times money is to be spent, and at other times it should be saved. Whenever the decision is made to spend it, the money can come directly from the company treasury, that is, out of capital, or it can be "rented," that is, borrowed.

7.1 Why Interest?

The decision is always between alternatives, and should be based on the total profit that can be made by judicious usage of a certain sum of money. For example, suppose that your construction company had a job which seemed to require a tower crane. If you did not have the tower crane, you could perhaps find other ways of getting the building completed, but the job would take much longer and would be more costly. In other words, the tower crane would make extra money for the company. However, if you did not buy a tower crane, you could put the same money to work in some other way, such as having more capital so that you could take on another job and make more money. Or perhaps you would put the money in the hands of someone, such as a banker or a stockbroker, who would invest it for you so that it would make money for you. The choice, then, is to put the money to work in such a way that it makes the most money for you. But in any case the money is not at all productive unless it is put to work, and this means that the decision must be made just as soon as the money is in hand. If the cash is buried in a tin can in your backyard, it can never be worth more than its face value. In fact, it can depreciate because of inflation.

Money therefore has a timely value. You can invest it yourself in some productive way, or you can let some agent, such as a bank, invest it for you. Whoever uses it gains something. If you or your agent lets someone else use your money to buy a house or an automobile, that third person has obtained a concrete economic gain, for he has added to his worth by the value of his purchase. But, if you have not used the money in your own business to make more money (by buying and using a tower crane, for example), then you must make at least as much extra cash when you invest it elsewhere. Therefore the third party who bought the house or automobile must pay you for the use of your money. You are, in effect, paid for giving up the use of your money for personal purposes. Of course, if you borrow the money to buy the crane, then you must pay "rent" for the use of the money. This premium that money brings to itself for using it over a stipulated period of time is called *interest*.

7.2 Interest Defined

More formally, interest may be defined as money paid for the use of borrowed money. Or, in a broad sense, interest can be said to be the return obtainable by the productive investment of capital. The rate of interest is the ratio between the interest chargeable or payable at the end of a period of time and the money owed at the beginning of that period. The rate is always based on a 1-year period unless a shorter time is stipulated, such as 1% per month. Thus, if \$8 of interest is payable annually on a debt of \$100, the interest rate is \$8/\$100 = 0.08 per year. This is described as an interest rate of 8%, the "per year" being understood.

7.2.1 Rate of Interest

Sometimes interest is payable oftener then once each year, but the interest rate per year is usually what is meant when the interest rate is quoted, unless specifically stated otherwise. In this way, 0.00667 payable monthly, 0.02 payable quarterly, or 0.04 payable semiannually are all described as 8%. There is a slight difference among these four percentages, but the difference between the nominal rate of 8% and the effective rate produced by each of the others is not large enough to affect a decision in the economic analysis of any construction project. (The monthly rate of 0.00667 is equal to 8.3%; quarterly, 0.02 = 8.24%; and semiannually, 0.04 = 8.16%.)

7.3 Plans for Paying Back a Loan

Consider the four plans shown in Table 7.1 by which a loan of $10,000 is paid back in 10 years with interest at 8%. The date at which the loan is made is considered time 0, and the time is measured in years from that date. The $10,000 is called the *principal* of the loan.

7.3.1 Short Term Notes

Plan 1 is typical of a scheme of repayment often used with short-term notes. Suppose that you borrow some money on a 30-day note in order to meet your payroll. At the end of the month you could pay back the principal and the interest out of your draw, but then you would find that you had to borrow the same amount again. To save bookkeeping and certain other finance charges, the bank could be induced to continue the note, and you would pay only the interest due at that time. This process could be repeated until the end of the job, when you would pay off the note plus the interest for the last month. Notice that in Plan 1 no money is paid on the principal until the very end of the total time period, but interest is paid at the end of each year.

7.3.2 Uniform Principal Payments

Plan 2 is another scheme often used in repaying short-term notes. It differs from Plan 1 in that periodic payments are made on the principal, in addition to paying the interest due at the end of each period of time. But in this case, because the principal amount is being steadily reduced, each of the interest payments is less than the

Table 7.1 Four Plans for Repayment of $10,000 in 10 Years with Interest at 8%

End of Year	Interest Due (8% of Money Owed at Start of Year)	Total Money Owed before Year-End Payment	Year-End Payment	Money Owed after Year-End Payment
Plan 1				
0				$10,000.00
1	$ 800.00	$10,800.00	$ 800.00	10,000.00
2	800.00	10,800.00	800.00	10,000.00
3	800.00	10,800.00	800.00	10,000.00
4	800.00	10,800.00	800.00	10,000.00
5	800.00	10,800.00	800.00	10,000.00
6	800.00	10,800.00	800.00	10,000.00
7	800.00	10,800.00	800.00	10,000.00
8	800.00	10,800.00	800.00	10,000.00
9	800.00	10,800.00	800.00	10,000.00
10	800.00	10,800.00	10,800.00	0
Plan 2				
0				$10,000.00
1	$ 800.00	$10,800.00	$ 1800.00	9,000.00
2	720.00	9,720.00	1720.00	8,000.00
3	640.00	8,640.00	1640.00	7,000.00
4	560.00	7,560.00	1560.00	6,000.00
5	480.00	6,480.00	1480.00	5,000.00
6	400.00	5,400.00	1400.00	4,000.00
7	320.00	4,320.00	1320.00	3,000.00
8	240.00	3,240.00	1240.00	2,000.00
9	160.00	2,160.00	1160.00	1,000.00
10	80.00	1,080.00	1080.00	0
Plan 3				
0				$10,000.00
1	$ 800.00	$10,800.00	$ 1490.29	9,309.71
2	744.78	10,054.49	1490.29	8,564.20
3	685.14	9,249.34	1490.29	7,759.05
4	620.72	8,379.77	1490.29	6,889.48
5	551.16	7,440.64	1490.29	5,950.35
6	476.03	6,426.38	1490.29	4,936.09
7	394.89	5,330.98	1490.29	3,840.69

(Continued)

Table 7.1 (*Continued*)

End of Year	Interest Due (8% of Money Owed at Start of Year)	Total Money Owed before Year-End Payment	Year-End Payment	Money Owed after Year-End Payment
8	307.25	4,147.94	1490.29	2,657.65
9	212.61	2,870.26	1490.29	1,379.97
10	110.32	1,490.29	1490.29	0
Plan 4				
0				$10,000.00
1	$ 800.00	$10,800.00	$ 0.00	10,800.00
2	864.00	11,664.00	0.00	11,664.00
3	933.12	12,597.12	0.00	12,597.12
4	1007.27	13,604.89	0.00	13,604.89
5	1088.39	14,693.28	0.00	14,693.28
6	1175.46	15,868.74	0.00	15,868.74
7	1269.50	17,138.24	0.00	17,138.24
8	1371.06	18,509.30	0.00	18,509.30
9	1480.74	19,990.04	0.00	19,990.04
10	1599.20	21,589.24	21,589.24	0

preceding one. Thus the amount of dollars paid on each installment is a steadily decreasing number. In fact, the total number of dollars paid in Plan 1 is $18,000, but the total number of dollars paid in Plan 2 is $14,400.

7.3.3 *Level Constant Payments*

The scheme used in Plan 3 is the usual way of paying off a mortgage. The amount of $1490.29 is called the *level constant payment*. Out of this payment comes, first, all the interest due at that time; the remainder is applied toward reducing the principal. For example, out of the first payment, $800 is used to pay the interest, and $1490.29 − $800.00 = $690.29 is paid on the principal, reducing it from $10,000 to $9309.71. From the second payment $744.78 is paid on interest, leaving $1490.29 − $744.78 = $745.51 to be paid on the principal, which reduces it from $9309.71 to $8564.20. Notice that at first more than half of the level constant payment was used to pay interest, but as time goes on more is applied to the principal and less to the interest, until at the end only $110.32 is due on interest, while $1379.97 is applied to the principal. But the number of dollars paid each time remains the same. The total number of dollars actually paid back is $14,902.90.

7.3.4 Paying off a Loan

One last observation should be made concerning Plan 3. Unless you have agreed to a penalty clause such as that shown in the commitment described in Chapter 1, you can pay off the principal amount remaining due at any time and thus discharge your debt. For example, after making the fifth payment of $1490.29 there remains an unpaid balance of $5950.35. At that time, you can make an additional payment of $5950.35 and the debt will be canceled. You do not owe any further interest. You must pay interest only on money that is in your possession for the time during which you have it, if it is borrowed money. You do not owe interest on money that you have not received, nor do you owe interest on money that you have paid back.

7.3.5 Compound Interest

Plan 4 is an example of what is called *compound interest*. It is typical of what happens to a sum of money left untouched in a bank account. If considered as a debt, it is often called a *balloon note*. (Plan 1 is another form of balloon note.) Because no payments whatsoever are made between the time the money is borrowed (or placed in the bank) and the end of a specified time period, interest begets interest. For instance, at the end of the first year, because no payments are made, the total amount owed is the principal of $10,000 plus the interest of $800 for a total of $10,800. At the beginning of the second year, then, $10,800 is owed and interest is charged against this amount during the course of the year. At the end of the second year the interest due is $864 instead of $800, the additional $64 being the interest on the interest ($0.08 \times \$800 = \$64$). This means that interest is compounding. In the third year interest will be charged on $10,800 + \$864 = \$11,664$, and so on. At the end of 10 years the total compound amount of $21,589.24 must be paid to discharge the debt. If you want to pay off the debt sooner, say at the end of 5 years, the total amount due at that time must be paid ($14,693.28 for 5 years).

7.4 Equivalence

Surprisingly, all of the four plans of repayment are equivalent, one to the other, with respect to the time period and the rate of interest. This is true from the standpoint of both the lender and the borrower, but it is easier to see by considering the lender's position. For example, compare Plan 1 with Plan 4. At the end of the first year the bank receives $800, which it can immediately lend to some third party (call him Jones) at the same rate of interest. During the second year that $800 will earn 0.08 × $800 = $64 for the bank. At the end of the second year the bank receives $800 from the borrower using Plan 1, plus an additional $64 from Jones, for a total of $864, the same as the interest shown in Plan 4. The bank, having lent $800 to Jones, now lends $864 to Smith, and receives as interest at the end of the third year $800 from the first borrower, $64 from Jones, and 0.08 × $864 = $69.12 from Smith, for a total of $800 + $64 + $69.12 = $933.12, the same amount as shown in Plan 4. This process can be repeated all the way down the line for 10 years, so that Plan 1 is equivalent to Plan 4.

7.4.1 Commonality of Plans

It is not difficult to see that the same line of reasoning can be applied when comparing Plan 2 with Plan 4, and that it will also hold true when considering Plan 3 in relation to Plan 4. In other words, each one of the first three plans is equivalent to Plan 4 from the lender's viewpoint. Now there is a law in mathematics which states that, if $a = d$ and $b = d$ and $c = d$, then $a = b = c = d$. In other words, all four plans are equivalent, one to the other. The bank will make the same amount of money on the loan no matter which one of the four plans is adopted for repayment. There are three things common to each one of the plans: the principal of $10,000, the interest rate of 8%, and the total time of 10 years.

7.4.2 The Borrower's Viewpoint

From the borrower's viewpoint also, the plans are equivalent. Again consider Plan 1 versus Plan 4. The money you have to work with should make money for you, or you should not have borrowed it in the first place. In fact, it must earn at least as much as it costs to borrow. Therefore the borrowed $10,000 should earn at least $800 for you during the first year. At the end of that year, if you do not pay $800 to the bank, you should be able to put the money to work so that it earns at least $0.08 \times $800 = 64 for you during the second year. Simultaneously, the original $10,000 is earning at least $800 for you during the second year, so that at the end of that year you should have a capital of $10,000 + $800 + $64 + $800 = $11,664$, the same as the amount shown in Plan 4. It is simply a question of which pocket the money goes into. Therefore Plan 1 is equivalent to Plan 4 from the borrower's viewpoint, and it can be seen that, in a similar way all the plans are equivalent to one another.

7.4.3 Superiority of Plans

There is no single answer as to which plan is superior. The lender might demand a specific one of the methods of repayment, in which case, if the borrower wants the money, he will have to agree to the terms. If the option is with the borrower, the decision depends on how he thinks he will best be able to pay the money back, and what use he has for the money. In the final analysis, the actual true cost to the borrower and the total income to the bank are the same, no matter which plan is adopted. The total number of dollars changing hands is not the same:

$18,000   for Plan 1
$14,400   for Plan 2
$14,902.90 for Plan 3
$21,589.24 for Plan 4

but because the four plans are equivalent, the difference is only apparent, not real. The true cost is the same for every one of the plans.

7.5 Present Worth

But, again, in order for the four plans to be equivalent, each must have the same interest rate and the same total time for repayment, and each must be based on the same principal amount. Therefore the principal amount can be borrowed provided that there is a promise to repay it at a given interest rate for a stipulated time period in accordance with some definite plan. That principal can be called the *present worth* of the money. For example, if there is a promise to pay $21,589.24 10 years from now, and if the interest is 8%, then the present worth of that $21,589.24 is $10,000. Or, if there is a promise to pay $1490.29 for each of 10 years and the interest is 8%, the present worth of all that money is $10,000.

7.5.1 Interest Rate vs Present Worth

If the interest rate changes, the present worth is also altered. For instance, if the interest rate were 10% instead of 8%, then a promise to pay $21,589.24 10 years from now would produce a loan of only $8323.59. However, under the same conditions, an interest rate of 6% would yield a loan of $12,055.32. (Notice that these are not direct relationships:

$$\frac{0.08}{0.10} \times \$10,000 = \$8000, \textit{ not } \$8,323.59$$

and

$$\frac{0.08}{0.06} \times \$10,000 = \$13,333.33, \textit{ not } \$12,055.32$$

Direct ratios do not give the correct answer. The correct method of solution will be shown later.)

Similarly, if the interest were 10%, a promise to pay $1490.29 per year for 10 years could obtain a loan of only $9157.19. And if the interest were reduced from 8% to 6%, the same $1490.29 per year for 10 years would obtain $10,968.66.

7.5.2 Time vs Present Worth

Furthermore, if the time for repayment changes, the loan amount is also changed. Suppose that the interest rate remained at 8%, but

$21,589.24 was to be paid at the end of 20 years instead of at the end of 10 years. Then the amount that could be borrowed would be only $4631.93. But if that same $21,589.24 were paid back in 5 years, the loan would be for $14,692.27. In other words, if the interest is 8%, the present worth of $21,589.24 paid 20 years from now is $4631.93; paid 10 years from now, it is $10,000; and paid 5 years from now, it is $14,693.27. Similarly, if the interest were 8%, the present worth of $1490.29 paid each year for 20 years would be $14,631.89; for 10 years it would be $10,000; and for 5 years it would be only $5950.29. Thus it is seen that the amount that can be borrowed depends on the interest rate and on the time of repayment, so both of these are extremely important in computing mortgages and the income approach to value.

7.5.3 Meaning of "Present"

The word "present" in "present worth" refers to the date on which the loan is made. Thus, if money had been borrowed in the year 1426 with a promise to pay it back in 1492, then for purposes of computation 1426 becomes the present, even though that date is more than 500 years ago, Or, if a loan is going to be made in the year 2437, to be paid back by 2447, the loan amount in 2437 is its present worth. The rules of interest computation are immutable and have nothing to do with inflation or deflation.

7.6

$$S = P(1 + i)^n$$

The rules of interest lead to six useful formulas, which will be designated as equations I through VI. The first of these can be derived by the application of logic.

Suppose that a loan has a principal amount P. If the interest *rate* is i, then at the end of the first year the *amount* of interest owed will be iP. The total amount owed will be $P + iP = P(1 + i)$. If none of this is paid, at the end of the second year the amount of interest owed will be the rate of interest times the total amount owed at the beginning of the second year, which comes to $iP(1 + i)$. The total amount owed at the end of the second year will be the total owed at the beginning of the year plus the accrued interest for the year, which is

$$P(1 + i) + iP(1 + i) = (P + iP) (1 + i)$$
$$= P(1 + i) (1 + i)$$
$$= P(1 + i)^2$$

At the end of the third year the interest owed will be $iP(1 + i)^2$. Add this to the amount owed at the beginning of the third year, and you get

$$P(1 + i)^2 + iP(1 + i)^2 = (P + iP) (1 + i)^2$$
$$= P(1 + i) (1 + i)^2$$
$$= P(1 + i)^3$$

By extension, the rule now becomes obvious. If S is the total sum owed at the end of n years, then

$$S = P(1 + i)^n \qquad \text{(I)}$$

The expression $(1 + i)^n$ is called the *single payment compound amount factor* (see Table 7.2). For example, if the interest is 8% and $10,000 is borrowed for a period of 10 years, then

$$S = \$10,000 (1 + 0.08)^{10}$$
$$= \$10,000 \times 2.158924$$
$$= \$21,589.24$$

will be the total amount owed at the end of 10 years, if no payments are made before then (see Plan 4, Table 7.1). Notice that the interest rate must be put into decimal form to use in the formula. By dividing both sides of equation I by $(1 + i)^n$, you obtain P in terms of S:

$$P = \frac{S}{(1 + i)^n} \qquad \text{(II)}$$

The term $1/(1 + i)^n$ is called the *single payment present worth factor*.

Table. 7.2 Value of $(1 + i)^n$ for Various Interest Rates.

VALUE OF $(1 + i)^n$ FOR VARIOUS INTEREST RATES

n	1/2%	1%	1-1/2%	2%	3%	4%	5%	6%	7%	.8%	9%	10%	11%	12%
1	1.005	1.010	1.015	1.020	1.030	1.040	1.050	1.060	1.070	1.080	1.090	1.100	1.110	1.120
2	1.010	1.020	1.030	1.040	1.061	1.082	1.103	1.124	1.145	1.166	1.188	1.210	1.232	1.254
3	1.015	1.030	1.046	1.061	1.093	1.125	1.158	1.191	1.225	1.260	1.295	1.331	1.368	1.405
4	1.020	1.041	1.061	1.082	1.126	1.170	1.216	1.262	1.311	1.360	1.412	1.464	1.518	1.574
5	1.025	1.051	·1.077	1.104	1.159	1.217	1.276	1.338	1.403	1.469	1.539	1.611	1.685	1.762
6	1.030	1.062	1.093	1.126	1.194	1.265	1.340	1.419	1.501	1.587	1.677	1.772	1.870	1.974
7	1.036	1.072	1.110	1.149	1.230	1.316	1.407	1.504	1.606	1.714	1.828	1.949	2.076	2.211
8	1.041	1.083	1.126	1.172	1.267	1.369	1.477	1.594	1.718	1.851	1.993	2.144	2.305	2.476
9	1.046	1.094	1.143	1.195	1.305	1.423	1.551	1.689	1.838	1.999	2.172	2.358	2.558	2.773
10	1.051	1.105	1.161	1.219	1.344	1.480	1.629	1.791	1.967	2.159	2.367	2.594	2.839	3.106
11	1.056	1.116	1.178	1.243	1.384	1.539	1.710	1.898	2.105	2.332	2.580	2.853	3.152	3.479
12	1.062	1.127	1.196	1.268	1.426	1.601	1.796	2.012	2.252	2.518	2.813	3.138	3.498	3.896
13	1.067	1.138	1.214	1.294	1.469	1.665	1.886	2.133	2.410	2.720	3.066	3.452	3.883	4.363
14.	1.072	1.149	1.232	1.319	1.513	1.732	1.980	2.261	2.579	2.937	3.342	3.797	4.310	4.887
15	1.078	1.161	1.250	1.346	1.558	1.801	2.079	2.397	2.759	3.172	3.642	4.177	4.785	5.474
16	1.083	1.173	1.269	1.373	1.605	1.873	2.183	2.540	2.952	3.426	3.970	4.595	5.311	6.130
17	1.088	1.184	1.288	1.400	1.653	1.948	2.292	2.693	3.159	3.700	4.328	5.054	5.895	6.866
18	1.094	1.196	1.307	1.428	1.702	2.026	2.407	2.854	3.380	3.996	4.717	5.560	6.544	7.690
19	1.099	1.208	1.327	1.457	1.754	2.107	2.527	3.026	3.617	4.316	5.142	6.116	7.263	8.613
20	1.105	1.220	1.347	1.486	1.806	2.191	2.653	3.207	3.870	4.661	5.604	6.727	8.062	9.646
21	1.110	1.232	1.367	1.516	1.860	2.279	2.786	3.400	4.141	5.034	6.109	7.400	8.949	10.804
22	1.116	1.245	1.388	1.546	1.916	2.370	2.925	3.604	4.430	5.437	6.659	8.140	9.934	12.100
23	1.122	1.257	1.408	1.577	1.974	2.465	3.072	3.820	4.741	5.871	7.258	8.954	11.026	13.552
24	1.127	1.270	1.430	1.608	2.033	2.563	3.225	4.049	5.072	6.341	7.911	9.850	12.239	15.179
25	1.133	1.282	1.451	1.641	2.094	2.666	3.386	4.292	5.427	6.848	8.623	10.835	13.585	17.000
26	1.138	1.295	1.473	1.673	2.157	2.772	3.556	4.549	5.807	7.396	9.399	11.918	15.080	19.040
27	1.144	1.308	1.495	1.707	2.221	2.883	3.733	4.822	6.214	7.988	10.245	13.110	16.739	21.325
28	1.150	1.321	1.517	1.741	2.288	2.999	3.920	5.112	6.649	8.627	11.167	14.421	18.580	23.884
29	1.156	1.335	1.540	1.776	2.357	3.119	4.116	5.418	7.114	9.317	12.172	15.863	20.624	26.750
30	1.161	1.348	1.563	1.811	2.427	3.243	4.322	5.743	7.612	10.063	13.268	17.449	22.892	29.960
36	1.197	1.431	1.709	2.040										
48	1.270	1.612	2.043	2.587										
60	1.349	1.817	2.443	3.281										

For example, what is the present worth of \$21,589.24 10 years hence if money is worth 8%?

$$P = \frac{\$21,589.24}{(1 + 0.08)^{10}}$$

$$= \frac{\$21,589.24}{2.158924}$$

$$= \$10,000.00$$

7.7 *Level Constant Payments*

Suppose that you want to have S dollars in the bank at the end of n years, and you want to make a deposit of R dollars at the end of each year such that the deposits will compound to S. You make no deposit at the beginning of the time period, and you make your first deposit at the end of the first year. Then that first deposit will accumulate interest, not for n years, but for $(n - 1)$ years, since it earns no interest during the first year, because it was deposited, not at time 0, but rather at the end of the first year. At the end of n years, if the interest rate is i, the first deposit will amount to

$$R(1 + i)^{n-1}$$

The second deposit is of the same R dollars, but it is made at the end of the second year, so that it will amount to

$$R(1 + i)^{n-2}$$

The third year's deposit will accumulate to

$$R(1 + i)^{n-3}$$

and so on. The deposit just before the last one will be

$$R(1 + i)$$

and the last deposit will earn no interest—it will simply be equal to R dollars.

The total in the bank will be the sum of all the future sums:

$$S = R(1 + i)^{n-1} + R(1 + i)^{n-2} + R(1 + i)^{n-3} + \cdots$$
$$+ R(1 + i) + R$$

Reversing the order and factoring gives

$$S = R[1 + (1 + i) + (1 + i)^2 + \cdots + (1 + i)^{n-3}$$
$$+ (1 + i)^{n-2} + (1 + i)^{n-1}]$$

Now multiply both sides of the equation by $(1 + i)$ to get

$$S + iS = R[(1 + i) + (1 + i)^2 + \cdots + (1 + i)^{n-3}$$
$$+ (1 + i)^{n-2} + (1 + i)^{n-1} + (1 + i)^n]$$

Subtract the first equation from the second, and the only terms remaining are

$$iS = R[-1 + (1 + i)^n]$$

or

$$iS = R[(1 + i)^n - 1]$$

Then

$$R = S\left[\frac{i}{(1 + i)^n - 1}\right] \tag{III}$$

The quantity $i/[(1 + i)^n - 1]$ is called the *sinking fund deposit factor*.

For example, how much must be deposited at the end of each year for 10 years in order to accumulate \$21,589.24 if the interest is 8%?

$$
\begin{aligned}
R &= S\left[\frac{i}{(1 + i)^n - 1}\right] \\[2mm]
&= \$21,589.24\left[\frac{0.08}{(1 + 0.08)^{10} - 1}\right] \\[2mm]
&= \$21,589.24 \times \frac{0.08}{(2.158924 - 1)} \\[2mm]
&= \$21,589.34 \times 0.0690295 \\[2mm]
&= \$1490.29
\end{aligned}
$$

(See Plan 3, Table 7.1, and note that it is indeed equivalent to Plan 4.)

7.7.1 Capital Recovery Factor

Because $S = P(1 + i)^n$, it is possible to substitute in equation III and get

$$R = P(1 + i)^n\left[\frac{i}{(1 + i)^n - 1}\right]$$

or

$$R = P\left[\frac{i\,(1 + i)^n}{(1 + i)^n - 1}\right] \tag{IVa}$$

Another form of equation IV which gives exactly the same answer is

$$R = P\left[\frac{i}{(1 + i)^n - 1} + i\right] \tag{IVb}$$

Equation IV answers the question: How much must be paid at the end of each year so as to pay off a debt of P dollars in n years if interest is at rate i? Alternatively, the question can be asked as follows:

How much must I get at the end of each year for n years to justify
and investment of P dollars if I want an i rate of return on my investment? As used with mortgages, the expression

$$\frac{i(1 + i)^n}{(1 + i)^n - 1}$$

was herein called *the constant*, but in many textbooks it is referred to
as the *capital recovery factor*. Because both forms of equation IV produce exactly the same answer, the capital recovery factor is always
equal to the sinking fund factor plus the interest rate:

$$\frac{i}{(1 + i)^n - 1} + i$$

As an example, what are the payments on a 10-year mortgage of
$10,000 if the interest is 8%? The yearly payment would be

$$R = P\left[\frac{i(1 + i)^n}{(1 + i)^n - 1}\right]$$

$$= \$10,000\left[\frac{0.08\ (1 + 0.08)^{10}}{(1 + 0.08)^n - 1}\right]$$

$$= \$10,000\left(\frac{0.08 \times 2.158924}{2.158924 - 1}\right)$$

$$= \$10,000\left(\frac{0.1727139}{1.158924}\right)$$

$$= \$10,000 \times 0.149029$$

$$= \$1490.29$$

(The constant would be 0.149029 and would be called 14.9). The
monthly payments become

$$\frac{\$1490.29}{12} = \$124.19$$

Equations III and IV can be reversed to obtain

$$S = R\left[\frac{(1 + i)^n - 1}{i}\right] \qquad \text{(V)}$$

and

$$P = R \left[\frac{(1 + i)^n - 1}{i(1 + i)^n} \right] \tag{VI}$$

which show S and P in terms of R. The expression

$$\frac{(1 + i)^n - 1}{i}$$

is the *uniform annual series compound amount factor*, and the expression

$$\frac{(1 + i)^n - 1}{i(1 + i)^n}$$

is the *uniform annual series present worth factor*. As an example, find how great a loan can be obtained upon a promise to pay $1490.29 per year for 10 years if the interest is 8%.

$$\begin{aligned}
P &= R \left[\frac{(1 + i)^n - 1}{i(1 + i)^n} \right] \\
&= \$1490.29 \left[\frac{(1 + 0.08)^{10} - 1}{0.08 \, (1 + 0.08)^{10}} \right] \\
&= \$1490.29 \left(\frac{2.158924 - 1}{0.08 \times 2.158924} \right) \\
&= \$1490.29 \times \frac{1.158924}{0.1727139} \\
&= \$1490.29 \times 6.7100795 \\
&= \$10,000
\end{aligned}$$

To facilitate the solution of problems, tables of all six factors are given in the Appendix (Tables A.1 through A.12).

7.8 *Nominal and Effective Rates*

Interest is not always computed on a yearly basis. Corporate bonds generally pay interest semiannually, while finance charges on credit cards are figured on a monthly basis. In each of these cases the true or effective rate of interest is not the same as the nominal rate. If interest is paid at the rate of 4% every six months, it is said to be 8% interest, or 8% per year compounded semiannually. But if the time value of money is considered, the payment made at the middle of the year will earn interest on itself for the second 6 months. For example, on a debt of $10,000 the interest at 8% would be $800 for 1 year, or $400 every 6 months. However, if the first payment of $400 could be invested at 8% it would earn $\frac{1}{2}$ × 0.08 × $400 = $16 during the second half of the year, and the total true, or effective, interest would be $400 + $400 + $16 = $816, which is 8.16% of $10,000. Thus, paying interest at the rate of 8% semiannually is the same as paying 8.16% annually. In this case the *nominal* rate is 8% per year, and the *effective* rate is 8.16% per year.

7.8.1 Periods Shorter Than One Year

All six formulas (equations I through VI) were developed on the basis that the periods of time considered were multiples of whole years. To use the formulas with shorter periods of time, make the following adjustments:

n = number of *periods*

i = interest rate *per period*

R = amount paid at end of *each period*

S = sum of money at end of the total *number of periods*

P remains the present worth, to be measured at the beginning of the reckoning. For example, if interest is 8% compounded semiannually, how much must be paid back at the end of 1 year if $10,000 is borrowed at the beginning of that year? Here n = 2; therefore i = 0.08 ÷ 2 = 0.04.

$$S = P (1 + i)^n$$
$$= \$10,000 (1 + 0.04)^2$$
$$= \$10,000 \times 1.0816$$
$$= \$10,816.00$$

Similarly, to find how much must be paid back at the end of 10 years under the same terms and conditions, we have n = 10 × 2 = 20, i = 0.08 ÷ 2 = 0.04, and

$$S = \$10,000 (1 + 0.04)^{20}$$
$$= \$10,000 \times 2.1911221$$
$$= \$21,911.22$$

This is somewhat higher than $21,589.24, the former answer, which was based on 8% annual rate.

7.8.2 Effective Rate

The effective rate of interest can be found by using the expression

$$(1 + i)^n - 1$$

where i and n are the numbers obtained from the procedure of Section 7.8.1. For instance, the effective rate of interest for 8% compounded semiannually becomes

$$(1 + 0.04)^2 - 1 = 1.0816 - 1 = 0.0816$$

or 8.16%. Similarly, the true annual rate corresponding to 1% per month would be

$$(1 + 0.01)^{12} - 1 = 1.1268 - 1 = 0.1268 \text{ or } 12.68\%$$

not 12%.

7.9 Examples of Problems

1. If $3000 is invested now at 5%, how much will it accumulate to in 20 years?

or

What is the compound amount of $3000 for 20 years with interest at 5%?

or

How much must be saved 20 years from now in order to justify a present expenditure of $3000 if money is worth 5%?

Solution:
$$i = 0.05$$
$$n = 20$$
$$P = \$3000$$
$$S = ?$$
$$S = P(1 + i)^n$$
$$= \$3000 (1 + 0.05)^{20}$$

The compound amount factor $(1.05)^{20}$ is given in the 5% table (Table A.7) as 2.653, so that

$$S = \$3000 \times 2.653$$
$$= \$7959$$

2. If $3000 is invested now, $2000 3 years from now, and $1000 6 years from now, all at 6%, what will be the total amount 15 years from now?

Solution: The formulas involving R cannot be used because the amounts are not all the same, the time intervals are not 1 year or less, and the first investment was made at the beginning of the time instead of at the end of the first time interval. The solution therefore requires three separate calculations involving P and S. The first "present" is now; the second "present" starts 3 years from now; and the third "present" begins 6 years from now.

$$P_1 = \$3000, \quad P_2 = \$2000, \quad P_3 = \$1000$$
$$n_1 = 15, \quad n_2 = 12, \quad n_3 = 9$$
$$i_1 = 0.06, \quad i_2 = 0.06, \quad i_3 = 0.06$$
$$S = S_1 + S_2 + S_3$$
$$= P_1(1 + i)^{n_1} + P_2(1 + i)^{n_2} + P_3(1 + i)^{n_3}$$
$$= \$3000(1.06)^{15} + \$2000(1.06)^{12} + \$1000(1.06)^9$$
$$= \$3000 \times 2.379 + \$2000 \times 2.012 + \$1000 \times 1.689$$
$$= \$7191 + \$4024 + \$1689$$
$$= \$12,904$$

3. What is the compound amount of $500 for 10 years with interest at 7% compounded semiannually?

Solution: The interest rate per period is $7\%/2 = 3\frac{1}{2}\%$. The number of periods is $10 \times 2 = 20$. From the $3\frac{1}{2}\%$ table (Table A.4) the compound amount factor is found to be 1.990.

$$i = 0.035$$
$$n = 20$$
$$P = \$500$$
$$S = \,?$$
$$S = P(1 + i)^n$$
$$= \$500(1.034)^{20}$$
$$= \$500 \times 1.990$$
$$= \$995$$

4. What is the present worth of $10,000 10 years hence if interest is 8%?

or

How much can you afford to spend now to avoid spending $10,000 10 years from now if the interest rate is 8%?

or

If the bank's interest rate is 8%, how much must you deposit to accumulate $10,000 in 10 years?

or

How much can be borrowed upon a promise to pay $10,000 in 10 years if the interest is 8%?

Solution: $i = 0.08$

$n = 10$

$S = \$10,000$

$P = ?$

$$P = \frac{S}{(1 + i)^n}$$

$$= \frac{\$10,000}{(1 + 0.08)^{10}} \quad \text{or} \quad \$10,000 \times \frac{1}{(1.08)^{10}}$$

$$= \frac{\$10,000}{2.159} \quad \text{or} \quad \$10,000 \times 4.632$$

$$= \$4632$$

where 0.4632 is the present worth factor found in the 8% table (Table A.11). Using the more exact figure of $(1.08)^{10} = 2.158924$ gives

$$P = \frac{\$10,000}{2.158924}$$

$$= \$4631.94$$

a difference of only 6 cents from the previous answer of $4632. Such a small difference can easily be neglected in planning the finances of a construction project, which means that Tables A.1 through A.12 in the Appendix are quite satisfactory for the solution of practical problems.

5. What loan at 6% could be completely paid back by payments of $1000 at the end of 5, 10, 15, and 20 years?

or

How much is it justifiable to spend now in order to save prospective expenditures of $1000 at the end of 5, 10, 15, and 20 years if money is worth 6%?

or

How much invested now at 6% would produce exactly $1000 in 5 years, another $1000 in 10 years, yet another $1000 in 15 years, and a final $1000 in 20 years?

or

What is the present worth of $1000 at the end of each 5 years for the next 20 years if the interest is at 6%?

Solution: $i = 0.06$

$$n_1 = 5, \quad n_2 = 10, \quad n_3 = 15, \quad n_4 = 20$$
$$S_1 = \$1000, \quad S_2 = \$1000, \quad S_3 = \$1000, \quad S =_4 \$1000$$
$$P = P_1 + P_2 + P_3 + P_4$$

Using the present worth factors from the 6% table (Table A.9) gives

$$P_1 = \$1000 \times 0.7473 = \$\ 747.30$$
$$P_2 = 1000 \times 0.5584 = 558.40$$
$$P_3 = 1000 \times 0.4173 = 417.30$$
$$P_4 = 1000 \times 0.3118 = 311.80$$
$$P = \$2034.80$$

This problem could not be solved by the use of a formula involving R because the time periods were greater than 1 year, even though all the payments were the same.

6. What is the present worth of $5800 due 8 years from now if interest is 10% compounded quarterly?

Solution: The rate per interest period is $\frac{1}{4} \times 10\% = 2\frac{1}{2}\%$. The number of periods is $8 \times 4 = 32$.

$$i = 0.025$$

$$n = 32$$

$$S = \$5800$$

$$P = ?$$

$$P = S \left[\frac{1}{(1 + i)^n} \right]$$

$$= \$5800 \left[\frac{1}{(1.025)^{32}} \right]$$

$$= \$5800 \times 0.4538 \text{ (from } 2\tfrac{1}{2}\% \text{ Table A.2)}$$

$$= \$2632.04 \text{ or } \$2632 \text{ for all practical purposes}$$

7. How many years will it take for money to double itself with the interest at 6%?

or

How long will it take an investment of $1000 to increase to $2000 if the interest is 6%?

$$i = 0.06$$

$$\frac{S}{P} = \frac{\$2000}{\$1000} = 2$$

$$n = ?$$

$$S = P(1 + i)^n$$

$$\frac{S}{P} = (1 + i)^n$$

$$2 = (1.06)^n$$

From the 6% table (Table A.9), the compound amount factors that can solve this problem are

$$n = 11, \quad (1.06)^{11} = 1.898$$
$$n = 12, \quad (1.06)^{12} = 2.012$$
$$n = 11.9 \text{ years, approximately}$$

8. An approximate solution can also be found for the preceding problem by applying the rule of 72. The number 0.72 divided by the interest rate will give the number of years required for capital to double at that rate. If the interest is 6%,

$$\frac{0.72}{0.06} = \frac{72}{6} = 12 \text{ years}$$

If the interest is 3%,

$$\frac{0.72}{0.03} = \frac{72}{3} = 24 \text{ years, and so forth}$$

9. A savings certificate that costs $75 now will pay $100 in 6 years. What is the interest rate?

Solution:

$$\frac{S}{P} = \frac{100}{75} = 1.333$$

$$n = 6$$

$$i = ?$$

$$\frac{S}{P} = (1 + i)^n$$

Therefore

$$(1 + i)^6 = 1.333$$

From the tables, the closest answers are the compound amount factors for $4\frac{1}{2}\%$ and for 5%:

$$(1.045)^6 = 1.302, \qquad (1.05)^6 = 1.340$$

Interpolation gives

$$i = 0.045 + \left(\frac{1.333 - 1.302}{1.340 - 1.302}\right) \times 0.005$$

$$= 0.045 + \left(\frac{0.031}{0.038}\right) \times 0.005$$

$$= 0.0491 \text{ or } 4.91\%$$

10. It is desired to establish a sinking fund that will amount to $600,000 in 25 years. If interest is at 5%, how much must be invested at the end of each of those 25 years?

or

What uniform annual expenditure, such as on preventive maintenance, is justifiable for each of 25 years in order to avoid spending $600,000 at the end of that time, if money is worth 5%?

or

What annual investment must be made at 5% to replace a $600,000 structure 25 years from now?

Solution:

$i = 0.05$

$n = 25$

$S = \$600,000$

$R = ?$

$$R = S\left[\frac{i}{(1 + i)^n - 1}\right]$$

$$= \$600,000\left[\frac{0.05}{(1 + 0.05)^{25} - 1}\right]$$

The 5% table (Table A.7) gives the sinking fund factor as 0.02095 for $n = 25$. It is not necessary to work out the fraction in the brackets.

$$R = \$600,000 \times 0.02095$$
$$= \$12,570 \text{ per year}$$

11. How much would be accumulated in the sinking fund of Problem 10 at the end of 15 years?

Solution:

$i = 0.05$

$n = 15$

$R = \$12,570$

$S = ?$

The 5% table gives the uniform annual series compound amount factor for $n = 15$ as 21.579:

$$S = \$12,570 \times 21.579$$
$$= \$271,248$$

12. What quarterly deposit must be made into a sinking fund to amount to $5,000 in 7 years if interest is at 8% compounded quarterly?

Solution: Here the interest rate per period is one-quarter of the nominal yearly rate, and the number of periods is four times the number of years.

$$i = \tfrac{1}{4} \times 0.08 = 0.02$$

$$n = 4 \times 7 = 28$$

$$S = \$5000$$

$$R = ?$$

From the 2% table (Table A.1) the sinking fund deposit factor for $n = 28$ is found to be 0.02699.

$$R = \$5000 \times 0.02699$$
$$= \$134.95$$

Notice that this is a quarterly, not a yearly, deposit.

13. What annual year-end payment for 10 years is necessary to repay a loan of $10,000 if interest is at 8%?

or

If $10,000 is deposited now at 8% interest, what uniform amount could be withdrawn at the end of each year for 10 years, and have nothing left in the account at the beginning of the eleventh year?

or

What is the annual cost of capital recovery of $10,000 in 10 years if money is worth 8%?

Solution:
$$i = 0.08$$
$$n = 10$$
$$P = \$10,000$$
$$R = ?$$

$$R = P\left[\frac{i(1+i)^n}{(1+i)^n - 1}\right]$$

The capital recovery factor for $i = 0.08$ and $n = 10$ is found in the 8% table (Table A.11) to be 0.14903:

$$R = \$10,000 \times 0.14903$$
$$= \$1490.30$$

This answer is certainly very close to the exact answer of $1490.295, given in Table 7.1 as $1490.29.

14. How much will be owed on the loan of Problem 13 after three payments have been made?

As previously explained, only the remaining principal of the loan is owed at that point. No further interest is owed unless the loan is not paid off. Therefore it is necessary to find the present worth of the loan at that time, which is 3 years after the loan has been made. By its definition, present worth cannot exist after a period of time; it must be determined for the beginning of some time interval. Thus the solution of Problem 14 is the answer to this question: What is the present worth of $1490.30 for 7 years with interest at 8%?

Solution:

$$i = 0.08$$
$$n = 7$$
$$R = \$1490.30$$
$$P = ?$$

$$P = R\left[\frac{(1 + i)^n - 1}{i(1 + i)^n}\right]$$

From the 8% table (Table A.11), the uniform annual series present worth factor is seen to be 5.206, so that

$$P = \$1490.30 \times 5.206$$
$$= \$7,758.50$$

which is quite close to the value of $7759.05 given in Table 7.1. The difference is negligible for practical purposes.

15. A construction manager has completed a certain job on which his fee was to have been $100,000. The owner offers to pay him $30,000 at once, and the remaining $70,000 in five yearly installments of $14,000 each. If the construction manager has to pay 7% interest on any money he borrows, how much is he losing by accepting the owner's offer?

Solution: The loss must be computed on the basis of what is owed now, not on what might happen in the future. True, the construction manager will have to pay 7% interest if he has to borrow the money, but if he had the money in hand, he ought to be able to invest it so as to earn 7%. Therefore

$$i = 0.07$$
$$n = 5$$
$$R = \$14,000$$
$$P = ?$$

From the 7% table (Table A.10), the uniform annual series present worth factor is found to be 4.100:

$$P = R\left[\frac{(1 + i)^n - 1}{i(1 + i)^n}\right]$$
$$= \$14,000 \times 4.100$$
$$= \$57,400$$

Therefore the loss would be $70,000 - $57,400 = $12,600$, in present dollars.

16. What would be the proper payments for the owner to make under the conditions of Problem 15?

Solution:
$$i = 0.07$$
$$n = 5$$
$$P = \$70,000$$
$$R = ?$$

From the 7% table (Table A.10), the capital recovery factor is found to be 0.24389, so the payments should be as follows:

$$R = \$70,000 \times 0.24389$$
$$= \$17,072.30$$

instead of the $14,000 offered.

17. A certain 20-year $10,000 coupon bond pays 5% annually, that is to say, the owner receives $500 each year for 20 years and an additional $10,000 at the end of the twentieth year, in return for lending the company $10,000 (buying a $10,000 bond). After 8 years the owner wants to sell the bond, but a prospective buyer wants to receives 7% return on his money. How much will the buyer pay the owner?

Solution: The buyer will receive $500 for each of 12 years. In addition he will receive $10,000 at the end of that time. Since he wants a 7% return,

$$i = 0.07$$
$$n = 12$$
$$R = \$500$$
$$S = \$10,000$$
$$P = P_1 + P_2 = ?$$

$$P_1 = \frac{S}{(1 + i)^n}, \qquad P_2 = R\left[\frac{(1 + i)^n - 1}{i(1 + i)^n}\right]$$

Using the appropriate factors in the 7% table (Table A.10) gives

$$P = \$10,000 \times 0.4440 + \$500 \times 7.943$$
$$= \$4440 + \$3971.50 = \$8411.50$$

7.9.1 Add-On Interest

Suppose that a $500 truck is purchased with a down payment of $1000, and the balance is financed for 3 years at 6% add-on interest; what are the monthly payments? What is the true rate of interest?

Solution: The bank computes add-on interest as time × rate × principal. In this example,

$$3 \times 0.06 \times \$4000 = 0.18 \times \$4000$$
$$= \$720$$

The total principal plus "interest" is then divided by the number of payments to find the monthly payment:

$$\frac{\$4720}{36} = \$131.11, \text{ the monthly payment}$$

The true rate of interest can be found only by trial and error. Trying 1% per month gives

$$i = 0.01$$
$$n = 36$$
$$P = \$4000$$
$$R = ?$$
$$R = P \left[\frac{i(1 + i)^n}{(1 + i)^n - 1} \right]$$
$$= \$4000 \left[\frac{0.01 \, (1.01)^{36}}{(1.01)^{36} - 1} \right]$$
$$= \$4000 \left(\frac{0.01 \times 1.4308}{1.4038 - 1} \right)$$
$$= \$132.85$$

which is close enough to $131.11.

If the rate of interest were in fact 1% per month, the effective yearly rate would be

$$(1.01)^{12} - 1 = 1.1268 - 1$$
$$= 0.1268 \text{ or } 12.68\% \text{ per year}$$

However, since 1% per month is a trifle high in this problem,the true rate is close to 12% per year, which is twice the rate of 6% used by the bank in computing the monthly payments.

In fairness to the bank, it should be pointed out that administrative costs are much higher in connection with small loans and monthly payments.

7.10 Loss of Interest as a Cost

When comparing four methods of repaying a loan in Section 7.3, it was seen that they were all equivalent even though the payments and frequency of payments were different. From the viewpoint of the borrower, then, the true cost of a loan lies not in the number of dollars paid back, but rather in the interest rate and the total time of repayment. The same concept holds true for a lender or an investor. The lender must get interest for his money, and the value of the loan is determined by the interest rate and the time of the loan. An investor can always choose between two alternatives: Shall I put my money into this investment, or shall I put it in a nice safe bank account where it will draw interest? If the money is put into the investment, it must return more interest than would be received in the bank because of the risk element that exists in an investment. (Every investment has a risk element. Some risks are very slight, but they are there, nonetheless.)

7.10.1 Risk Profit

If money is put into an investment, then only the extra gain above and beyond bank interest will be a true profit to compensate for risk and for certain other economic factors. Since the investor has decided to give up the interest his money could have earned him in the bank, that interest must be considered to be a cost of the investment.

7.10.2 Example

As an example, suppose that a savings account would earn 5%, but a piece of land could be bought for $10,000. After paying $200 per year taxes on the land for 10 years, it might be sold for $20,000. Should the money be put in the bank or in the land?

Solution: If the $10,000 is put into the bank in 10 years' time it will have accumulated to

$$S = P (1 + i)^n$$
$$= \$10,000 (1 + 0.05)^{10}$$
$$= \$16,288.94$$

For a true comparison, the $200 per year must also be considered as being put into the bank. In that case, at the end of 10 years, because of compound interest, the yearly deposits will accumulate to

$$S = R \left[\frac{(1 + i)^n - 1}{i} \right]$$

$$= \$200 \left[\frac{(1 + 0.05)^{10} - 1}{0.05} \right]$$

$$= \$2515.58$$

The total sum that would be in the bank would be

$$\$16,288.94 + \$2515.58 = \$18,804.52$$

In other words, for a total cash outlay of

$$\$10,000 + 10 \times \$200 = \$10,000 + \$2000$$
$$= \$12,000$$

the amount returned from the land would be $20,000, but the amount returned from the bank would be $18,804.52, and the difference between the two, $20,000 − $18,804.52 = $1195.48, would be the profit covering the risk factor. It is interesting to note that, if money is worth 6% instead of 5%, the selling price of $20,000 will actually turn out to represent a loss, even though the initial cost and the cost per year (taxes) come to the same total cash outlay of only $12,000.

7.10.3 Equipment Costs

Cash in the bank produces not only interest, but also the ability to do business. It is a general rule of thumb that liquid assets should amount to about 10% of the dollar volume of work of a construction company. Many companies have been successful with much smaller ratios of cash to dollar volume, but 10% seems like a reasonable figure for a well-managed company. Therefore, for the purpose of the next problem, assume that the volume of business in any one year will be ten times the number of dollars in the bank at the beginning of that year. Furthermore, assume that the net profit before taxes will be 4% of the dollar volume of business, and that the bank pays 5% interest.

Suppose that your company wants to buy a piece of equipment that can be purchased for $40,000 cash, or $10,000 down and the balance at 6% add-on for 3 years. Should you pay cash or buy on terms?

Solution: Before solving the problem in detail, consider what happens to $100 in the bank.

Year	$ in Bank	× 10 = $ Business	×0.04 = $ Profit	5% Interest	$ in Bank at End of Year
0–1	100.00	1000.00	40.00	5.00	145.00
1–2	145.00	1450.00	58.00	7.25	210.26

Notice that, during the first year, the total additional cash that the company has is $40 + $5 = $45: $40 from profit, and $5 from interest. The profit amounts to $10 \times 0.04 = 0.40$ of the initial capital in the bank. During the second year, the company will make a profit on the original $100, which has not been touched, and will also make a profit on the interest and on the profit of the first year. It will also receive interest on the first year's profit and the first year's interest. In other words, the profit margin acts like a compound interest rate, provided that it is left in the bank. Therefore, the total "interest" rate becomes $0.05 + (10 \times 0.04) = 0.05 + 0.40 = 0.45$, or 45%.

Now the alternatives become clear. Over a 3-year period, the cash price "cost" becomes

$$S = P(1 + i)^n$$
$$= \$40,000 (1 + 0.45)^3$$
$$= \$40,000 \times 3.0486$$
$$= \$121,945$$

If bought on terms, the "cost" of the down payment becomes

$$S = P(1 + i)^n$$
$$= \$10,000 (1 + 0.45)^3$$
$$= \$30,486$$

The payments on the balance would actually be made monthly, but to simplify the problem suppose that they are made at the end of each year. The remaining balance is $40,000 − \$10,000 = \$30,000$. The cost of financing is 3 (years) × 0.06 (per year) = 0.18 of the balance; $\$30,000 \times 0.18 = \$5400$. The three yearly payments would then be $(\$30,000 + \$5400)/3 = \$35,400/3 = \$11,800$. At the end of 3 years the "cost" of these payments would be

$$S = R \left[\frac{(1 + i)^n - 1}{i} \right]$$

$$= \$11,800 \left[\frac{(1 + 0.45)^3 - 1}{0.45} \right]$$

$$= \$11,800 \left(\frac{3.0486 - 1}{0.45} \right)$$

$$= \$11,800 \times \frac{2.0486}{0.45}$$

$$= \$53,719$$

The total "cost" of buying on terms becomes $\$30,486 + \$53,719 = \$84,205$, which is less than $121,945; hence the equipment should be bought on terms.

Many factors were omitted in this problem in order to simplify it—for example, insurance, taxes, maintenance, obsolescence, and depreciation—but in, general, the solution indicates that it is best to preserve your capital and use borrowed money to make money.

7.11 Leasing

Any piece of construction equipment must be charged off to each job on an hourly basis. If that piece of equipment costs the company $5 for every useful hour of its life, the job must be charged at least $5 per hour, plus the cost of labor. In a sense, the job is paying the company for the use of the equipment, and is thus leasing the equipment from the company. Of course the total cost of ownership per hour must include oil, fuel, tires, storage, and set-up or delivery, plus all the factors mentioned at the end of Problem 7.10.3, but for the present consider only the cost of purchasing.

7.11.1 Cost Per Hour

The cost of purchasing includes the first cost, which in turn covers delivery, sales tax, and make-ready costs, plus the cost of interest charged or chargeable, but does not include "lost" profit. In the example of Section 7.10.3 the cash price cost, including lost interest, would become

$$S = P(1 + i)$$
$$= \$40,000 (1 + 0.05)^3$$
$$= \$46,305$$

for a 3-year period. At the end of that time, suppose that the machine has a trade-in value (called the *salvage value*) of $14,000. Then the purchasing cost would be $46,305 − $14,000 = $32,305. If it is believed that the machine will be used 15,000 hours per year or 45,000 hours in a 3-year period, this portion of the cost of ownership becomes $32,305/45,000 = $0.72 or 72 cents per hour.

The cost of buying on terms is computed as follows:

Down payment cost: $S = P(1 + i)^n$
$$= \$10,000 (1 + 0.05)^3$$
$$= \$11,576$$

Yearly payments cost: $S = R\left[\dfrac{(1 + i)^n - 1}{i}\right]$
$$= \$11,800\left[\dfrac{(1 + 0.05)^3 - 1}{0.05}\right]$$
$$= \$37,200$$

Total purchasing cost $= \$11,576 + 37,200$
$$= \$48,776$$

Subtracting the salvage value gives

$$\$48,776 - \$14,000 = \$34,776$$

$$\text{Cost per hour} = \frac{\$34,776}{45,000} = \$0.77 \text{ or 77 cents per hour}$$

7.11.2 Consideration of Alternatives

It would be a most unusual accounting procedure to include "lost" interest as a cost. Generally, the purchase cost basis is simply the replacement cost, including any interest paid out, but not "lost" profit or "lost" interest. The reason these factors were included in Sections 7.10.3 and 7.11.1 is simply that they are influences in making a decision between alternatives. One alternative is to buy a piece of equipment; a second is to put the money in the bank; and a third is to put the money into the business. The final decision depends on where the money will produce the most profit.

7.12 Applications to Real Estate Problems

In Chapter 1, Section 1.1.5.12, the idea of the level constant payment was developed. In that example, the interest rate was $7\frac{1}{2}\%$, and the term of the mortgage was 22 years and 4 months. Each yearly payment was to be \$134,124, and the mortgage was for \$1,450,000. The constant, then, is 9.25, and can be determined by the use of formula IV:

$$R = P(1 + i)^n \left[\frac{i}{(1 + i)^n - 1} \right]$$

$$\frac{R}{P} = (1 + i)^n \left[\frac{i}{(1 + i)^n - 1} \right]$$

On a monthly basis, $i = 0.075/12 = 0.00625$, and $n = 268$ months. Then

$$\frac{R}{P} = (1 + 0.00625)^{268} \left[\frac{0.00625}{(1 + 0.00625)^{268} - 1} \right] \text{per month} \times 12$$

and

$$\frac{R}{P} = 0.0925, \text{ the constant}$$

7.12.1 *Equity Build-Up*

As each mortgage payment is made, part goes to pay interest and the rest of the payment is applied against the principal, so that the debt is reduced somewhat, as shown in Plan 3 of Table 7.1. The cash that is used to pay off the actual debt, not the interest but the principal, is increasing the owner's equity. If he had not borrowed anything, he would have had to put an amount equal to the loan into the project at the beginning of it. By paying off the debt, he is putting the same amount in gradually, over a long period of time. Now a problem arises: At what point does the equity become so large, and the rate of return on the investment so small, that the project should be sold?

7.12.1.1 EXAMPLE: PICANOS VILLA.   Consider the example of Picanos Villa (Chapter 4). In Section 4.5 the cash equity was shown as $185,700. The mortgage of $927,000 was to be at $7\frac{1}{2}\%$ for 22 years 4 months, giving a constant of 9.25, and yearly payments of $85,748. What will the equity be at the end of 10 years 4 months?

To solve this problem it is necessary to work backwards. After 10 years 4 months there will remain exactly 12 years on the life of the mortgage. The amount remaining on the debt at that time is the present worth of the mortgage at that time. Then

$$R = \$85{,}748$$

$$i = 0.075$$

$$n = 12$$

$$P = ?$$

$$R = P(1 + i)^n \left[\frac{i}{(1 + i)^n - 1} \right]$$

$$\$85{,}748 = P(1 + 0.075)^{12} \left[\frac{0.075}{(1 + 0.075)^{12} - 1} \right]$$

$$\$85{,}748 = P(2.3818) \left(\frac{0.075}{2.3818 - 1} \right)$$

$$\$85{,}748 = P \times 0.12928$$

$P = \$663{,}273.51$, the balance remaining on the principal of the mortgage

Since the original mortgage was for $927,000, the amount that was paid off was $927,000 − $663,273 = $263,726. With an original cash equity of $185,700, the total equity has become $263,726 + $185,700 = $449,426. Of course the rents may increase in 10 years 4 months, but suppose that expenses increase just as fast. Then the net cash flow per year will still be $28,698 (Chapter 4, Section 4.5.2), and

$$\frac{\text{Return}}{\text{Equity}} = \frac{\$28,698}{\$449,426} = 6.4\%$$

which is really not satisfactory. The project should, at that time, either be sold or refinanced. In fact, most projects are usually ready for sale or refinance after about 7 years.

7.12.2 Depreciation

Tax laws permit three kinds of depreciation of real estate: straight line (SL), sum of the years' digits (SYD), and declining balance (DB). On construction equipment a fourth method is usually used. It is in a sense a SL method, but here the depreciation is taken per hour of use, based on the estimated life of the machine in hours of use. Each of the methods used for real estate projects is based on an estimated life in years, and depreciation is figured early. Thus, if a $20,000 house has 20 years of life ahead of it, the first year's depreciation, using SL, will be 1/20 of $20,000, or $1000. The same depreciation of $1000 is used in each succeeding year in SL computations, including the twentieth. However, it is known that the property will have some remaining value at the end of 20 years; if nothing else, the land will have some value. This residual value is called the *salvage value*. For the house in question, if the salvage value were $20,000, the depreciation could only total $20,000 − $2000 = $18,000, and each year's depreciation would be 1/20 of $18,000 = $900.

Over the long haul it will be found that SL depreciation gives about the same results as any of the more elaborate methods. Furthermore, it avoids the grief and aggravation associated with the recapture provisions of the tax laws, as any competent accountant can verify. Therefore it seems advisable to use SL depreciation.

7.12.2.1 EXAMPLE: PICANOS VILLA. The replacement cost of Picanos Villa was $1,124,990, according to Section 4.4 of Chapter 4. Suppose that the salvage values lies only in the land, which would be $94,000. Then the amount to be depreciated is $1,124,990 − $94,000 = $1,030,990. What follows is a simplification, and is given only for purposes of illustration.

If a 20-year life is assumed, each year's depreciation will be 1/20 × $1,030,990 = $51,549.50, say $51,550. During the first year the owner will receive $28,698 in cash, plus an equity build-up of $16,223, for a total profit of $28,698 + $16,223 = $44,921. Because the depreciation is $51,550, the project will show a net book loss of $51,550 − $44,921 = $6629. If the project is owned individually or in some sort of partnership, the "loss" can be taken out and applied against other income, thus reducing the income tax on the other income. The cash flow of $28,698 is tax free. Alternatively, the "loss" of $6629 can be left on the books and carried forward for as many as 5 years. This is often done because, whereas the SL depreciation remains steady, the equity build-up gets larger each year, so that each year's profit becomes greater, and within a few years the depreciation no longer covers the total profit. Thus taxes are avoided while a net cash flow continues.

7.12.3 Time-Adjusted Return

The present worth or economic value of Picanos Villa as given in Chapter 4, Section 4.3.4.17, was determined by a type of simplification that is generally used by real estate brokers. It was there assumed that the mortgage was never paid off. A more accurate calculation of present worth should include the value of the equity build-up, as well as the value of the tax shelters resulting from depreciation. Inclusion of these factors leads to a higher cash flow and thus a higher present worth. This same increased cash flow can be used to compute the time-adjusted rate of return. The effect of equity build-up and depreciation can be computed by the use of the formulas in this chapter. However, since the simplified method gives satisfactory results for the purpose of construction funding, the time-adjusted rate of return is used only in considering the purchase of a completed and established project.

7.12.4 Depreciation Fallacies

Some investors who have large incomes from other sources put their money into projects solely to get a tax loss from depreciation. They do not particularly want any cash income. This seems to be a serious error. They often find, when they sell the property, that they have suffered a true loss. The conservative investor will always look for a positive cash flow and accept a tax loss as a bonus. He will look at each investment as though it must stand on its own feet, so that, in case his other income is suddenly shut off for any reason, he will still receive a cash return from his project.

Basically, it is not depreciation that benefits an investor, it is the cash return for the use of his money.

Appendix

Table A.1   2% Compound Interest Factors

	SINGLE PAYMENT		UNIFORM ANNUAL SERIES				
	Compound Amount Factor	Present Worth Factor	Sinking Fund Factor	Capital Recovery Factor	Compound Amount Factor	Present Worth Factor	
n	Given P To find S $(1+i)^n$	Given S To find P $\dfrac{1}{(1+i)^n}$	Given S To find R $\dfrac{i}{(1+i)^n-1}$	Given P To find R $\dfrac{i(1+i)^n}{(1+i)^n-1}$	Given R To find S $\dfrac{(1+i)^n-1}{i}$	Given R To find P $\dfrac{(1+i)^n-1}{i(1+i)^n}$	n
1	1.020	0.9804	1.00000	1.02000	1.000	0.980	1
2	1.040	0.9612	0.49505	0.51505	2.020	1.942	2
3	1.061	0.9423	0.32675	0.34675	3.060	2.884	3
4	1.082	0.9238	0.24262	0.26262	4.122	3.808	4
5	1.104	0.9057	0.19216	0.21216	5.204	4.713	5
6	1.126	0.8880	0.15853	0.17853	6.308	5.601	6
7	1.149	0.8706	0.13451	0.15451	7.434	6.472	7
8	1.172	0.8535	0.11651	0.13651	8.583	7.325	8
9	1.195	0.8368	0.10252	0.12252	9.755	8.162	9
10	1.219	0.8203	0.09133	0.11133	10.950	8.983	10
11	1.243	0.8043	0.08218	0.10218	12.169	9.787	11
12	1.268	0.7885	0.07456	0.09456	13.412	10.575	12
13	1.294	0.7730	0.06812	0.08812	14.680	11.348	13
14	1.319	0.7579	0.06260	0.08260	15.974	12.106	14
15	1.346	0.7430	0.05783	0.07783	17.293	12.849	15
16	1.373	0.7284	0.05365	0.07365	18.639	13.578	16
17	1.400	0.7142	0.04997	0.06997	20.012	14.292	17
18	1.428	0.7002	0.04670	0.06670	21.412	14.992	18
19	1.457	0.6864	0.04378	0.06378	22.841	15.678	19
20	1.486	0.6730	0.04116	0.06116	24.297	16.351	20
21	1.516	0.6598	0.03878	0.05878	25.783	17.011	21
22	1.546	0.6468	0.03663	0.05663	27.299	17.658	22
23	1.577	0.6342	0.03467	0.05467	28.845	18.292	23
24	1.608	0.6217	0.03287	0.05287	30.422	18.914	24
25	1.641	0.6095	0.03122	0.05122	32.030	19.523	25
26	1.673	0.5976	0.02970	0.04970	33.671	20.121	26
27	1.707	0.5859	0.02829	0.04829	35.344	20.707	27
28	1.741	0.5744	0.02699	0.04699	37.051	21.281	28
29	1.776	0.5631	0.02578	0.04578	38.792	21.844	29
30	1.811	0.5521	0.02465	0.04465	40.568	22.396	30
31	1.848	0.5412	0.02360	0.04360	42.379	22.938	31
32	1.885	0.5306	0.02261	0.04261	44.227	23.468	32
33	1.922	0.5202	0.02169	0.04169	46.112	23.989	33
34	1.961	0.5100	0.02082	0.04082	48.034	24.499	34
35	2.000	0.5000	0.02000	0.04000	49.994	24.999	35
40	2.208	0.4529	0.01656	0.03656	60.402	27.355	40
45	2.438	0.4102	0.01391	0.03391	71.893	29.490	45
50	2.692	0.3715	0.01182	0.03182	84.579	31.424	50
55	2.972	0.3365	0.01014	0.03014	98.587	33.175	55
60	3.281	0.3048	0.00877	0.02877	114.052	34.761	60
65	3.623	0.2761	0.00763	0.02763	131.126	36.197	65
70	4.000	0.2500	0.00667	0.02667	149.978	37.499	70
75	4.416	0.2265	0.00586	0.02586	170.792	38.677	75
80	4.875	0.2051	0.00516	0.02516	193.772	39.745	80
85	5.383	0.1858	0.00456	0.02456	219.144	40.711	85
90	5.943	0.1683	0.00405	0.02405	247.157	41.587	90
95	6.562	0.1524	0.00360	0.02360	278.085	42.380	95
100	7.245	0.1380	0.00320	0.02320	312.232	43.098	100

Table A.2 $2\frac{1}{2}\%$ Compound Interest Factors

n	SINGLE PAYMENT		UNIFORM ANNUAL SERIES				n
	Compound Amount Factor	Present Worth Factor	Sinking Fund Factor	Capital Recovery Factor	Compound Amount Factor	Present Worth Factor	
	Given P To find S $(1+i)^n$	Given S To find P $\dfrac{1}{(1+i)^n}$	Given S To find R $\dfrac{i}{(1+i)^n-1}$	Given P To find R $\dfrac{i(1+i)^n}{(1+i)^n-1}$	Given R To find S $\dfrac{(1+i)^n-1}{i}$	Given R To find P $\dfrac{(1+i)^n-1}{i(1+i)^n}$	
1	1.025	0.9756	1.00000	1.02500	1.000	0.976	1
2	1.051	0.9518	0.49383	0.51883	2.025	1.927	2
3	1.077	0.9286	0.32514	0.35014	3.076	2.856	3
4	1.104	0.9060	0.24082	0.26582	4.153	3.762	4
5	1.131	0.8839	0.19025	0.21525	5.256	4.646	5
6	1.160	0.8623	0.15655	0.18155	6.388	5.508	6
7	1.189	0.8413	0.13250	0.15750	7.547	6.349	7
8	1.218	0.8207	0.11447	0.13947	8.736	7.170	8
9	1.249	0.8007	0.10046	0.12546	9.955	7.971	9
10	1.280	0.7812	0.08926	0.11426	11.203	8.752	10
11	1.312	0.7621	0.08011	0.10511	12.483	9.514	11
12	1.345	0.7436	0.07249	0.09749	13.796	10.258	12
13	1.379	0.7254	0.06605	0.09105	15.140	10.983	13
14	1.413	0.7077	0.06054	0.08554	16.519	11.691	14
15	1.448	0.6905	0.05577	0.08077	17.932	12.381	15
16	1.485	0.6736	0.05160	0.07660	19.380	13.055	16
17	1.522	0.6572	0.04793	0.07293	20.865	13.712	17
18	1.560	0.6412	0.04467	0.06967	22.386	14.353	18
19	1.599	0.6255	0.04176	0.06676	23.946	14.979	19
20	1.639	0.6103	0.03915	0.06415	25.545	15.589	20
21	1.680	0.5954	0.03679	0.06179	27.183	16.185	21
22	1.722	0.5809	0.03465	0.05965	28.863	16.765	22
23	1.765	0.5667	0.03270	0.05770	30.584	17.332	23
24	1.809	0.5529	0.03091	0.05591	32.349	17.885	24
25	1.854	0.5394	0.02928	0.05428	34.158	18.424	25
26	1.900	0.5262	0.02777	0.05277	36.012	18.951	26
27	1.948	0.5134	0.02638	0.05138	37.912	19.464	27
28	1.996	0.5009	0.02509	0.05009	39.860	19.965	28
29	2.046	0.4887	0.02389	0.04889	41.856	20.454	29
30	2.098	0.4767	0.02278	0.04778	43.903	20.930	30
31	2.150	0.4651	0.02174	0.04674	46.000	21.395	31
32	2.204	0.4538	0.02077	0.04577	48.150	21.849	32
33	2.259	0.4427	0.01986	0.04486	50.354	22.292	33
34	2.315	0.4319	0.01901	0.04401	52.613	22.724	34
35	2.373	0.4214	0.01821	0.04321	54.928	23.145	35
40	2.685	0.3724	0.01484	0.03984	67.403	25.103	40
45	3.038	0.3292	0.01227	0.03727	81.516	26.833	45
50	3.437	0.2909	0.01026	0.03526	97.484	28.362	50
55	3.889	0.2572	0.00865	0.03365	115.551	29.714	55
60	4.400	0.2273	0.00735	0.03235	135.992	30.909	60
65	4.978	0.2009	0.00628	0.03128	159.118	31.965	65
70	5.632	0.1776	0.00540	0.03040	185.284	32.898	70
75	6.372	0.1569	0.00465	0.02965	214.888	33.723	75
80	7.210	0.1387	0.00403	0.02903	248.383	34.452	80
85	8.157	0.1226	0.00349	0.02849	286.279	35.096	85
90	9.229	0.1084	0.00304	0.02804	329.154	35.666	90
95	10.442	0.0958	0.00265	0.02765	377.664	36.169	95
100	11.814	0.0846	0.00231	0.02731	432.549	36.614	100

191

Table A.3 3% Compound Interest Factors

	SINGLE PAYMENT		UNIFORM ANNUAL SERIES				
	Compound Amount Factor	Present Worth Factor	Sinking Fund Factor	Capital Recovery Factor	Compound Amount Factor	Present Worth Factor	
n	Given P To find S $(1+i)^n$	Given S To find P $\dfrac{1}{(1+i)^n}$	Given S To find R $\dfrac{i}{(1+i)^n-1}$	Given P To find R $\dfrac{i(1+i)^n}{(1+i)^n-1}$	Given R To find S $\dfrac{(1+i)^n-1}{i}$	Given R To find P $\dfrac{(1+i)^n-1}{i(1+i)^n}$	n
1	1.030	0.9709	1.00000	1.03000	1.000	0.971	1
2	1.061	0.9426	0.49261	0.52261	2.030	1.913	2
3	1.093	0.9151	0.32353	0.35353	3.091	2.829	3
4	1.126	0.8885	0.23903	0.26903	4.184	3.717	4
5	1.159	0.8626	0.18835	0.21835	5.309	4.580	5
6	1.194	0.8375	0.15460	0.18460	6.468	5.417	6
7	1.230	0.8131	0.13051	0.16051	7.662	6.230	7
8	1.267	0.7894	0.11246	0.14246	8.892	7.020	8
9	1.305	0.7664	0.09843	0.12843	10.159	7.786	9
10	1.344	0.7441	0.08723	0.11723	11.464	8.530	10
11	1.384	0.7224	0.07808	0.10808	12.808	9.253	11
12	1.426	0.7014	0.07046	0.10046	14.192	9.954	12
13	1.469	0.6810	0.06403	0.09403	15.618	10.635	13
14	1.513	0.6611	0.05853	0.08853	17.086	11.296	14
15	1.558	0.6419	0.05377	0.08377	18.599	11.938	15
16	1.605	0.6232	0.04961	0.07961	20.157	12.561	16
17	1.653	0.6050	0.04595	0.07595	21.762	13.166	17
18	1.702	0.5874	0.04271	0.07271	23.414	13.754	18
19	1.754	0.5703	0.03981	0.06981	25.117	14.324	19
20	1.806	0.5537	0.03722	0.06722	26.870	14.877	20
21	1.860	0.5375	0.03487	0.06487	28.676	15.415	21
22	1.916	0.5219	0.03275	0.06275	30.537	15.937	22
23	1.974	0.5067	0.03081	0.06081	32.453	16.444	23
24	2.033	0.4919	0.02905	0.05905	34.426	16.936	24
25	2.094	0.4776	0.02743	0.05743	36.459	17.413	25
26	2.157	0.4637	0.02594	0.05594	38.553	17.877	26
27	2.221	0.4502	0.02456	0.05456	40.710	18.327	27
28	2.288	0.4371	0.02329	0.05329	42.931	18.764	28
29	2.357	0.4243	0.02211	0.05211	45.219	19.188	29
30	2.427	0.4120	0.02102	0.05102	47.575	19.600	30
31	2.500	0.4000	0.02000	0.05000	50.003	20.000	31
32	2.575	0.3883	0.01905	0.04905	52.503	20.389	32
33	2.652	0.3770	0.01816	0.04816	55.078	20.766	33
34	2.732	0.3660	0.01732	0.04732	57.730	21.132	34
35	2.814	0.3554	0.01654	0.04654	60.462	21.487	35
40	3.262	0.3066	0.01326	0.04326	75.401	23.115	40
45	3.782	0.2644	0.01079	0.04079	92.720	24.519	45
50	4.384	0.2281	0.00887	0.03887	112.797	25.730	50
55	5.082	0.1968	0.00735	0.03735	136.072	26.774	55
60	5.892	0.1697	0.00613	0.03613	163.053	27.676	60
65	6.830	0.1464	0.00515	0.03515	194.333	28.453	65
70	7.918	0.1263	0.00434	0.03434	230.594	29.123	70
75	9.179	0.1089	0.00367	0.03367	272.631	29.702	75
80	10.641	0.0940	0.00311	0.03311	321.363	30.201	80
85	12.336	0.0811	0.00265	0.03265	377.857	30.631	85
90	14.300	0.0699	0.00226	0.03226	443.349	31.002	90
95	16.578	0.0603	0.00193	0.03193	519.272	31.323	95
100	19.219	0.0520	0.00165	0.03165	607.288	31.599	100

Table A.4 $3\frac{1}{2}\%$ Compound Interest Factors

	SINGLE PAYMENT		UNIFORM ANNUAL SERIES				
n	Compound Amount Factor	Present Worth Factor	Sinking Fund Factor	Capital Recovery Factor	Compound Amount Factor	Present Worth Factor	n
	Given P To find S $(1+i)^n$	Given S To find P $\dfrac{1}{(1+i)^n}$	Given S To find R $\dfrac{i}{(1+i)^n-1}$	Given P To find R $\dfrac{i(1+i)^n}{(1+i)^n-1}$	Given R To find S $\dfrac{(1+i)^n-1}{i}$	Given R To find P $\dfrac{(1+i)^n-1}{i(1+i)^n}$	
1	1.035	0.9662	1.00000	1.03500	1.000	0.966	1
2	1.071	0.9335	0.49140	0.52640	2.035	1.900	2
3	1.109	0.9019	0.32193	0.35693	3.106	2.802	3
4	1.148	0.8714	0.23725	0.27225	4.215	3.673	4
5	1.188	0.8420	0.18648	0.22148	5.362	4.515	5
6	1.229	0.8135	0.15267	0.18767	6.550	5.329	6
7	1.272	0.7860	0.12854	0.16354	7.779	6.115	7
8	1.317	0.7594	0.11048	0.14548	9.052	6.874	8
9	1.363	0.7337	0.09645	0.13145	10.368	7.608	9
10	1.411	0.7089	0.08524	0.12024	11.731	8.317	10
11	1.460	0.6849	0.07609	0.11109	13.142	9.002	11
12	1.511	0.6618	0.06848	0.10348	14.602	9.663	12
13	1.564	0.6394	0.06206	0.09706	16.113	10.303	13
14	1.619	0.6178	0.05657	0.09157	17.677	10.921	14
15	1.675	0.5969	0.05183	0.08683	19.296	11.517	15
16	1.734	0.5767	0.04768	0.08268	20.971	12.094	16
17	1.795	0.5572	0.04404	0.07904	22.705	12.651	17
18	1.857	0.5384	0.04082	0.07582	24.500	13.190	18
19	1.923	0.5202	0.03794	0.07294	26.357	13.710	19
20	1.990	0.5026	0.03536	0.07036	28.280	14.212	20
21	2.059	0.4856	0.03304	0.06804	30.269	14.698	21
22	2.132	0.4692	0.03093	0.06593	32.329	15.167	22
23	2.206	0.4533	0.02902	0.06402	34.460	15.620	23
24	2.283	0.4380	0.02727	0.06227	36.667	16.058	24
25	2.363	0.4231	0.02567	0.06067	38.950	16.482	25
26	2.446	0.4088	0.02421	0.05921	41.313	16.890	26
27	2.532	0.3950	0.02285	0.05785	43.759	17.285	27
28	2.620	0.3817	0.02160	0.05660	46.291	17.667	28
29	2.712	0.3687	0.02045	0.05545	48.911	18.036	29
30	2.807	0.3563	0.01937	0.05437	51.623	18.392	30
31	2.905	0.3442	0.01837	0.05337	54.429	18.736	31
32	3.007	0.3326	0.01744	0.05244	57.335	19.069	32
33	3.112	0.3213	0.01657	0.05157	60.341	19.390	33
34	3.221	0.3105	0.01576	0.05076	63.453	19.701	34
35	3.334	0.3000	0.01500	0.05000	66.674	20.001	35
40	3.959	0.2526	0.01183	0.04683	84.550	21.355	40
45	4.702	0.2127	0.00945	0.04445	105.782	22.495	45
50	5.585	0.1791	0.00763	0.04263	130.998	23.456	50
55	6.633	0.1508	0.00621	0.04121	160.947	24.264	55
60	7.878	0.1269	0.00509	0.04009	196.517	24.945	60
65	9.357	0.1069	0.00419	0.03919	238.763	25.518	65
70	11.113	0.0900	0.00346	0.03846	288.938	26.000	70
75	13.199	0.0758	0.00287	0.03787	348.530	26.407	75
80	15.676	0.0638	0.00238	0.03738	419.307	26.749	80
85	18.618	0.0537	0.00199	0.03699	503.367	27.037	85
90	22.112	0.0452	0.00166	0.03666	603.205	27.279	90
95	26.262	0.0381	0.00139	0.03639	721.781	27.484	95
100	31.191	0.0321	0.00116	0.03616	862.612	27.655	100

Table A.5 4% Compound Interest Factors

	SINGLE PAYMENT		UNIFORM ANNUAL SERIES				
	Compound Amount Factor	Present Worth Factor	Sinking Fund Factor	Capital Recovery Factor	Compound Amount Factor	Present Worth Factor	
n	Given P To find S $(1+i)^n$	Given S To find P $\dfrac{1}{(1+i)^n}$	Given S To find R $\dfrac{i}{(1+i)^n-1}$	Given P To find R $\dfrac{i(1+i)^n}{(1+i)^n-1}$	Given R To find S $\dfrac{(1+i)^n-1}{i}$	Given R To find P $\dfrac{(1+i)^n-1}{i(1+i)^n}$	n
1	1.040	0.9615	1.00000	1.04000	1.000	0.962	1
2	1.082	0.9246	0.49020	0.53020	2.040	1.886	2
3	1.125	0.8890	0.32035	0.36035	3.122	2.775	3
4	1.170	0.8548	0.23549	0.27549	4.246	3.630	4
5	1.217	0.8219	0.18463	0.22463	5.416	4.452	5
6	1.265	0.7903	0.15076	0.19076	6.633	5.242	6
7	1.316	0.7599	0.12661	0.16661	7.898	6.002	7
8	1.369	0.7307	0.10853	0.14853	9.214	6.733	8
9	1.423	0.7026	0.09449	0.13449	10.583	7.435	9
10	1.480	0.6756	0.08329	0.12329	12.006	8.111	10
11	1.539	0.6496	0.07415	0.11415	13.486	8.760	11
12	1.601	0.6246	0.06655	0.10655	15.026	9.385	12
13	1.665	0.6006	0.06014	0.10014	16.627	9.986	13
14	1.732	0.5775	0.05467	0.09467	18.292	10.563	14
15	1.801	0.5553	0.04994	0.08994	20.024	11.118	15
16	1.873	0.5339	0.04582	0.08582	21.825	11.652	16
17	1.948	0.5134	0.04220	0.08220	23.698	12.166	17
18	2.026	0.4936	0.03899	0.07899	25.645	12.659	18
19	2.107	0.4746	0.03614	0.07614	27.671	13.134	19
20	2.191	0.4564	0.03358	0.07358	29.778	13.590	20
21	2.279	0.4388	0.03128	0.07128	31.969	14.029	21
22	2.370	0.4220	0.02920	0.06920	34.248	14.451	22
23	2.465	0.4057	0.02731	0.06731	36.618	14.857	23
24	2.563	0.3901	0.02559	0.06559	39.083	15.247	24
25	2.666	0.3751	0.02401	0.06401	41.646	15.622	25
26	2.772	0.3607	0.02257	0.06257	44.312	15.983	26
27	2.883	0.3468	0.02124	0.06124	47.084	16.330	27
28	2.999	0.3335	0.02001	0.06001	49.968	16.663	28
29	3.119	0.3207	0.01888	0.05888	52.966	16.984	29
30	3.243	0.3083	0.01783	0.05783	56.085	17.292	30
31	3.373	0.2965	0.01686	0.05686	59.328	17.588	31
32	3.508	0.2851	0.01595	0.05595	62.701	17.874	32
33	3.648	0.2741	0.01510	0.05510	66.210	18.148	33
34	3.794	0.2636	0.01431	0.05431	69.858	18.411	34
35	3.946	0.2534	0.01358	0.05358	73.652	18.665	35
40	4.801	0.2083	0.01052	0.05052	95.026	19.793	40
45	5.841	0.1712	0.00826	0.04826	121.029	20.720	45
50	7.107	0.1407	0.00655	0.04655	152.667	21.482	50
55	8.646	0.1157	0.00523	0.04523	191.159	22.109	55
60	10.520	0.0951	0.00420	0.04420	237.991	22.623	60
65	12.799	0.0781	0.00339	0.04339	294.968	23.047	65
70	15.572	0.0642	0.00275	0.04275	364.290	23.395	70
75	18.945	0.0528	0.00223	0.04223	448.631	23.680	75
80	23.050	0.0434	0.00181	0.04181	551.245	23.915	80
85	28.044	0.0357	0.00148	0.04148	676.090	24.109	85
90	34.119	0.0293	0.00121	0.04121	827.983	24.267	90
95	41.511	0.0241	0.00099	0.04099	1012.785	24.398	95
100	50.505	0.0198	0.00081	0.04081	1237.624	24.505	100

Table A.6 $4\frac{1}{2}\%$ Compound Interest Factors

	SINGLE PAYMENT		UNIFORM ANNUAL SERIES				
	Compound Amount Factor	Present Worth Factor	Sinking Fund Factor	Capital Recovery Factor	Compound Amount Factor	Present Worth Factor	
n	Given P To find S $(1+i)^n$	Given S To find P $\dfrac{1}{(1+i)^n}$	Given S To find R $\dfrac{i}{(1+i)^n-1}$	Given P To find R $\dfrac{i(1+i)^n}{(1+i)^n-1}$	Given R To find S $\dfrac{(1+i)^n-1}{i}$	Given R To find P $\dfrac{(1+i)^n-1}{i(1+i)^n}$	n
1	1.045	0.9569	1.00000	1.04500	1.000	0.957	1
2	1.092	0.9157	0.48900	0.53400	2.045	1.873	2
3	1.141	0.8763	0.31877	0.36377	3.137	2.749	3
4	1.193	0.8386	0.23374	0.27874	4.278	3.588	4
5	1.246	0.8025	0.18279	0.22779	5.471	4.390	5
6	1.302	0.7679	0.14888	0.19388	6.717	5.158	6
7	1.361	0.7348	0.12470	0.16970	8.019	5.893	7
8	1.422	0.7032	0.10661	0.15161	9.380	6.596	8
9	1.486	0.6729	0.09257	0.13757	10.802	7.269	9
10	1.553	0.6439	0.08138	0.12638	12.288	7.913	10
11	1.623	0.6162	0.07225	0.11725	13.841	8.529	11
12	1.696	0.5897	0.06467	0.10967	15.464	9.119	12
13	1.772	0.5643	0.05828	0.10328	17.160	9.683	13
14	1.852	0.5400	0.05282	0.09782	18.932	10.223	14
15	1.935	0.5167	0.04811	0.09311	20.784	10.740	15
16	2.022	0.4945	0.04402	0.08902	22.719	11.234	16
17	2.113	0.4732	0.04042	0.08542	24.742	11.707	17
18	2.208	0.4528	0.03724	0.08224	26.855	12.160	18
19	2.308	0.4333	0.03441	0.07941	29.064	12.593	19
20	2.412	0.4146	0.03188	0.07688	31.371	13.008	20
21	2.520	0.3968	0.02960	0.07460	33.783	13.405	21
22	2.634	0.3797	0.02755	0.07255	36.303	13.784	22
23	2.752	0.3634	0.02568	0.07068	38.937	14.148	23
24	2.876	0.3477	0.02399	0.06899	41.689	14.495	24
25	3.005	0.3327	0.02244	0.06744	44.565	14.828	25
26	3.141	0.3184	0.02102	0.06602	47.571	15.147	26
27	3.282	0.3047	0.01972	0.06472	50.711	15.451	27
28	3.430	0.2916	0.01852	0.06352	53.993	15.743	28
29	3.584	0.2790	0.01741	0.06241	57.423	16.022	29
30	3.745	0.2670	0.01639	0.06139	61.007	16.289	30
31	3.914	0.2555	0.01544	0.06044	64.752	16.544	31
32	4.090	0.2445	0.01456	0.05956	68.666	16.789	32
33	4.274	0.2340	0.01374	0.05874	72.756	17.023	33
34	4.466	0.2239	0.01298	0.05798	77.030	17.247	34
35	4.667	0.2143	0.01227	0.05727	81.497	17.461	35
40	5.816	0.1719	0.00934	0.05434	107.030	18.402	40
45	7.248	0.1380	0.00720	0.05220	138.850	19.156	45
50	9.033	0.1107	0.00560	0.05060	178.503	19.762	50
55	11.256	0.0888	0.00439	0.04939	227.918	20.248	55
60	14.027	0.0713	0.00345	0.04845	289.498	20.638	60
65	17.481	0.0572	0.00273	0.04773	366.238	20.951	65
70	21.784	0.0459	0.00217	0.04717	461.870	21.202	70
75	27.147	0.0368	0.00172	0.04672	581.044	21.404	75
80	33.830	0.0296	0.00137	0.04637	729.558	21.565	80
85	42.158	0.0237	0.00109	0.04609	914.632	21.695	85
90	52.537	0.0190	0.00087	0.04587	1145.269	21.799	90
95	65.471	0.0153	0.00070	0.04570	1432.684	21.883	95
100	81.589	0.0123	0.00056	0.04556	1790.856	21.950	100

Table A.7 5% Compound Interest Factors

n	SINGLE PAYMENT		UNIFORM ANNUAL SERIES				n
	Compound Amount Factor	Present Worth Factor	Sinking Fund Factor	Capital Recovery Factor	Compound Amount Factor	Present Worth Factor	
	Given P To find S $(1+i)^n$	Given S To find P $\dfrac{1}{(1+i)^n}$	Given S To find R $\dfrac{i}{(1+i)^n-1}$	Given P To find R $\dfrac{i(1+i)^n}{(1+i)^n-1}$	Given R To find S $\dfrac{(1+i)^n-1}{i}$	Given R To find P $\dfrac{(1+i)^n-1}{i(1+i)^n}$	
1	1.050	0.9524	1.00000	1.05000	1.000	0.952	1
2	1.103	0.9070	0.48780	0.53780	2.050	1.859	2
3	1.158	0.8638	0.31721	0.36721	3.153	2.723	3
4	1.216	0.8227	0.23201	0.28201	4.310	3.546	4
5	1.276	0.7835	0.18097	0.23097	5.526	4.329	5
6	1.340	0.7462	0.14702	0.19702	6.802	5.076	6
7	1.407	0.7107	0.12282	0.17282	8.142	5.786	7
8	1.477	0.6768	0.10472	0.15472	9.549	6.463	8
9	1.551	0.6446	0.09069	0.14069	11.027	7.108	9
10	1.629	0.6139	0.07950	0.12950	12.578	7.722	10
11	1.710	0.5847	0.07039	0.12039	14.207	8.306	11
12	1.796	0.5568	0.06283	0.11283	15.917	8.863	12
13	1.886	0.5303	0.05646	0.10646	17.713	9.394	13
14	1.980	0.5051	0.05102	0.10102	19.599	9.899	14
15	2.079	0.4810	0.04634	0.09634	21.579	10.380	15
16	2.183	0.4581	0.04227	0.09227	23.657	10.838	16
17	2.292	0.4363	0.03870	0.08870	25.840	11.274	17
18	2.407	0.4155	0.03555	0.08555	28.132	11.690	18
19	2.527	0.3957	0.03275	0.08275	30.539	12.085	19
20	2.653	0.3769	0.03024	0.08024	33.066	12.462	20
21	2.786	0.3589	0.02800	0.07800	35.719	12.821	21
22	2.925	0.3418	0.02597	0.07597	38.505	13.163	22
23	3.072	0.3256	0.02414	0.07414	41.430	13.489	23
24	3.225	0.3101	0.02247	0.07247	44.502	13.799	24
25	3.386	0.2953	0.02095	0.07095	47.727	14.094	25
26	3.556	0.2812	0.01956	0.06956	51.113	14.375	26
27	3.733	0.2678	0.01829	0.06829	54.669	14.643	27
28	3.920	0.2551	0.01712	0.06712	58.403	14.898	28
29	4.116	0.2429	0.01605	0.06605	62.323	15.141	29
30	4.322	0.2314	0.01505	0.06505	66.439	15.372	30
31	4.538	0.2204	0.01413	0.06413	70.761	15.593	31
32	4.765	0.2099	0.01328	0.06328	75.299	15.803	32
33	5.003	0.1999	0.01249	0.06249	80.064	16.003	33
34	5.253	0.1904	0.01176	0.06176	85.067	16.193	34
35	5.516	0.1813	0.01107	0.06107	90.320	16.374	35
40	7.040	0.1420	0.00828	0.05828	120.800	17.159	40
45	8.985	0.1113	0.00626	0.05626	159.700	17.774	45
50	11.467	0.0872	0.00478	0.05478	209.348	18.256	50
55	14.636	0.0683	0.00367	0.05367	272.713	18.633	55
60	18.679	0.0535	0.00283	0.05283	353.584	18.929	60
65	23.840	0.0419	0.00219	0.05219	456.798	19.161	65
70	30.426	0.0329	0.00170	0.05170	588.529	19.343	70
75	38.833	0.0258	0.00132	0.05132	756.654	19.485	75
80	49.561	0.0202	0.00103	0.05103	971.229	19.596	80
85	63.254	0.0158	0.00080	0.05080	1245.087	19.684	85
90	80.730	0.0124	0.00063	0.05063	1594.607	19.752	90
95	103.035	0.0097	0.00049	0.05049	2040.694	19.806	95
100	131.501	0.0076	0.00038	0.05038	2610.025	19.848	100

Table A.8 $5\frac{1}{2}\%$ Compound Interest Factors

	SINGLE PAYMENT		UNIFORM ANNUAL SERIES				
	Compound Amount Factor	Present Worth Factor	Sinking Fund Factor	Capital Recovery Factor	Compound Amount Factor	Present Worth Factor	
n	Given P To find S $(1+i)^n$	Given S To find P $\dfrac{1}{(1+i)^n}$	Given S To find R $\dfrac{i}{(1+i)^n-1}$	Given P To find R $\dfrac{i(1+i)^n}{(1+i)^n-1}$	Given R To find S $\dfrac{(1+i)^n-1}{i}$	Given R To find P $\dfrac{(1+i)^n-1}{i(1+i)^n}$	n
1	1.055	0.9479	1.00000	1.05500	1.000	0.948	1
2	1.113	0.8985	0.48662	0.54162	2.055	1.846	2
3	1.174	0.8516	0.31565	0.37065	3.168	2.698	3
4	1.239	0.8072	0.23029	0.28529	4.342	3.505	4
5	1.307	0.7651	0.17918	0.23418	5.581	4.270	5·
6	1.379	0.7252	0.14518	0.20018	6.888	4.996	6
7	1.455	0.6874	0.12096	0.17596	8.267	5.683	7
8	1.535	0.6516	0.10286	0.15786	9.722	6.335	8
9	1·619	0.6176	0.08884	0.14384	11.256	6.952	9
10	1.708	0.5854	0.07767	0.13267	12.875	7.538	10
11	1.802	0.5549	0.06857	0.12357	14.583	8.093	11
12	1.901	0.5260	0.06103	0.11603	16.386	8.619	12
13	2.006	0.4986	0.05468	0.10968	18.287	9.117	13
14	2.116	0.4726	0.04928	0.10428	20.293	9.590	14
15	2.232	0.4479	0.04463	0.09963	22.409	10.038	15
16	2.355	0.4246	0.04058	0.09558	24.641	10.462	16
17	2.485	0.4024	0.03704	0.09204	26.996	10.865	17
18	2.621	0.3815	0.03392	0.08892	29.481	11.246	18
19	2.766	0.3616	0.03115	0.08615	32.103	11.608	19
20	2.918	0.3427	0.02868	0.08368	34.868	11.950	20
21	3.078	0.3249	0.02646	0.08146	37.786	12.275	21
22	3.248	0.3079	0.02447	0.07947	40.864	12.583	22
23	3.426	0.2919	0.02267	0.07767	44.112	12.875	23
24	3.615	0.2767	0.02104	0.07604	47.538	13.152	24
25	3.813	0.2622	0.01955	0.07455	51.153	13.414	25
26	4.023	0.2486	0.01819	0.07319	54.966	13.662	26
27	4.244	0.2356	0.01695	0.07195	58.989	13.898	27
28	4.478	0.2233	0.01581	0.07081	63.234	14.121	28
29	4.724	0.2117	0.01477	0.06977	67.711	14.333	29
30	4.984	0.2006	0.01381	0.06881	72.435	14.534	30
31	5.258	0.1902	0.01292	0.06792	77.419	14.724	31
32	5.547	0.1803	0.01210	0.06710	82.677	14.904	32
33	5.852	0.1709	0.01133	0.06633	88.225	15.075	33
34	6.174	0.1620	0.01063	0.06563	94.077	15.237	34
35	6.514	0.1535	0.00997	0.06497	100.251	15.391	35
40	8.513	0.1175	0.00732	0.06232	136.606	16.046	40
45	11.127	0.0899	0.00543	0.06043	184.119	16.548	45
50	14.542	0.0688	0.00406	0.05906	246.217	16.932	50
55	19.006	0.0526	0.00305	0.05805	327.377	17.225	55
60	24.840	0.0403	0.00231	0.05731	433.450	17.450	60
65	32.465	0.0308	0.00175	0.05675	572.053	17.622	65
70	42.430	0.0236	0.00133	0.05633	753.271	17.753	70
75	55.454	0.0180	0.00101	0.05601	990.076	17.854	75
80	72.476	0.0138	0.00077	0.05577	1299.571	17.931	80
85	94.724	0.0106	0.00059	0.05559	1704.069	17.990	85
90	123.800	0.0081	0.00045	0.05545	2232.731	18.035	90
95	161.802	·0.0062	0.00034	0.05534	2923.671	18.069	95
100	211.469	0.0047	0.00026	0.05526	3826.702	18.096	100

Table A.9 6% Compound Interest Factors

	SINGLE PAYMENT		UNIFORM ANNUAL SERIES				
	Compound Amount Factor	Present Worth Factor	Sinking Fund Factor	Capital Recovery Factor	Compound Amount Factor	Present Worth Factor	
n	Given P To find S $(1+i)^n$	Given S To find P $\dfrac{1}{(1+i)^n}$	Given S To find R $\dfrac{i}{(1+i)^n-1}$	Given P To find R $\dfrac{i(1+i)^n}{(1+i)^n-1}$	Given R To find S $\dfrac{(1+i)^n-1}{i}$	Given R To find P $\dfrac{(1+i)^n-1}{i(1+i)^n}$	n
1	1.060	0.9434	1.00000	1.06000	1.000	0.943	1
2	1.124	0.8900	0.48544	0.54544	2.060	1.833	2
3	1.191	0.8396	0.31411	0.37411	3.184	2.673	3
4	1.262	0.7921	0.22859	0.28859	4.375	3.465	4
5	1.338	0.7473	0.17740	0.23740	5.637	4.212	5
6	1.419	0.7050	0.14336	0.20336	6.975	4.917	6
7	1.504	0.6651	0.11914	0.17914	8.394	5.582	7
8	1.594	0.6274	0.10104	0.16104	9.897	6.210	8
9	1.689	0.5919	0.08702	0.14702	11.491	6.802	9
10	1.791	0.5584	0.07587	0.13587	13.181	7.360	10
11	1.898	0.5268	0.06679	0.12679	14.972	7.887	11
12	2.012	0.4970	0.05928	0.11928	16.870	8.384	12
13	2.133	0.4688	0.05296	0.11296	18.882	8.853	13
14	2.261	0.4423	0.04758	0.10758	21.015	9.295	14
15	2.397	0.4173	0.04296	0.10296	23.276	9.712	15
16	2.540	0.3936	0.03895	0.09895	25.673	10.106	16
17	2.693	0.3714	0.03544	0.09544	28.213	10.477	17
18	2.854	0.3503	0.03236	0.09236	30.906	10.828	18
19	3.026	0.3305	0.02962	0.08962	33.760	11.158	19
20	3.207	0.3118	0.02718	0.08718	36.786	11.470	20
21	3.400	0.2942	0.02500	0.08500	39.993	11.764	21
22	3.604	0.2775	0.02305	0.08305	43.392	12.042	22
23	3.820	0.2618	0.02128	0.08128	46.996	12.303	23
24	4.049	0.2470	0.01968	0.07968	50.816	12.550	24
25	4.292	0.2330	0.01823	0.07823	54.865	12.783	25
26	4.549	0.2198	0.01690	0.07690	59.156	13.003	26
27	4.822	0.2074	0.01570	0.07570	63.706	13.211	27
28	5.112	0.1956	0.01459	0.07459	68.528	13.406	28
29	5.418	0.1846	0.01358	0.07358	73.640	13.591	29
30	5.743	0.1741	0.01265	0.07265	79.058	13.765	30
31	6.088	0.1643	0.01179	0.07179	84.802	13.929	31
32	6.453	0.1550	0.01100	0.07100	90.890	14.084	32
33	6.841	0.1462	0.01027	0.07027	97.343	14.230	33
34	7.251	0.1379	0.00960	0.06960	104.184	14.368	34
35	7.686	0.1301	0.00897	0.06897	111.435	14.498	35
40	10.286	0.0972	0.00646	0.06646	154.762	15.046	40
45	13.765	0.0727	0.00470	0.06470	212.744	15.456	45
50	18.420	0.0543	0.00344	0.06344	290.336	15.762	50
55	24.650	0.0406	0.00254	0.06254	394.172	15.991	55
60	32.988	0.0303	0.00188	0.06188	533.128	16.161	60
65	44.145	0.0227	0.00139	0.06139	719.083	16.289	65
70	59.076	0.0169	0.00103	0.06103	967.932	16.385	70
75	79.057	0.0126	0.00077	0.06077	1300.949	16.456	75
80	105.796	0.0095	0.00057	0.06057	1746.600	16.509	80
85	141.579	0.0071	0.00043	0.06043	2342.982	16.549	85
90	189.465	0.0053	0.00032	0.06032	3141.075	16.579	90
95	253.546	0.0039	0.00024	0.06024	4209.104	16.601	95
100	339.302	0.0029	0.00018	0.06018	5638.368	16.618	100

Table A.10 7% Compound Interest Factors

	SINGLE PAYMENT		UNIFORM ANNUAL SERIES				
	Compound Amount Factor	Present Worth Factor	Sinking Fund Factor	Capital Recovery Factor	Compound Amount Factor	Present Worth Factor	
n	Given P To find S $(1+i)^n$	Given S To find P $\dfrac{1}{(1+i)^n}$	Given S To find R $\dfrac{i}{(1+i)^n-1}$	Given P To find R $\dfrac{i(1+i)^n}{(1+i)^n-1}$	Given R To find S $\dfrac{(1+i)^n-1}{i}$	Given R To find P $\dfrac{(1+i)^n-1}{i(1+i)^n}$	n
1	1.070	0.9346	1.00000	1.07000	1.000	0.935	1
2	1.145	0.8734	0.48309	0.55309	2.070	1.808	2
3	1.225	0.8163	0.31105	0.38105	3.215	2.624	3
4	1.311	0.7629	0.22523	0.29523	4.440	3.387	4
5	1.403	0.7130	0.17389	0.24389	5.751	4.100	5
6	1.501	0.6663	0.13980	0.20980	7.153	4.767	6
7	1.606	0.6227	0.11555	0.18555	8.654	5.389	7
8	1.718	0.5820	0.09747	0.16747	10.260	5.971	8
9	1.838	0.5439	0.08349	0.15349	11.978	6.515	9
10	1.967	0.5083	0.07238	0.14238	13.816	7.024	10
11	2.105	0.4751	0.06336	0.13336	15.784	7.499	11
12	2.252	0.4440	0.05590	0.12590	17.888	7.943	12
13	2.410	0.4150	0.04965	0.11965	20.141	8.358	13
14	2.579	0.3878	0.04434	0.11434	22.550	8.745	14
15	2.759	0.3624	0.03979	0.10979	25.129	9.108	15
16	2.952	0.3387	0.03586	0.10586	27.888	9.447	16
17	3.159	0.3166	0.03243	0.10243	30.840	9.763	17
18	3.380	0.2959	0.02941	0.09941	33.999	10.059	18
19	3.617	0.2765	0.02675	0.09675	37.379	10.336	19
20	3.870	0.2584	0.02439	0.09439	40.995	10.594	20
21	4.141	0.2415	0.02229	0.09229	44.865	10.836	21
22	4.430	0.2257	0.02041	0.09041	49.006	11.061	22
23	4.741	0.2109	0.01871	0.08871	53.436	11.272	23
24	5.072	0.1971	0.01719	0.08719	58.177	11.469	24
25	5.427	0.1842	0.01581	0.08581	63.249	11.654	25
26	5.807	0.1722	0.01456	0.08456	68.676	11.826	26
27	6.214	0.1609	0.01343	0.08343	74.484	11.987	27
28	6.649	0.1504	0.01239	0.08239	80.698	12.137	28
29	7.114	0.1406	0.01145	0.08145	87.347	12.278	29
30	7.612	0.1314	0.01059	0.08059	94.461	12.409	30
31	8.145	0.1228	0.00980	0.07980	102.073	12.532	31
32	8.715	0.1147	0.00907	0.07907	110.218	12.647	32
33	9.325	0.1072	0.00841	0.07841	118.933	12.754	33
34	9.978	0.1002	0.00780	0.07780	128.259	12.854	34
35	10.677	0.0937	0.00723	0.07723	138.237	•12.948	35
40	14.974	0.0668	0.00501	0.07501	199.635	13.332	40
45	21.002	0.0476	0.00350	0.07350	285.749	13.606	45
50	29.457	0.0339	0.00246	0.07246	406.529	13.801	50
55	41.315	0.0242	0.00174	0.07174	575.929	13.940	55
60	57.946	0.0173	0.00123	0.07123	813.520	14.039	60
65	81.273	0.0123	0.00087	0.07087	1146.755	14.110	65
70	113.989	0.0088	0.00062	0.07062	1614.134	14.160	70
75	159.876	0.0063	0.00044	0.07044	2269.657	14.196	75
80	224.234	0.0045	0.00031	0.07031	3189.063	14.222	80
85	314.500	0.0032	0.00022	0.07022	4478.576	14.240	85
90	441.103	0.0023	0.00016	0.07016	6287.185	14.253	90
95	618.670	0.0016	0.00011	0.07011	8823.854	14.263	95
100	867.716	0.0012	0.00008	0.07008	12381.662	14.269	100

Table A.11 8% Compound Interest Factors

n	SINGLE PAYMENT		UNIFORM ANNUAL SERIES				n
	Compound Amount Factor	Present Worth Factor	Sinking Fund Factor	Capital Recovery Factor	Compound Amount Factor	Present Worth Factor	
	Given P To find S $(1+i)^n$	Given S To find P $\dfrac{1}{(1+i)^n}$	Given S To find R $\dfrac{i}{(1+i)^n-1}$	Given P To find R $\dfrac{i(1+i)^n}{(1+i)^n-1}$	Given R To find S $\dfrac{(1+i)^n-1}{i}$	Given R To find P $\dfrac{(1+i)^n-1}{i(1+i)^n}$	
1	1.080	0.9259	1.00000	1.08000	1.000	0.926	1
2	1.166	0.8573	0.48077	0.56077	2.080	1.783	2
3	1.260	0.7938	0.30803	0.38803	3.246	2.577	3
4	1.360	0.7350	0.22192	0.30192	4.506	3.312	4
5	1.469	0.6806	0.17046	0.25046	5.867	3.993	5
6	1.587	0.6302	0.13632	0.21632	7.336	4.623	6
7	1.714	0.5835	0.11207	0.19207	8.923	5.206	7
8	1.851	0.5403	0.09401	0.17401	10.637	5.747	8
9	1.999	0.5002	0.08008	0.16008	12.488	6.247	9
10	2.159	0.4632	0.06903	0.14903	14.487	6.710	10
11	2.332	0.4289	0.06008	0.14008	16.645	7.139	11
12	2.518	0.3971	0.05270	0.13270	18.977	7.536	12
13	2.720	0.3677	0.04652	0.12652	21.495	7.904	13
14	2.937	0.3405	0.04130	0.12130	24.215	8.244	14
15	3.172	0.3152	0.03683	0.11683	27.152	8.559	15
16	3.426	0.2919	0.03298	0.11298	30.324	8.851	16
17	3.700	0.2703	0.02963	0.10963	33.750	9.122	17
18	3.996	0.2502	0.02670	0.10670	37.450	9.372	18
19	4.316	0.2317	0.02413	0.10413	41.446	9.604	19
20	4.661	0.2145	0.02185	0.10185	45.762	9.818	20
21	5.034	0.1987	0.01983	0.09983	50.423	10.017	21
22	5.437	0.1839	0.01803	0.09803	55.457	10.201	22
23	5.871	0.1703	0.01642	0.09642	60.893	10.371	23
24	6.341	0.1577	0.01498	0.09498	66.765	10.529	24
25	6.848	0.1460	0.01368	0.09368	73.106	10.675	25
26	7.396	0.1352	0.01251	0.09251	79.954	10.810	26
27	7.988	0.1252	0.01145	0.09145	87.351	10.935	27
28	8.627	0.1159	0.01049	0.09049	95.339	11.051	28
29	9.317	0.1073	0.00962	0.08962	103.966	11.158	29
30	10.063	0.0994	0.00883	0.08883	113.283	11.258	30
31	10.868	0.0920	0.00811	0.08811	123.346	11.350	31
32	11.737	0.0852	0.00745	0.08745	134.214	11.435	32
33	12.676	0.0789	0.00685	0.08685	145.951	11.514	33
34	13.690	0.0730	0.00630	0.08630	158.627	11.587	34
35	14.785	0.0676	0.00580	0.08580	172.317	11.655	35
40	21.725	0.0460	0.00386	0.08386	259.057	11.925	40
45	31.920	0.0313	0.00259	0.08259	386.506	12.108	45
50	46.902	0.0213	0.00174	0.08174	573.770	12.233	50
55	68.914	0.0145	0.00118	0.08118	848.923	12.319	55
60	101.257	0.0099	0.00080	0.08080	1253.213	12.377	60
65	148.780	0.0067	0.00054	0.08054	1847.248	12.416	65
70	218.606	0.0046	0.00037	0.08037	2720.080	12.443	70
75	321.205	0.0031	0.00025	0.08025	4002.557	12.461	75
80	471.955	0.0021	0.00017	0.08017	5886.935	12.474	80
85	693.456	0.0014	0.00012	0.08012	8655.706	12.482	85
90	1018.915	0.0010	0.00008	0.08008	12723.939	12.488	90
95	1497.121	0.0007	0.00005	0.08005	18701.507	12.492	95
100	2199.761	0.0005	0.00004	0.08004	27484.516	12.494	100

Table A.12   10% Compound Interest Factors

	Single Payment		Uniform Annual Series				
	Compound Amount Factor	Present Worth Factor	Sinking Fund Factor	Capital Recovery Factor	Compound Amount Factor	Present Worth Factor	
n	Given P To find S $(1+i)^n$	Given S To find P $\dfrac{1}{(1+i)^n}$	Given S To find R $\dfrac{i}{(1+i)^n-1}$	Given P To find R $\dfrac{i(1+i)^n}{(1+i)^n-1}$	Given R To find S $\dfrac{(1+i)^n-1}{i}$	Given R To find P $\dfrac{(1+i)^n-1}{i(1+i)^n}$	n
1	1.100	0.9091	1.00000	1.10000	1.000	0.909	1
2	1.210	0.8264	0.47619	0.57619	2.100	1.736	2
3	1.331	0.7513	0.30211	0.40211	3.310	2.487	3
4	1.464	0.6830	0.21547	0.31547	4.641	3.170	4
5	1.611	0.6209	0.16380	0.26380	6.105	3.791	5
6	1.772	0.5645	0.12961	0.22961	7.716	4.355	6
7	1.949	0.5132	0.10541	0.20541	9.487	4.868	7
8	2.144	0.4665	0.08744	0.18744	11.436	5.335	8
9	2.358	0.4241	0.07364	0.17364	13.579	5.759	9
10	2.594	0.3855	0.06275	0.16275	15.937	6.144	10
11	2.853	0.3505	0.05396	0.15396	18.531	6.495	11
12	3.138	0.3186	0.04676	0.14676	21.384	6.814	12
13	3.452	0.2897	0.04078	0.14078	24.523	7.103	13
14	3.797	0.2633	0.03575	0.13575	27.975	7.367	14
15	4.177	0.2394	0.03147	0.13147	31.772	7.606	15
16	4.595	0.2176	0.02782	0.12782	35.950	7.824	16
17	5.054	0.1978	0.02466	0.12466	40.545	8.022	17
18	5.560	0.1799	0.02193	0.12193	45.599	8.201	18
19	6.116	0.1635	0.01955	0.11955	51.159	8.365	19
20	6.727	0.1486	0.01746	0.11746	57.275	8.514	20
21	7.400	0.1351	0.01562	0.11562	64.002	8.649	21
22	8.140	0.1228	0.01401	0.11401	71.403	8.772	22
23	8.954	0.1117	0.01257	0.11257	79.543	8.883	23
24	9.850	0.1015	0.01130	0.11130	88.497	8.985	24
25	10.835	0.0923	0.01017	0.11017	98.347	9.077	25
26	11.918	0.0839	0.00916	0.10916	109.182	9.161	26
27	13.110	0.0763	0.00826	0.10826	121.100	9.237	27
28	14.421	0.0693	0.00745	0.10745	134.210	9.307	28
29	15.863	0.0630	0.00673	0.10673	148.631	9.370	29
30	17.449	0.0573	0.00608	0.10608	164.494	9.427	30
31	19.194	0.0521	0.00550	0.10550	181.943	9.479	31
32	21.114	0.0474	0.00497	0.10497	201.138	9.526	32
33	23.225	0.0431	0.00450	0.10450	222.252	9.569	33
34	25.548	0.0391	0.00407	0.10407	245.477	9.609	34
35	28.102	0.0356	0.00369	0.10369	271.024	9.644	35
40	45.259	0.0221	0.00226	0.10226	442.593	9.779	40
45	72.890	0.0137	0.00139	0.10139	718.905	9.863	45
50	117.391	0.0085	0.00086	0.10086	1163.909	9.915	50
55	189.059	0.0053	0.00053	0.10053	1880.591	9.947	55
60	304.482	0.0033	0.00033	0.10033	3034.816	9.967	60
65	490.371	0.0020	0.00020	0.10020	4893.707	9.980	65
70	789.747	0.0013	0.00013	0.10013	7887.470	9.987	70
75	1271.895	0.0008	0.00008	0.10008	12708.954	9.992	75
80	2048.400	0.0005	0.00005	0.10005	20474.002	9.995	80
85	3298.969	0.0003	0.00003	0.10003	32979.690	9.997	85
90	5313.023	0.0002	0.00002	0.10002	53120.226	9.998	90
95	8556.676	0.0001	0.00001	0.10001	85556.760	9.999	95
100	13780.612	0.0001	0.00001	0.10001	137796.123	9.999	100

THE LOAN APPLICATION

APPLICATION FOR LOAN ON RESIDENTIAL PROPERTY
(INCLUDING APPRAISAL REPORT)

Branch _____ Loan Officer_____ Date _____

Loan Desired $_____ Term _____ Rate _____%

PROPERTY DESCRIPTION

Address _____ City _____ State _____

Legal Description _____

Owner of record _____

Lot size _____ X _____ Age ____ Date Purchased _____ Purchase Price $ _____

(include additions or improvements) _____

Proposed Construction: Land Cost $ _____ Estimated Construction Cost $_____

Present Loan: Original Amount $ _____ Balance $ _____ Int. paid to _____

From whom _____ Rate _____ % Date Due _____

Occupied by: Owner_____ Tenant _____ Rented for $_____ per month

APPLICANT'S HISTORY

Name _____ Age [   ] Wife's Name _____

Address _____ Phone Number _____

Employed by _____ For _____ years. Position _____

Business Address _____ Business Phone Number _____

Annual Income: Salary $_____ Other $ _____ Total $ _____

Source of Income Other Than Salary or Business _____

_____ Credit References_____

_____

Loan Proceeds to be used for _____

Amount collected to apply on Appraisal Fee $ _____

_____

Signature of Applicant

Lending Officer's Comment — Recommendations _____

_____

[Reverse Side]

RESIDENTIAL APPRAISAL REPORT

Street Address _____ LEGAL DESCRIPTION: Lot_____

City _____ State_____ Floors: _____

_____ Side of _____ St. Block _____

_____ Feet _____ of _____ St. Addition _____

Paved _____Gravel _____ Ground Size _____

Walks and Curbs _____

Fig. A.1

Figures A.1—A.9 are reproduced by the courtesy of Warren, Gorham & Lamont, Inc.

202

Sewer _____ Cesspool _____ Septic Tank_____ Plantings _____

Water Supply_____ Electricity ____ Gas _____ Sprinkling System_____

Above or Below Grade _____

BUILDING IMPROVEMENTS

  (DESCRIBE):

NEIGHBORHOOD:

Year Built_____ Size _____   Age of typical Property_____

Kind_____   Distance to Schools _____

No. of Stories _____   Distance to Shopping _____

Foundation _____   Distance to Car or Bus _____

Basement Size _____ _____   Zone Restrictions_____

Heating Plan _____   Declining _____

Built-in Equipment _____   Static _____

Water Heater _____   Improving_____

Laundry Trays _____   Quality_____

Recreation Room_____   Adverse Influences _____

Rooms: 1st Floor _____   Walls: _____

Details: 2nd Floor Basement _____

Living Room   _____ _____   Fireplace _____

Dining Room and Halls   _____ _____   Linen Closet_____

Bedrooms   _____ _____   Closets _____

Kitchen   _____ _____   Cabinets _____

Bath   _____ _____   Shower _____

2nd Floor Bedrooms   _____ _____   Closets _____

Plumbing and Light Fixtures: Modern _____   Semi-Modern _____ Old _____

Garage Size _____   Drives and Walks _____

General Condition: Exterior _____   Interior_____ Roof_____

Grounds _____   Improvements Required _____

_____

_____ Cost $ _____

USE FOR INCOME DWELLINGS No. of Rental Units_____ Rooms each Unit _____

    Vacancy Allowance _____ % $ _____ Gross Yearly Rental Furnished $ _____

    Operating Expense $ _____ Gross Yearly Rental Unfurnished $ _____

       Total $ _____ Less Operating and Vacancy $ _____

                                Net Return $ _____

   ASSESSED VALUE: RENTAL VALUE: APPRAISEMENT:

LAND $ _____   LAND $ _____

IMPROVEMENTS $ _____   IMPROVEMENTS $ _____

TOTAL $ _____ $ _____ TOTAL $ _____

Remarks: _____

Date _____ Appraiser _____

Courtesy of The First National Bank of Portland, Oregon

Fig. A.1 (*Continued*)

APPLICATION FOR LOAN ON COMMERCIAL PROPERTY
(INCLUDING APPRAISAL REPORT)

Branch _____ Loan Officer _____ Date _____

Applicant _____ Address _____

Loan Desired $ _____ Term _____ _____ Rate _____%

PROPERTY DESCRIPTION

Address _____ City _____ State_____

Legal Description _____

Land Size _____ x _____Date Purchased_____ Cost $_____

BUILDING IMPROVEMENTS

Existing _____ Size _____ No. Stories _____ Age _____

To be built _____

Construction _____ Basement Size _____

Date Purchased _____ Purchase Price $ _____

No. of Rentals _____ Annual Gross Income $ _____

Annual Rental Value of Owner Occupied Space $ _____

Annual Operating Cost Including Taxes $ _____

Space Under Lease	*Term of Lease*	*Date Expires*

Holder of Present Mortgage _____ Address_____

Original Amt. $ _____ Bal. Due $ _____ Rate _____% Ins. Amt. $ _____

Financial Statement: Attached [ ]   In File [ ]

_____

Signature of Applicant

Loan Officer's Recommendations _____

_____ _____

_____

[Reverse Side]

APPRAISER'S REPORT

Date _____

Address of Property _____

Legal Description :_____

_____

Fig. A.2

204 ·

THE LOAN APPLICATION

Land Size _____ Size of Bldg. _____

No. of Stories _____ Type of Construction _____ Year Built____

Foundation _____ Basement Size _____

Heating Plant _____

Plumbing _____ Elevators _____

Fire Escapes _____ Type of Roof _____

Use/Type of Building _____

OCCUPANCY	Gross per Month	Termination of Lease
1st Floor _____	$ _____	_____
2nd Floor _____	$ _____	_____
3rd Floor _____	$ _____	_____
4th Floor _____	$ _____	_____
Additional Space _____	$ _____	_____

Total Gross Annual Income 100% Occupancy $ _____

Less _____ % Predicted Vacancy $ _____

Effective Gross Annual Income Total $ _____

ANNUAL OPERATING EXPENSE

Total General Taxes	$ _____	Repairs — Decorating	$ _____
Special Assessments	$ _____	Equipment Replacement	$ _____
Insurance	$ _____	Supplies	$ _____
Pay Roll	$ _____	Management	$ _____
Heat	$ _____	Advertising	$ _____
Water/Electricity/Gas	$ _____	Miscellaneous	$ _____

Total Operating Expense $ _____

Net Annual Income $ _____

Land value $ _____ Capitalization Rate _____ % $ _____

Annual Net Building Return $ _____

LOCATION INFORMATION

Is the area improving ( )   Static ( )   Declining ( )

Predicted economic life   years.

Likelihood of competitive construction: Strong ( )   Moderate ( ) , Little ( )

Percentage of occupancy in competitive buildings _____%

Is the site developed to its highest and best use _____

_____

Remarks: _____

_____

ASSESSED VALUE:		APPRAISEMENT:	
LAND	$ _____	LAND	$ _____
BUILDINGS	$ _____	BUILDINGS	$ _____
TOTAL	$ _____	TOTAL	$ _____

Appraiser

Fig. A.2   (*Continued*)

THE LOAN APPLICATION

PROJECT DATA CHECK LIST FOR
OFFICE BUILDING LOAN

I. Brief Statement of Project
- what type building to be built (e.g., 4 story, 44,000 sq. ft.)
- where building is to be located
- in some instances, statement might conclude with amount only of loan requested.

II. Location and Physical Description
  A. General economic factors of metropolitan area
    1. Brief history of city
    2. City's major attractions
    3. Transportation network
      a. Highways
      b. Airlines
      c. Railroads
      d. Trucking
      e. Bus lines
      f. Water transportation (if applicable)
    4. Trade area
      a. Number of square miles
      b. Population
      c. Buying income
    5. Industry
      a. Number of manufacturing establishments
      b. Number of persons employed in these
      c. Annual payroll
      d. Type products manufactured — are they diversified?
      e. Primary economy of town
    6. Natural resources of area
  B. Population
    1. Rate of growth past five years
    2. Anticipated growth or factors or conditions likely to influence future growth
    3. Breakdown of population
      - what percent industrialized, etc.
      - number of doctors
      - number of dentists
      - number of lawyers
      - number of insurance companies
      - average per capita income
  C. Site location
    1. Brief statement of immediate area around building location
    2. Transportation relative to building
      a. City bus lines nearby — percent of total passengers these lines carry

Fig. A.3.

b. Airport
- time and distance from building
- is it convenient to building occupants/customers
c. Train terminals (in cities where passenger train load is sufficient to warrant discussion)
3. Relation to banks, post office, shops, downtown area
4. Relation to restaurants and other eating facilities
5. Relation to hospitals
6. Relation to predominant residential area for managers, executives, professional people who would be potential occupants.
7. Number of nearby small towns or communities, and time and distance factors relative to building.
8. Outlook for the future for location with particular regard to directional trends of city's present and potential expansion.
9. Existing buildings in area — number, age, height, type, condition, rental rate, and parking facilities
D. Legal description of property
E. Land value
1. Recent sales of comparable property in surrounding area
a. Address
b. Location — relative to proposed building location
c. Dimensions of property
d. Sales price
e. Price per square foot
f. Nature of property, i.e., land, land with improvements taken into consideration, land with improvements not considered.
F. Title to property

III. Proposed Building
A. Detailed description
B. Services (from brochure)
C. Management
D. Type of tenants desired/obtained
E. Description of leases being executed
F. Zoning
G. Taxes
1. City real estate tax — assessment ratio
2. State and county real estate tax
3. Other taxes (where applicable)
a. Franchise and excise tax rates
b. Personalty tax rate
c. Income tax rate
4. Special assessments and charges e.g., garbage pick-up, sewage disposal
H. Insurance rates
I. Average utility costs for building

Fig. A.3 (*Continued*)

IV. Estimated Income and Basis of Estimates
    A. Proposed rental rate for building
        • ground floor
        • upper floors
        • comparison with rates of existing buildings — favorable or unfavorable and why
    B. Projections (with comparative operating ratios)
        1. Income statement
        2. Cash flow

V. Economic Feasibility of the Project
    A. Relationship of site to area development
    B. Anticipated factors likely to influence future growth — demand
    C. Results of interviews
        • Standard set of questions employed
    D. Conclusions

VI. Loan Requested
    A. Amount
    B. Term
    C. Interest rate

VII. Information Concerning Applicant
    A. Company background (including profit-sharing plan)
    B. Principals

VIII. Exhibits
    A. Plans and specifications
    B. City map
    C. Office building brochure
    D. Company brochure
    E. Photographs (aerial and ground) of site
    F. Sample lease
    G. Typical office layout
    H. Pictures of surrounding properties

Fig. A.3 *(Continued)*

ANALYSIS OF THE TRANSACTION

ANALYSIS OF DRIVE-IN RESTAURANT SITE

DATE _____   REPORTED BY: _____

I. LOCATION: _____
   (Street address, City, County and State)

II. SITE DATA & ACCESSIBILITY: *(ATTACH PLOT PLAN; PHOTOGRAPH-LEFT SIDE, RIGHT SIDE, DIRECTLY IN FRONT OF, ACROSS STREET FROM; LEGAL DESCRIPTION; CITY MAP WITH LOCATION PINPOINTED.)*

	Yes	No	Comment
Lot is level	[ ]	[ ]	_____
Drainage	[ ]	[ ]	_____
Curbs	[ ]	[ ]	_____
Gutters	[ ]	[ ]	_____
Sidewalk	[ ]	[ ]	_____
Sewer	[ ]	[ ]	_____
Water	[ ]	[ ]	_____
Gas	[ ]	[ ]	_____
Electricity	[ ]	[ ]	_____
Utility poles to be relocated	[ ]	[ ]	_____
Good street condition	[ ]	[ ]	_____
Traffic signal (if at intersection)	[ ]	[ ]	_____
Bus stop nearby	[ ]	[ ]	_____
Offsite parking available	[ ]	[ ]	_____
Proposed street changes or repairs	[ ]	[ ]	_____
Congested traffic	[ ]	[ ]	_____

Character of traffic: neighborhood _____ % Business _____ % Tourist _____ %.
Speed zone of traffic in front of site _____ mph, adjacent street _____ mph.
Site is right-hand _____ or left-hand _____ outbound.
How far back are buildings on adjacent property? (in feet) _____ .
Visibility distance approaching site street:
    From left: Sign _____ yds.   Bldg._____ yds.
    From right: Sign _____ yds.   Bldg._____ yds.

III. FAST FOODS COMPETITION WITHIN ONE MILE OF SITE

Name	*Type*	*Distance from our site*
_____	_____	_____
_____	_____	_____
_____	_____	_____
_____	_____	_____

(If more room needed, attach separate sheet.)

Fig. A.4

Supermarkets in Area: _____

Distance from Site: _____ Hours: _____

Churches in Area: _____

Distance from Site: _____

Department Stores in Area: _____

Distance from Site:_____

Schools in Area: _____

Distance from Site: _____

Shopping Centers within one mile: Yes [ ]   No [ ] .   Size: Major [ ]
                                   Neighborhood [ ]   Small [ ] .

IV. POPULATION AND INCOME DATA:

1.   Show population by quadrant on Diagram 2. Use (m) for thousands.

2.   Indicate income level by quadrant on Diag. 2. Source _____

3.   Indicate residential value by quadrant on back. Source _____

4.   Age of homes range from _____ yrs. to _____ yrs. Source _____

5.   No. of homes within 1 mile _____ ; 2 miles _____

6.   Major industry firms in this area are _____ .

V.   ZONING DATA:

1.   Is property zoned for a restaurant? Yes [ ];   No [ ] . If "yes", what is classification of
     zoning?_____ . If "no", rezoning feasibility _____ and time
     required? _____

2.   Front set-back required: _____ ft. Side yard inset must be _____ ft. Rear yard inset must
     be _____ ft.
     Source of zoning data (give official name & phone number): _____
     _____

3.   Our sign permitted? Yes [ ]   No   [ ] . If yes, zoning class existing _____
     Maximum Sq. ft. sign area _____ Maximum height on sign _____
     Set-back on sign (in feet) _____

4.   How many curb cuts permitted? _____ Maximum width of curb cuts _____ Min. _____
     Traffic count, 24 hour period _____ and _____
                        Front of Site (street)   Adjacent (street)

5.   Owner _____ Address _____
     City _____ State · _____ Phone _____

6.   Realtor _____ Address _____
     City _____ State _____ Phone _____
     Attorney _____ Address _____
     City _____ State _____ Phone _____

Fig. A.4   *(Continued)*

210

ANALYSIS OF THE TRANSACTION

7. Improved Lease _____
   Asking Rental with improvements: _____
   What will the taxes be with improvements: _____
   Will landlord give 15 year lease and options _____ . Will landlord give option to purchase _____

8. Land Lease _____ Asking Rental _____ Term _____ Tax Rate is _____ __

9. Purchase _____ Asking Price _____ Cash _____ Contract _____
   Taxes are: _____ Assessed Valuation: _____

VI. LAND INFORMATION:
   1. Lot size _____ . Is it a corner lot? _____ Is alley next to property? _____
      Size _____ . Attach plot plan or drawing of property.
   2. Is land at street level _____ . If not, give facts on _____
   3. Type of fill used _____ . When filled _____
   4. Improvements on property are: _____
      _____
   5. Is land clear of trees and all other conditions regarding site work? _____
      Give facts, size and number of trees, type of fill on lot _____

DIAGRAM NO. 1
(Show North)

VII. COMMENTS:
_____
_____
_____
_____

Fig. A.4   *(Continued)*

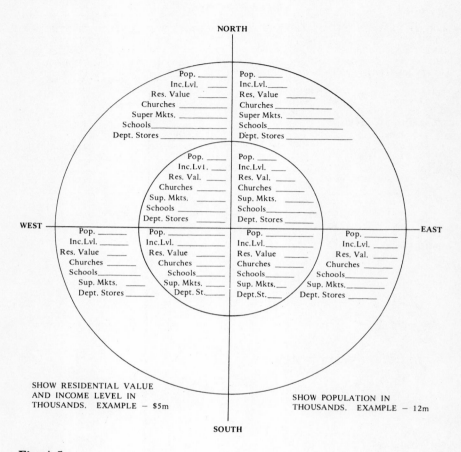

SHOW RESIDENTIAL VALUE
AND INCOME LEVEL IN
THOUSANDS. EXAMPLE — $5m

SHOW POPULATION IN
THOUSANDS. EXAMPLE — 12m

Fig. A.5

212

ANALYSIS OF THE TRANSACTION

DIAGRAM OF PLOT

MUST BE DRAWN IN DETAIL, SHOWING DIRECTIONS AND SIDE OF ROAD: NORTH, SOUTH, EAST OR WEST; PROPOSED LOCATION OF STORE; CURB CUTS OR BREAKS ALREADY ON PROPERTY – GIVE NUMBER OF CURB CUTS PERMITTED: SIDEWALKS AND WHO MAINTAINS. SHOW ANY TREES, BUILDINGS, POLES, FIRE HYDRANTS, TRAFFIC LIGHTS, BUS STOPS. ATTACH TO SURVEY.

Courtesy of John H. Noel, III, Nashville, Tennessee

Fig. A.6

THE LOAN COMMITMENT

CHECK LIST OF DOCUMENTS TO BE RECEIVED

BROKER OR SPONSOR _____

[ ] Construction
[ ] Permanent
[ ] Construction & Permanent
[ ] Stand-By

BORROWER _____

LOCATION _____

Date Requested	Documentation	Date Received	Remarks
	Loan Submission:		
	Financial Statement — Borrower		
	Financial Statement — Guarantors		
	Financial Statement — General Contractors		
	D. & B. Report		
	Reference Checks (Personal, Retail, Banks, etc.)		
	Plot Plan		
	Plans and Specifications — Preliminary		
	Cost Breakdown		
	Proposed Annual Income and Operating Statement		
	Appraisal (By: _____)		
	Market Analysis (By: _____)		
	Photographs		
	Take-Out (Who: _____)		
	Lease Agreements		
	Lessee Rated (_____) and Term (_____ yrs.)		
	Committee Brief		
	Approved by Committee		
	Commitment Letter Mailed or Delivered		
	Commitment Letter Accepted		
	Loan Approved:		
	Fee Payable — Cash		
	Fee Payable — Note Due _____ , 19_____		
	Partnership or Trust Agreement		
	Corporate Resolution		
	Corporate Borrowing Authority		
	Corporate Articles		

Fig. A.7

Date Requested	Documentation	Date Received	Remarks
	Guaranty Agreement		
	Note		
	Mortgage		
	Construction Loan Agreement		
	Hazard Insurance (Builders Risk)		
	Final Policies of Insurance — Premiums Prepaid		
	Liability Insurance		
	Guaranteed Rental Scale, Lease Insurance		
	Title Policy		
	Escrow Letter (Transfer Title Only)		
	Letter of Instructions — Title Company (Disburse)		
	Schedule "B" Title Exceptions Approved by Legal Department		
	Participation Agreement		
	(Who: _____)		
	Buy/Sell Agreement		
	Construction Contract		
	Interest Equalization Tax Agreement		
	Draw Schedule		
	Financing Statements and Security Agreements — Chattels		
	Inventory of Personal Property Identified by Make, Model and Serial Number		
	Financing Statements and Security Agreements — Receivables		

	Evidence That Personal Property, Fixtures
	    and Equipment Are Free and Clear of All
	    Liens and Encumbrances		

	Certificate of Occupancy or Other Govern-
	    ment Certificate re: Zoning, Ordinances,
	    etc.		

	Evidence Showing Compliance With Zoning
	    Laws and Ordinances As Of The
	    Completion Date		

	Plans & Specifications — Final		
	Plat of Survey on Construction Completion		
	Architect's Certificates of Completion Per Plans and Specifications		
	Original Building Permit From City, County or Other Governing Authority		

Fig. A.7   *(Continued)*

215

THE LOAN COMMITMENT

Date Requested	Documentation	Date Received	Remarks
	Evidence of Compliance With Government Regulations in Connection With Sale of Electricity, Utilities or Other Unique Functions		
	Verify Accuracy of Interim Interest Charges Through Closing		
	Certificates of Occupancy For All Tenants		
	Tentant Space Acceptances		
	Subordination Agreement		
	Assignment of Mortgage (If Previously Held by Interim Lender)		
	Original Prime Leases as Recorded		
	Lease Assignments (recorded prior to mortgage)		
	Assignment of Assignment of Lessor's In Interest (If previously held by Interim Lender)		
	Compliance With All Lease and Leasing Requirements Prior to Completion Date, Per Borrower's Affidavit		
	Evidence of Compliance with Parking Index of Gross Leaseable Area to be Maintained		
	Establish Tickler Fire Quarterly & Annual Statements re: Kicker		
	Legal Department Memo Conditions Fulfilled		

The foregoing action has been completed this _____ day of _____ , 19_____ .

_____

Fig. A.7   (*Continued*)

Financial Statement for Individual Partnership or Corporation

To_____Bank

_____City_____State

DATE _____

Name_____

Address_____   Character of Business_____

For the purpose of obtaining credit from the above Bank, I hereby tender the following statement of my business as of_____

_____19_____ and agree to notify you promptly of any change affecting my ability to pay.

Every schedule on this report must be filled out. Where there are no amounts to enter, write the word "None".

ASSETS				LIABILITIES			
Cash in hand and in banks				Notes Payable, due within one year { For merchandise			
Notes receivable, not due, but maturing within six months { For merchandise sold				{ For real estate			
{ For money loaned				{ To banks			
{ For real estate sold				{ To others			
Accounts Receivable, current and considered good { For merchandise sold				Accounts Payable { For merchandise, not due.			
{ Other				{ For merchandise, past due			
Merchandise (INDICATE WHETHER COST OR REPLACEMENT VALUE)				{ Others, not due			
United States Bonds or Notes				{ Others, past due			
Other Listed Securities (Give detailed list on back)				Other current liabilities			
TOTAL QUICK				TOTAL CURRENT			
Notes Receivable, past due or maturing in over six months { For merchandise sold				Notes Payable, not due within twelve months from date of this statement { Real estate mortgage (List on reverse side)			
{ For money loaned				{ Other			
{ For real estate sold				Other mortgages, judgments or liens not within twelve months from date of this statement (List in detail)			
Accounts Receivable, past due { For merchandise sold							
{ Other							
Real Estate (List on reverse side)							
Buildings (List on reverse side)				TOTAL LIABILITIES			
Machinery and tools $				NET WORTH			
less depreciation_____net				This section to be used only if a corporation to show distribution of net worth			
Stocks and bonds other than U. S. (See reverse side)							
Other assets (Itemize)				Capital Stock, common			
				Capital Stock, preferred			
				Surplus			
				Undivided Profits			
TOTAL ASSETS				TOTAL			

Total sales last calendar or fiscal year $_____. Cost of sales $_____. Profit or loss $_____

Have endorsed notes of others amounting to $_____, In present business_____years. Carry $_____

insurance on merchandise $_____on buildings, and $_____on machinery and equipment.

Carry $_____life insurance payable to_____. Have pledged $_____

of above accounts and notes as collateral.

Form No. A-1   OVER

Fig. A.8

SCHEDULE OF REAL ESTATE OWNED AND MORTGAGES PAYABLE

Location and Description	Improvements	Value		Mortgages	Equity
		Assessed	Cash		

NOTE--If you have ever failed in business give particulars below and how and on what basis you settled with creditors.

_____

_____

_____

_____

_____

Listed Stocks and Bonds other than U. S. Bonds--See opposite side

DESCRIPTION	MARKET VALUE

PLEASE ANSWER FULLY:

1. Are you a partner in any firm?_____Name of firm_____

2. Is real estate as listed recorded in your name?_____

        If not, in whose name?_____

        If joint, state with whom_____

3. If this statement covers the business of a partnership list below the names and addresses of all partners.

_____

_____

    I certify that the above schedules and the statements on the opposite side are a true and correct account of the condition of my business and affairs on the day above stated.

    Witness my hand and seal, this_____day of_____19____

_____(Seal)

Fig. A.9

HUD-FHA PROGRAM
FOR MORTGAGE INSURANCE FOR NURSING HOMES AND RELATED FACILITIES

WHAT IT IS

- This program helps finance construction and improvement of nursing homes and related facilities. Providing rehabilitation, intermediate, and/or extended care services, it insures mortgages for a single health care facility or for a combination of related facilities, under Section 232 of the National Housing Act.

NATURE OF PROGRAM

- A nursing home or related facility may be either privately owned and operated for profit (proprietary) or owned by a private, nonprofit corporation or association.

- The facility serves people who need skilled nursing care and medical service but do not require acute inpatient hospital care. It may also provide a protective living environment and routine personal and health services for those who do not need skilled nursing care.

- The appropriate agency for the area in which the facility is located must certify the need and is responsible for assuring that State and Federal licensing and operating standards are enforced.

SPECIAL REQUIREMENTS

- The area FHA insuring office director determines the amount of working capital required for a private, proprietary facility. The director also determines the proportion of operating funds needed for expenses until the nursing home attains sustaining occupancy. FHA requires cost certification and adherence to prevailing wage standards.

ELIGIBLE MORTGAGOR

- The mortgagor for a proprietary facility may be a corporation, trust, partnership, or an individual approved by FHA. The nonprofit mortgagor may be a private corporation or association, but must be organized for purposes other than making a profit for itself or for its officers or members. Further, it

must not be controlled or directed in any way by persons or firms seeking to derive profit from the facility.

- Each mortgagor is subject to a regulatory agreement. A corporation mortgagor also may be regulated by charter provision.

- A mortgagor may lease the facility to an operator on terms approved by FHA. But whether the mortgagor directly operates or leases the facility to another, it must be operated under all necessary licenses and inspections required by Federal, State or local regulations.

MORTGAGE CONDITIONS

- The mortgage may cover costs of new construction or rehabilitation of existing buildings; it may not exceed a 20-year term. The project must include at least 20 beds and funds may be advanced during construction.

Maximum interest rate is variable.

Insurance Premium: ½ of 1% on declining scheduled balances.

Fees and Charges: Application and Commitment, $3 per $1,000 of mortgage amount. Inspection, not to exceed $5 per $1,000 of mortgage amount.

MORTGAGE LIMITS

- The mortgage amount includes cost of equipment for operating the nursing home, intermediate care facility or both.

The maximum mortgage amount established by law is $12.5 million per project. Within this limit, the highest insurable mortgage amount for proposed construction is 90 percent of the FHA-estimate of value. On most rehabilitation projects, the mortgage amount may not exceed 90 percent of the estimated value after rehabilitation.

Fig. A.10

219

APPLICATION AND PROCESSING

■ After consulting with lenders, prospective sponsors confer with local FHA insuring offices. A sponsor provides:

1. Full information about the property.

2. A definite plan outline for the care and service to be offered.

3. Evidence of title to the land, option to purchase, or owner's authorization to inspect the site for the purpose requested.

4. An acceptable Certificate of Need (FHA Form 2576) or assurance that it is forthcoming.

The FHA mortgage credit analysis of the sponsor covers:

1. Character and reputation.

2. Ability and experience in developing, building, and operating a nursing home or facility of the type or size proposed.

3. Financial capacity to complete, equip and furnish the facility according to FHA regulations and the needs of the occupants, as well as ability to provide the necessary operating capital.

The underwriting analysis determines whether the project will earn an adequate income. After the FHA analysis, the sponsor completes an FHA application form, attaches the requested exhibits and asks his lender to submit it to FHA for processing. FHA processes the application and issues a commitment for insurance.

INFORMATION SOURCE

HUD Area Office or HUD-FHA Insuring Office.

ADMINISTERING OFFICE

Assistant Secretary for Housing Production and Mortgage Credit—FHA Commissioner.

January 1971

HUD-130-F(2)
GPO 911-788

Fig. A.10 *(Continued)*

HUD-FHA PROGRAM
FOR UNSUBSIDIZED COOPERATIVE HOUSING

SECTION 213, SECTION 221(d)(3)(MARKET RATE), NATIONAL HOUSING ACT

WHAT IT IS

Mortgages on cooperative housing projects which require no assistance or subsidy may be insured under the provisions of Section 213 or 221(d)(3)(Market Rate) of the National Housing Act. These are market interest rate programs. No income limitations are imposed on the members of these cooperatives.

ELIGIBLE PROJECTS

- Five or more units—detached (need not be contiguous), semi-detached, row, elevator.
- Section 221(d)(3)(Market Rate): new, or rehabilitated structures.
- Section 213, new, existing, or rehabilitated structures: may include non-dwelling commercial—must be predominantly residential.
- Must be built in conformity with FHA minimum property standards.

ELIGIBLE SPONSORS AND MORTGAGORS

- **Pre-sold Management Type** cooperative corporations which restrict occupancy to the members of the cooperative. (Sections 213 and 221)
- **Investor Sponsored Type** developed by a profit corporation which has certified that it intends to construct the project and sell it to a cooperative within two years after completion of construction. (Section 213 and 221)
- **Nonprofit Sponsored Type** developed by a properly motivated nonprofit group intended for transfer to cooperative ownership after completion of construction and sale of the necessary cooperative memberships. The nonprofit sponsor must meet all requirements for nonprofit sponsorship and must demonstrate that the project will be operated successfully as a nonprofit rental project in the event the project is not successfully marketed on a cooperative basis. (Section 221)

PROCEDURES FOR SPONSORS

The sponsor of a proposed cooperative project should discuss the proposal with the local HUD/FHA insuring office. If the FHA feasibility findings are favorable, the sponsor will submit an application, along with the required fee and exhibits, through an approved lender. The application is for insurance of a blanket mortgage to cover the entire project.

FINANCED BY

- Private lenders (mortgages eligible for purchase by FNMA)

MORTGAGE LIMITS—Lesser of the following:

- Section 213—$20,000,000 ($25,000,000 in the case of public mortgagor)
- Section 221—$12,500,000
- Section 213—97% of FHA estimate of cost
- Section 221—100% of FHA estimate of cost

(Investor Sponsor Mortgagor under both 213 and 221 may obtain a 90% mortgage which is increased to the above limits upon sale to cooperative mortgagor)

The sum of the per-unit limit under the appropriate section of the National Housing Act.

COOPERATIVE PROCEDURES

- The members of a cooperative elect their own board of directors. The board of directors decides matters that concern management and maintenance of the project; but the management must meet standards of the lender and of FHA. The success of a cooperative depends on experienced and stable management.
- Each member pays to the cooperative a monthly carrying charge equal to his share of the sum required by the cooperative to meet expenses. Since operating costs may vary from time to time, the monthly charges paid by members may be adjusted up or down to reflect such changes.

SUBSIDIZED COOPERATIVE PROGRAMS

- Families and individuals who cannot afford to live in a cooperative without some form of assistance may be eligible for assistance under the HUD Rent Supplement Program; or they may be eligible for membership in a subsidized cooperative having a mortgage insured under Section 236 of the National Housing Act. Such members must be within prescribed income limits.

INFORMATION SOURCE
HUD Area Office or HUD-FHA Insuring Office.

ADMINISTERING OFFICE
Assistant Secretary for Housing Production and Mortgage Credit—FHA Commissioner.

May 1971

GPO 911-310 HUD-256-F

Fig. A.11

HUD-FHA NON-ASSISTED PROGRAM
FOR RENTAL HOUSING FOR MODERATE INCOME FAMILIES

SECTION 221(d)(4) NATIONAL HOUSING ACT

WHAT IT IS

- A program designed to aid in providing housing for families of moderate income.

ELIGIBLE PROJECTS

- Projects containing 5 or more units of detached, semi-detached, row, or walk-up or elevator-type multifamily structures, designed primarily for residential use in conformance with FHA Property Standards.
- Projects may vary widely in layout, size, and design, depending on the type of market to be served.
- FHA will regulate rents, rate of return and methods of operation.
- Family income limits are not a condition for occupancy.
- This program provides a 10 percent Builder's and Sponsor's Profit and Risk allowance.
- Not limited to new construction—considered appropriate for the rehabilitation of projects.

ELIGIBLE MORTGAGORS

- Individuals, partnerships, corporations, or other legal entities approved by the Commissioner, excluding nonprofit, limited dividend, cooperative, and public mortgagors.

PROPERTY REQUIREMENTS

- The project must be located on real estate held:
  (a) In fee simple.
  (b) On a leasehold for not less than 99 years, or having a period of 75 years to run from the date the mortgage is executed.
  (c) Leasehold for 50 years, provided the lessor is a government agency, Indian, or Indian tribe.

FINANCING

- FHA approved private lending institution. (Mortgages eligible for purchase by FNMA)

TENANT OCCUPANTS

- No income requirements.
- No restrictions due to race, creed, color or age of the prospective tenant or the composition of his family.

MORTGAGE LIMITS

- The maximum mortgage cannot exceed the lesser of:

  (1) $12,500,000

  (2) 90 percent FHA's estimate of the replacement cost of the project:

  (3) For such part of the property or project attributable to dwelling use an amount per family unit, depending on the number of bedrooms which may be within the dwelling:
  Elevator type:
  $10,925 no bedroom
  $15,525 one-bedroom
  $18,400 two-bedroom
  $23,000 three-bedroom
  $26,162 four-bedroom or more
  All other types:
  $ 9,200 no bedroom
  $12,937 one-bedroom
  $15,525 two-bedroom
  $19,550 three-bedroom
  $22,137 four-bedroom or more

- The sums mentioned in (3) above may be increased by up to 45 percent in high cost areas.
- Mortgage term is limited to 40 years.
- Maximum interest rate is variable.
- Repayment—level annuity monthly plan (equal monthly payments to principal and interest).

Fig. A.12

222

HOW SPONSOR SHOULD PROCEED

- Preliminary conference with FHA insuring office—identifying locality, general site, number of units and rents to be charged.
- If project appears feasible sponsor will be asked to submit application (FHA Form 2013) for feasibility analysis.
- After analysis FHA will advise the sponsor of its finding of feasibility and estimates upon which the feasibility is predicated; such as FHA land value, improvements, general requirements, estimated construction time, etc.
- Sponsor then submits a formal application with fee and exhibits, and if approved FHA will issue a conditional commitment.
- After the final submission is made by the sponsor in compliance with the guidelines established at the feasibility conference, a firm commitment will be issued.

FEES AND CHARGES

- 1. **FHA**
  —application fee (with formal application) is $1.50 per thousand of mortgage amount applied for
  —commitment fee, $3.00 per thousand dollars of commitment amount, less application fee previously paid
  —inspection fee, $5.00 per thousand dollars of commitment amount
  —mortgage insurance premium, first premium collected in advance at rate of ½ of 1 percent of the mortgage amount.

- 2. **Mortgagee**
  —service charge, not to exceed 2 percent of mortgage amount.

- 3. **FNMA**
  —1½ percent of mortgage amount.

INFORMATION SOURCE

HUD Area Office or HUD-FHA Insuring Office.

ADMINISTERING OFFICE

Assistant Secretary for Housing Production and Mortgage Credit—FHA Commissioner.

January 1971

HUD-143-F(3)
GPO 911-881

Fig. A.12   *(Continued)*

HUD-FHA NON-ASSISTED PROGRAM
SECTION 231 HOUSING FOR THE ELDERLY AND HANDICAPPED

SECTION 231—WHAT IT IS

A program to aid in development of rental housing for occupancy by elderly or handicapped families or individuals.

An elderly person is defined as one who is age 62 or over. A handicapped person is one whose physical impairment (a) is expected to be of continued and indefinite duration; (b) substantially impedes his ability to live independently; and (c) is such that his ability to live independently could be improved by more suitable housing.

ELIGIBLE PROJECTS

■ Projects containing eight or more units of detached, semi-detached, row, walk-up or elevator type multi-family structures designed primarily for residential use in conformance with HUD Property Standards for housing the elderly and handicapped. All local codes and zoning requirements must be met.

■ Projects may vary widely in layout, size, and design, depending on the type of market to be served.

■ HUD will regulate rents, rate of return and methods of operation.

■ Project must involve either new construction or rehabilitation.

■ This program provides a 10 percent builder's and sponsor's profit and risk allowance to profit-motivated sponsors.

SUBSIDY PAYMENTS

■ If project is owned by a nonprofit mortgagor, eligible tenants may receive rent supplement assistance.

ELIGIBLE MORTGAGORS

■ Individuals, partnerships, corporations including non-profits or other legal entities approved by the FHA Commissioner.

PROPERTY REQUIREMENTS

■ The project must be located on real estate held:
(a) In fee simple.
(b) On a leasehold for not less than 99 years, or having a period of 75 years to run from the date the mortgage is executed.

(c) On a leasehold for 50 years provided the lessor is a government agency, Indian, or Indian tribe.
■ Projects may contain central dining and other congregate facilities; units need not contain kitchens.

FINANCING

■ FHA approved private or public institutions. (Mortgages eligible for purchase by FNMA or GNMA).

TENANT OCCUPANTS

■ No income requirements, except in the case of persons receiving rent supplement assistance.

■ No restrictions due to race, creed, color.

■ Project must be designed for elderly or handicapped and they must be given priority in occupancy, but nonelderly or nonhandicapped may occupy units in the project.

MAXIMUM AMOUNT INSURABLE

$12,500,000 private mortgagor

$50,000,000 public mortgagor

LIMITS PER FAMILY UNIT

Elevator type building:

$10,450	no bedroom
14,850	one-bedroom
17,600	two-bedroom
22,000	three-bedroom
25,025	four-bedroom or more

All other types:

$8,800	no bedroom
12,375	one-bedroom
14,850	two-bedroom
18,700	three-bedroom
21,175	four bedroom or more

In areas where cost levels so require, limits per family unit may be increased up to 45 percent.

BASIS FOR CALCULATING THE LOAN

Nonprofit mortgagor: 100 percent of estimated replacement cost of the project.

Fig. A.13

Profit mortgagor: 90 percent of estimated replacement cost.

- Mortgage term is limited to 40 years or 3/4 of remaining economic life, whichever is less.

- The current maximum interest rate is 7 percent.

- Amortization is via the level annuity monthly payment plan (equal monthly payments to principal and interest).

HOW SPONSOR SHOULD PROCEED

- Preliminary conference with HUD area or HUD-FHA insuring office—identifying locality, general site, type of project contemplated, amenities to be offered, number of units and rents to be charged.

- If application is considered, sponsor will be asked to submit application (FHA Form 2013) for feasibility analysis.

- After analysis HUD will advise the sponsor of its finding of feasibility and the estimates upon which the feasibility is predicted, such as land value, improvements, general requirements, and estimated construction time.

- Sponsor then submits a formal application with fee and exhibits; if approved, HUD will issue a conditional commitment.

- After the final submission is made by the sponsor in compliance with the guidelines established at the feasibility conference, HUD will issue a firm commitment.

FEES AND CHARGES

1. FHA
   —application fee (with formal application) is $1.50 per thousand of mortgage amount applied for.

   —commitment fee is $3 per thousand dollars of commitment amount, less application fee previously paid.

   —inspection fee is $5 per thousand dollars of commitment amount.

   —mortgage insurance premium, first premium collected in advance at rate of ½ of one percent of the mortgage amount.

2. Mortgagee
   —service charge, not to exceed two percent of mortgage amount.

3. FNMA
   —1½ percent of mortgage amount.

ADMINISTERING OFFICE

Assistant Secretary for Housing Production and Mortgage Credit—FHA Commissioner.

INFORMATION SOURCE

HUD Area Office or HUD-FHA Insuring Office

Fig. A.13 (*Continued*)

HUD-FHA NON-ASSISTED PROGRAM
FOR MOBILE HOME PARKS

WHAT IT IS

- A program to finance the construction or rehabilitation of mobile home parks.
- The maximum interest rate is variable.

ELIGIBLE PROJECTS

- Projects may consist either of spaces to be built, or of existing parks to be rehabilitated.
- Projects may vary widely in layout, size, and design, depending on the type of market to be served.
- Must be built in conformity with FHA's Mobile Home Court Development Guide, FHA G4200.7.
- FHA will regulate rents, rate of return, methods of operation.

ELIGIBLE MORTGAGORS

- Individuals, partnerships, corporations, or other legal entity approved by the Commissioner.

PROPERTY REQUIREMENTS

- The park must be located in real estate held:
  (a) In fee simple.
  (b) On a leasehold for not less than 99 years, or having a period of 75 years to run from the date the mortgage is executed.
  (c) Leasehold for 50 years, provided the lessor is a government agency, Indian, or Indian tribe.

FINANCING

- Approved FHA private lending institutions. (Mortgages eligible for purchase by FNMA)

TENANT OCCUPANTS

- No income requirements.
- The mortgagor may not require as a condition of occupancy the purchase of a mobile home from a specific dealer or manufacturer.
- No space may be rented for a period of less than 30 days.
- No restrictions due to race, creed, color or age of the prospective tenant or the composition of his family.

MORTGAGE LIMITS

- The maximum mortgage cannot exceed the lesser of:
  (a) $1,000,000

  (b) 90 percent of FHA's estimate of the value of the park after the construction of improvements.

  (c) An amount equal to $2,500 per space.
- The sums mentioned in (a) and (c) above may be increased by up to 45 percent in high cost areas.
- Mortgage term is limited to 40 years.
- Maximum interest rate is 8 percent.
- Repayment—level annuity monthly plan (equal monthly payments to principal and interest).
- Special limitations apply when park is on leased land. FHA offices will explain how these affect a specific situation.

HOW SPONSOR SHOULD PROCEED

- Preliminary conference with FHA insuring office—identifying locality, general site, number of spaces and rents to be charged.
- If project appears feasible, sponsor will be asked to submit application (FHA Form 2013) for feasibility analysis.
- After analysis FHA will advise the sponsor of its finding of feasibility and the estimates upon which the feasibility is predicated, such as FHA land value, improvements, general requirements, estimated construction time, etc.
- Sponsor then submits a formal application with fee and exhibits, and if approved, FHA will issue a conditional commitment.
- After the final submission is made by the sponsor in compliance with the guidelines established at the feasibility conference, a firm commitment will be issued.

Fig. A.14

226

FEES AND CHARGES

■ 1. FHA
  —application fee (with formal application) is $1.50 per thousand of mortgage amount applied for
  —commitment fee, $3.00 per thousand dollars of commitment amount, less application fee previously paid
  —inspection fee, $5.00 per thousand dollars of commitment amount

  —mortgage insurance premium, first premium collected in advance at rate of ½ of 1 percent of the mortgage amount.

■ 2. Mortgagee
  —service charge, not to exceed 2 percent of mortgage amount.

■ 3. FNMA
  —1½ percent of mortgage amount.

INFORMATION SOURCE

HUD Area Office or HUD-FHA Insuring Office.

ADMINISTERING OFFICE

Assistant Secretary for Housing Production and Mortgage Credit—FHA Commissioner.

Fig. A.14 *(Continued)*

SECTION 234 NATIONAL HOUSING ACT

WHAT IT IS

- The Federal Housing Administration insures mortgages obtained by investors to finance construction or rehabilitation of housing projects of four or more single-family units.
- Later the individual units in such projects are released from the blanket mortgage, sold to individual owners, and financed separately. The single units, when sold, may be financed by the buyers with FHA-insured or non-FHA mortgages; or a buyer may purchase on an all-cash basis without a mortgage if he chooses to do so.

ELIGIBLE PROJECTS

- Projects containing four or more units of detached, semi-detached, row, or walk-up or elevator type multifamily structures.
- Projects may vary widely in layout, size and design, depending on the type of market to be served.
- May include non-dwelling commercial—must be predominately residential.
- May be new or rehabilitated structure.

ELIGIBLE MORTGAGORS

- Individuals, partnerships, corporations, or other legal entities approved by HUD.

PROJECT MORTGAGE LIMITS

Lesser of the following:
- $20,000,000 (maximum - private mortgagor).
- 90 percent of FHA estimate of cost.
- The sum of the per unit limit under Section 234.

FINANCING

- FHA-approved private lending institution.

FAMILY UNIT REQUIREMENTS

- Whether the project is new or existing, sale to condominium buyers can be made only after FHA has processed the case and found the plan of condominium ownership acceptable.

- All planned construction must be completed.
- Units amounting to 80 percent of the value of all units must have been sold to FHA-approved buyers.
- The mortgage on a family unit must be a first mortgage.
- One person may own as many as four units financed with FHA-insured mortgages, provided he lives in one of them. It is not required that all of the unit mortgages be FHA-insured. Some of the unit mortgages may be FHA-insured, some financed conventionally, and others purchased for cash.

FAMILY UNIT MORTGAGE LIMITATIONS

- The mortgage amount cannot exceed $33,000. The amount is further limited as follows:
  a. Based on the FHA value of the family unit, including common areas and facilities, it cannot exceed 97 percent of the first $15,000, plus 90 percent of the next $10,000, plus 80 percent of the value above $25,000 for an owner-occupant.
  b. For a unit owned by a person who does not live in it, the mortgage amount cannot exceed 85 percent of the amount computed for an owner-occupant.
- The maximum interest rate is variable. The FHA mortgage insurance premium is ½ of 1 percent a year on decreasing principal balances, without taking into account prepayments or delinquencies.

CHARACTERISTICS OF UNIT OWNERSHIP

- The extent of interest that the owner of a living unit has in the common areas and facilities is governed by the ratio of value of his unit to the total value of all the units. This ratio also represents his voting interest in the condominium owners' association. Along with the owners of other units in the project, he has the right to use the common areas and facilities and the obligation to maintain them. The owners make monthly contributions to the condominium association covering their proportionate share of the cost of maintaining these common areas and facilities.

INFORMATION SOURCE

HUD Area Office or HUD-FHA Insuring Office.

ADMINISTERING OFFICE

Assistant Secretary for Housing Production and Mortgage Credit—FHA Commissioner.

Fig. A.15

HUD-FHA NON-ASSISTED PROGRAM FOR SECTION 207 RENTAL HOUSING

SECTION 207 RENTAL HOUSING

WHAT IT IS

■ A program designed to aid in the development of rental housing for moderate- and middle-income families.

ELIGIBLE PROJECTS

■ Projects containing 8 or more units of detached, semi-detached, row, walk-up or elevator-type multi-family structures, designed primarily for residential use in conformance with FHA Property Standards.
■ Projects may vary widely in layout, size, and design, depending on the type of market to be served.
■ FHA will regulate rents, rate of return and methods of operation.

ELIGIBLE MORTGAGORS

■ Individuals, partnerships, corporations, or other legal entities approved by the Commissioner.

PROPERTY REQUIREMENTS

■ The project must be located on real estate held:
  (a) In fee simple.
  (b) On a leasehold for not less than 99 years, or having a period of 75 years to run from the date the mortgage is executed.
  (c) Leasehold for 50 years, provided the lessor is a government agency, Indian, or Indian tribe.

FINANCING

■ FHA approved private lending institutions. (Mortgages eligible for purchase by FNMA)

TENANT OCCUPANTS

■ No income requirements.
■ No restrictions due to race, creed, color or age of the prospective tenant or the composition of his family.

MORTGAGE LIMITS

■ The maximum mortgage cannot exceed the lesser of:
  (1) $20,000,000 if executed by a Private Mortgagor.
  (2) $50,000,000 if executed by a Public Mortgagor.
  (3) 90 percent FHA's estimate of the value of the project after the construction of improvements.
  (4) For such part of the property or project attributable to dwelling use, an amount per family unit, depending on the number of bedrooms which may be within the dwelling:

  Elevator type:
    $11,550 no bedroom
    $16,500 one-bedroom
    $19,800 two-bedroom
    $24,750 three-bedroom
    $28,050 four-bedroom or more

  All other types:
    $ 9,900 no bedroom
    $13,750 one-bedroom
    $16,500 two-bedroom
    $20,350 three-bedroom
    $23,100 four-bedroom or more
■ The sums mentioned in (4) above may be increased by up to 45 percent in high cost areas.
■ Mortgage term is limited to 40 years.
■ The maximum interest rate is variable.
■ Repayment—level annuity monthly plan (equal monthly payments to principal and interest).

HOW SPONSOR SHOULD PROCEED

■ Preliminary conference with FHA insuring office—identifying locality, general site, number of units

Fig. A.16

and rents to be charged.
- If project appears feasible sponsor will be asked to submit application (FHA Form 2013) for feasibility analysis.
- After analysis FHA will advise the sponsor of its finding of feasibility and the estimates upon which the feasibility is predicated; such as FHA land value, improvements, general requirements, estimated construction time, etc.
- Sponsor then submits a formal application with fee and exhibits, and if approved FHA will issue a conditional commitment.
- After the final submission is made by the sponsor in compliance with the guidelines established at the feasibility conference, a firm commitment will be issued.

FEES AND CHARGES

- **1. FHA**
   —application fee (with formal application) is $1.50 per thousand of mortgage amount

applied for
   —commitment fee, $3.00 per thousand dollars of commitment amount, less application fee previously paid

   —inspection fee, $5.00 per thousand dollars of commitment amount

   —mortgage . insurance premium, first premium collected in advance at rate of ½ of 1 percent of the mortgage amount.

- **2. Mortgagee**
   —service charge, not to exceed 2 percent of mortgage amount.

- **3. FNMA**
   —1½ percent of mortgage amount.

INFORMATION SOURCE	ADMINISTERING OFFICE
HUD Area Office or HUD-FHA Insuring Office.	Assistant Secretary for Housing Production and Mortgage Credit—FHA Commissioner.

January 1971

HUD-142-F(2)

GPO 911-882

Fig. A.16 (*Continued*)

HUD-FHA ASSISTED PROGRAM
FOR THE RENT SUPPLEMENT PROGRAM

WHAT IT IS

- Privately built housing for low-income families and individuals eligible for public housing and who are either displaced by governmental action, 62 years of age (or older), physically handicapped, living in substandard housing, or whose unit was damaged or destroyed by natural disaster.
- Provides assistance in the form of monthly Federal payment to owner in behalf of low-income tenants.

ELIGIBLE PROJECTS

- Only new housing projects *or* existing ones involving major rehabilitation.
- Five or more units—detached, semi-detached, row, walk-up, or elevator structures.
- Modest design suitable to the market and location.
- Must be built in conformity with FHA minimum property standards.
- Regulated by FHA established maximum rents, rate of return, methods of operation, rent supplement payments.
  Must be *either* part of a workable program for community improvement *or* have local official approval.

ELIGIBLE SPONSORS AND MORTGAGORS

- Private nonprofit organization, limited dividend mortgagor, or cooperative housing corporation.
- Consideration given to qualifications of sponsors—character, integrity, motivation, past successful participation in housing, demonstrable interest in this type of housing, recognition of continuing responsibility, financial ability, capacity to provide competent management.

PROJECT MANAGEMENT

- Success depends on competent project management.
- Housing owner expected to assist tenants in application preparation.
- Management has fiscal responsibilities—monthly statements, re-certifications of incomes.
- Management program must be approved by FHA at least 30 days prior to initial endorsement.

FINANCED BY

- Private lenders (nonprofit mortgagors eligible for GNMA Tandem Plan).

- By State or local governments, through loans, or under State or local program of loan insurance or tax abatement.

MORTGAGE LIMITS

- Limits and terms applicable to Section 221 (d)(3).
- Maximum amount—not in excess of $12,500,000.
- Repayment—level annuity monthly plan (equal monthly payments to principal & interest).

HOW ONE BEGINS

- Preliminary conference with local HUD-FHA area or insuring office—identifying locality, general site, proposed type and number of living units, need for housing, type of people to be served, plans for management.
- If project appears feasible—sponsor will be asked to submit application for analysis.
- Feasibility analysis and other forms and exhibits will not be executed until sponsor has been advised that rent supplement funds have been allocated.
- Favorable decision resulting from feasibility analysis will result in reservation of rent supplement funds if available.
- Formal application will be invited (accompanied by required fee).

ABOUT THE TENANTS

- Eligible tenants described in opening paragraph.
- Income limits comparable to those of public housing locally.
- Total assets cannot exceed $2,000 *unless* applicant is 62 years or older, in which case assets may total $5,000 (personal property excluded).
- Supplement for any tenant may not exceed 70% and must represent at least 10% of the FHA-approved rent for the unit.

RENT SUPPLEMENT AMOUNT

- Difference between 25% of gross income and FHA-approved rental for unit represents rent supplement amount.
- Re-certification of income required yearly (except for elderly).
- Local HUD-FHA area or insuring office will negotiate rent supplement contracts.
- It will provide that payment of rent supplements for eligible tenants will be made monthly, by voucher initiated by housing owner.

INFORMATION SOURCE

HUD Area Office or HUD-FHA Insuring Office.

ADMINISTERING OFFICE

Assistant Secretary for Housing Production and Mortgage Credit—FHA Commissioner.

January 1971

GPO 912-308   HUD-91-F(3)

Fig. A.17

HUD-FHA ASSISTED PROGRAM
FOR RENTAL AND CO-OP HOUSING FOR LOWER-INCOME FAMILIES

SECTION 236, NATIONAL HOUSING ACT

WHAT IT IS

- Privately built rental and cooperative housing for low- and moderate-income families.
- Provides assistance in the form of monthly Federal payments to mortgagee, reducing cost to occupant by paying part of interest on market rate project.

ELIGIBLE PROJECT

- Five or more units - detached (need not be contiguous), semi-detached, row, walk-up or elevator structures.
- Only new structures or existing ones involving major rehabilitation.
- May include non-dwelling commercial-must be predominantly residential.
- Designed so that basic rent is less than 25 percent of maximum income limits.
- An insured limited dividend project purchased by nonprofit organization or co-op.

ELIGIBLE SPONSORS AND MORTGAGORS

- Private, nonprofit organization, limited dividend mortgagor, or cooperative housing corporation.
- Consideration given to qualifications of sponsor's character, integrity, motivation, past successful participation in housing, demonstrable interest in this type of housing, recognition of continuing responsibility, financial ability, capacity to provide competent management.

PROJECT MANAGEMENT

- Sponsors must have management program - realistic plan for providing socially oriented management and related human services.
- Housing owner expected to assist tenants in application preparation.
- Management has fiscal responsibilities - monthly statements, re-certifications of incomes.
- Management program must be approved by FHA at least 30 days prior to initial endorsement.

FINANCING

- By private lenders, (nonprofit mortgagors eligible for GNMA Tandem Plan).
- By State or local governments through loans, or under State or local program of loan insurance or Tax abatement.

MORTGAGE LIMITS

Lesser of the following:
- $12,500,000 (maximum)
- 90 percent of FHA estimate of cost (100 percent for nonprofit or cooperative mortgagor).
- The sum of the per unit-limit under Section 221.

TENANTS AND COOPERATIVE OCCUPANTS

- Must meet specified income requirements and one of the following: be a family (two persons related by blood, marriage or operation of law), or single (at least 62 years of age), or handicapped persons (no age requirement).
- 10 percent of dwelling units may be for single people under 62 years of age.
- Priorities to those displaced by urban renewal, government action, national disaster.

TENANT INCOME LIMITS

- Adjusted income cannot exceed 135 percent of limits applicable to public housing locally.
- Adjusted income is current income from all sources before taxes of all members of the family occupying unit excluding a 5 percent deduction for unusual or temporary income, less $300 for each minor and less earnings of each minor.
- Income recertified every two years and needed adjustment in rental charges made.
- During initial rent-up tenants over-income are required to pay fair market rental.

MONTHLY RENTAL CHARGES

- After the initial rent-up eligible tenant pays basic rental or 25 percent of income whichever is greater; over-income tenant pays 25 percent of income but not in excess of fair market rental.
- Basic monthly rental charge is based on operation at 1 percent interest rate mortgage.
- HUD-FHA makes monthly assistance payments to mortgagee to reduce mortgage payments from market rate to an amount required for a 1 percent mortgage.
- Eligible tenant pays greater of basic rental charge or 25 percent of adjusted income (a limited number of tenants may also receive rent supplement assistance).
- Fair market rental (over-income tenants) based on operation at market interest rate.
- Will include all utilities except telephone.

INFORMATION SOURCE

HUD Area Office or HUD-FHA Insuring Office.

ADMINISTERING OFFICE

Assistant Secretary for Housing Production and Mortgage Credit—FHA Commissioner.

Fig. A.18

232

Index

Abscissa, 145
Absence of liens, 24
Abstract of title, 29
Add-on interest, 178, 179
Adverse changes, 26
Application loan requirements, 97
Appraisal of land, 90
Appraisers Institute, 90
Architect, 101
Architect's fee, 121
Architectural approval, 32, 33
Architectural requirements, 43
Assessments, 29
Assignability, 32
Auxiliary income, 106

Balloon note, 17, 156
Bank discount, 116
Bankruptcy, 26
Bar chart, 142, 143, 150
Bonds, 71
Borrowing on the construction contract, 57, 58
Brick and mortar cost, 61, 115
Budget feasibility study, 2, 121
Builder's fee, 120
Building budget, 125, 126
Building codes, 79
Business loan, 45

Capitalization rate, 111, 112, 113
Capital recovery factor, 165
Cap rate, 111, 112, 113
Cash flow, 119
Cash forecasting, 147
Cash profit, 119

Ceiling of the mortgage, 36, 49, 62
Certificate of occupancy, 29, 30
Certification, 129
Chattel mortgage, 25
Closing cost, discount, 5
  legal fee, 6
  note versus mortgage, 6-7
  origination fee, 6
  recording fees, 7
Commercial loans, 45
Commitment for a loan, 7-13
Company structure, 43
Compound interest, 156
Concessions, 37
Conformity of commitments, 46
Constant, the, 165
Constant payment, 16
Construction interest, 116
Construction loan, 1, 44, 76
  amount of, 48
  application, 50
  assignment, 23
  interest, 149
Construction payroll loans, 1
Contractor's estimate, 131
Conventional mortgage insurance, 54
Corporate structure, 42
Corporation, 71, 75
Covenants, 79
CPM, 150
Critical path method (CPM) diagrams, 142, 143

Date of maturity, 72
Debt service, 118
Declining vs balance(DB), 186

Default, 27
Department of Housing and Urban
    Development (HUD), 52
Depreciation, 186
Depreciation fallacies, 188
Developer's cost, 148
Developer's fee, 120
Draws, 51
Draw schedule, 135, 150

Effect of discount, 47
Effective rate of interest, 166-167
Entrepreneur, 46, 58
Entrepreneur's fee, 120
Equipment costs, 180, 181, 182
Equity, 19, 97, 114, 120
Equity build-up, 185
Escrow account, 24
Escrowed accounts, 17, 18
Escrow of taxes, 31
Estoppel, 30, 31
Extra holdback on subcontractors, 59-60

Feasibility analysis, 118
Federal Housing Administration (FHA),
    34, 44, 90, 91, 93, 94, 95, 96
FHA loans, 52, 53, 54, 55, 129
FHA small home loans, 54
Final payment, 148, 149
Financing, 1
First mortgage, 8, 13, 14
Floor of the mortgage, 36, 37, 48, 62
Front-end-loading, 140, 148, 150
"Front money," 1, 54, 55, 62, 76

Gantt diagram, 142
Gap, the, 49, 62
"Gap" financing, 1, 49, 76
Good faith deposit, 21, 91
Grace period, 17
Ground rent, 123

Hard market, 78
High-rise rentals, 104
Hold back on subcontractors, 59
Horizontal axis, 145

Income approach to value, 99
Income feasibility, 118
Increased equity, 126

Individual, 75
Individual ownership, 65-67
Inflation kicker, 41
Initial capital, 75
Initial offering, 71
Insurable value, 19, 20
Insurance, 27, 28
Interest, 51, 152
Interest equalization tax, 40
Interim financing, 58

Land acquisition loan, 92
Land development financing, 93
Land development loan, 1, 93
Land financing, 90
Land purchase loans, 1
Land purchasing, 90
Last draw, 56, 57
Leasing, 182, 183
Legal advice, 70, 76
"Legal instruments," 6
Lending institutions, 2
Level constant payments, 155, 162
Liability, 67, 68, 69, 72, 76
Lien release form, 130
Limited partnership, 75
Liquid assets, 64, 65, 92
Liquidated damages, 32
Loan application requirements, 91
Loan memorandum, 91, 92
Loan repayment, 156
Local ordinances, 79
Long-term funding, 1
Loss of interest, 179

Matrix analysis, 82
Minimum Property Standards (MPS),
    34, 53
Monthly draws, 131
Mortgage, 6-7
Mortgage broker, 2, 3, 7
"Mortgaged out," 19, 20
Mortgage loan, 1, 2, 7, 61, 62
Mortgage payments, 109, 110

Net actual cost, 147, 148
Nominal interest rate, 47, 166, 167
Not assignable, 22, 23
Note, 6, 7
"Number of units," 99, 101

Open note, 58-59
Operating expenses, 107
  maintenance and repairs, 107
  management, 108
  miscellaneous, 108
  payroll, 107
  replacement reserve, 108
  taxes, 108
  utilities, 107
Option agreement, 90
Ordinate, 145
Origination fee, 31, 116
Ownership change, 42

Participation, 41
Partnership, 67, 75
  active, 68
  general, 67, 68, 69
  limited, 68, 69, 70
  silent, 68
Permanent financing, 1, 23, 37
Permanent lender, 38, 44
Permanent loan, 19
Personality, 20
Prepayment privilege, 18, 19
Present worth of money, 159
Prime rate, 92
Principal of a loan, 153
Professional fees, 121
Public transportation, 80
Purchase of the loan, 31, 32
Purchasing costs, 182, 183

Rate of capitalization, 113
Rate of interest, 152
Rate of return, 119
Refinancing, 74, 75
REIT, 44, 90, 91, 92
Rent, 102, 104
Rent control, 53
Rent roll, 35, 36, 62
Repayment of loan, 92
Replacement cost, 19, 116, 120
Required capital, 57
Residential draws, 127
Residual value, 186
Retainage on construction draw, 56
Return on Investment (ROI), 124, 125,
  126
"Ride herd," 76

Risk profit, 179

Salvage value, 183, 186
Savings and loan bank, 4
S-curve, 145, 146, 156
Second mortgage, 8, 13, 14
Second offerings, 71
Securities and Exchange Commission, 71
Short-term funding, 1
Short-term lender, 38
Short-term loan, 45, 47, 92
Short-term notes, 153
Single-home loans, 51
Single payment compound amount
  factor, 161
Single payment present worth factor, 161
Sinking fund deposit factor, 164
Site selection, 77
  accessibility, 80
  adaptability, 79, 80
  community facilities, 81
  commuting time, 81
  location, 79
  transportation, 80, 81
Small loans, 4, 5
Speculative housing, 53
Stand-by commitment, 48
Start-up time, 39
State usury laws, 92
Step curve, 147, 150
Straight line depreciation (SL), 186
Street dedication, 38
Subcontractors, 59, 60
Subordination, 13, 14
Subsidiary companies, 23, 24
Sum of the years' digits (SYD) depreciation,
  186
Survey, 28

Taxes, 29
Tax loss, 70
Term of commitment, 32
Third mortgage, 8, 13
Time-adjusted return, 187
Time of completion, 21, 22
Title insurance, 28, 29
Trade fixtures, 25
Trade-in value, 183
True rate of interest,
  92

Uniform annual series compound amount
    factor, 168
Uniform annual series present worth
    factor, 166
Uniform principal payments,
    153
Usury laws, 72

Vacancy loss, 105
Value of a business, 97, 98
Value of income approach, 113
Vertical axis, 145
Veterans Administration (VA) loan, 129

Zoning regulations, 79